How It Works®

Science and Technology

Third Edition

Marshall Cavendish
99 White Plains Road
Tarrytown, NY 10591

Website: www.marshallcavendish.com

Third edition updated by Brown Reference Group plc.

Library of Congress Cataloging-in-Publication Data
How it works: science and technology.—3rd ed.
p. cm.
Includes index.
ISBN 0-7614-7314-9 (set)   ISBN 0-7614-7330-0 (Vol. 16)
1. Technology—Encyclopedias. 2. Science—Encyclopedias.
[1. Technology—Encyclopedias. 2. Science—Encyclopedias.]
T9 .H738 2003
603—dc21   2001028771

Consultant: Donald R. Franceschetti, Ph.D., University of Memphis

Brown Reference Group
Editor: Wendy Horobin
Associate Editors: Paul Thompson, Martin Clowes, Lis Stedman, Dawn Titmus
Managing Editor: Tim Cooke
Design: Alison Gardner
Picture Research: Becky Cox
Illustrations: Mark Walker, Darren Awuah

Marshall Cavendish
Project Editor: Peter Mavrikis
Production Manager: Alan Tsai
Editorial Director: Paul Bernabeo

Printed in Malaysia
Bound in the United States of America
08 07 06 05 04   6 5 4 3 2

Title picture: Submarines use special engines, see *Stirling Engine*

How It Works®

Science and Technology

Volume 16

Space Shuttle

Supercharger and Turbocharger

Marshall Cavendish

New York • London • Toronto • Sydney

Contents

Volume 16

Space Shuttle

A space shuttle is a reusable spacecraft that is launched vertically using rockets but which glides back to Earth and lands on a conventional runway without using its engines. Forming the main component of NASA's Space Transportation System (STS), this vehicle was developed in the 1970s to reduce the expense of launching astronauts and cargo into orbit around Earth. One of the reasons for the great expense is that space rockets are not reusable—they mostly burn away during or after launch. By contrast, most of a space shuttle is designed to be used up to 100 times, consequently saving large amounts of money. Initial shuttle plans were for a fully recoverable vehicle, consisting of a winged orbiter to carry payloads such as satellites into space and a system of rocket boosters to help launch it. One proposed design was for a 12-engine booster vehicle 230 ft. (70 m) long, carrying a 197 ft. (60 m) orbiter to a height of 47 miles (75 km), at which point the orbiter would propel itself on into space. The payload cost was expected to be very small in comparison with non-reusable launch vehicles, but the maximum payload was only about 11 tons (10 tonnes), and the development costs would have been prohibitive.

NASA therefore opted for a reusable orbiter with conventional rocket boosters. The size of the orbiter was reduced, and its carrying capacity was increased by more than 150 percent by storing its fuel in a disposable external tank. In place of the large piloted booster, two strap-on solid-fuel rockets were added. Thus the shuttle evolved to its current well-known configuration.

The orbiter itself is the size of a DC9 jet airliner, 122 ft. (37.2 m) long and with a wingspan of 78 ft. (23.8 m). The astronauts who pilot the shuttle ride in the nose of the orbiter, as in an ordinary aircraft. Half the orbiter's length is taken up by a cargo bay capable of carrying 29 tons (26 tonnes) into orbit and of bringing 14 tons (12.6 tonnes) back to Earth.

At the rear of the orbiter are three large rocket engines; during launch, they are fed with fuel from an external tank strapped to the orbiter's belly. This external tank, 159 ft. (47 m) long and 27.5 ft. (8.4 m) in diameter, falls away as the shuttle reaches orbit, burning up in the atmosphere. Weighing over 30 tons (27 tonnes), the empty tank is heavier than the orbiter's payload, and it is the only part of the system not designed for reuse.

▲ A view from space shuttle *Endeavour* of astronaut Pierre Thuot attempting to capture the *Intelsat VI* satellite by attaching it to the shuttle's remote manipulator system (RMS).

km/h), producing a temperature of 2700°F (1482°C) on the wing edges and on the nose of the space vehicle. The tiles were developed to resist this extreme heat, but each of the 31,000 needed to cover the shuttle had to be individually shaped and glued to the orbiter's surface: to do this job properly took longer than expected.

The approach and landing tests were carried out using a prototype space shuttle orbiter released from a carrier aircraft over the Mojave Desert in California and piloted down to the ground. For its atmospheric flight tests, the orbiter, named *Enterprise* after the spaceship in the TV series Star Trek, rode on the back of a modified Boeing 747 jumbo jet.

Enterprise was then taken to the Marshall Space Flight Center in Huntsville, Alabama, for vibration tests to confirm that the orbiter's structure would withstand the force of launching. Following these tests, it was ferried to Cape Canaveral, where it was mated with a dummy external tank and dummy rocket boosters. On

Getting away

To boost the shuttle at launch, two large solid-fuel rockets are strapped to the sides of the external tank. These strap-on boosters fall away as the shuttle ascends, parachuting into the sea to be recovered for reuse. Overall, the shuttle with its rockets stands 184 ft. (56 m) tall and weighs 2,000 tons (1,800 tonnes), and the engines produce around 6.6 million lbs. (3 million kg) of thrust.

Development costs for this design were estimated at around $5.5 billion, but problems and delays eventually increased this figure to $8 billion and resulted in the first shuttle flight occurring three years later than originally planned. One problem was that the engines, which burn liquid hydrogen and liquid oxygen, work at significantly higher pressures and temperatures than in previous rockets, and they have to withstand being fired for up to 100 missions. During the rigorous engine-testing program, cracks appeared in fuel pumps and in fuel pipelines, valves failed, and fires broke out.

Another problem lay in the heat-shield tiles that protect the orbiter during its reentry into the atmosphere. When the shuttle glides back from space, it reaches a speed of 17,000 mph (27,358

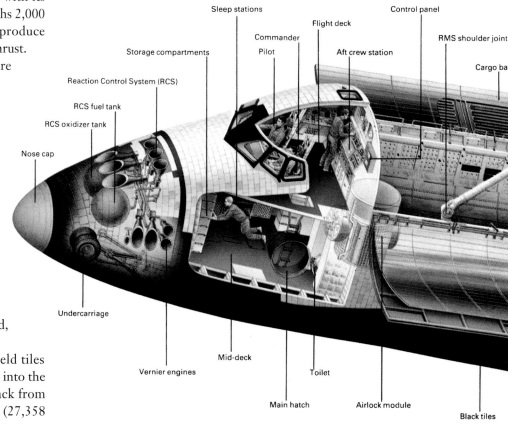

May 1, 1979, *Enterprise* was rolled out to the launch pad in a rehearsal of launch procedures.

At the same time that these tests were being carried out, the orbiter scheduled to make the first launch, *Columbia*, was undergoing the final stages of construction at Cape Canaveral. *Enterprise* itself never made a trip into space. A plan to bring it up to flight standard was abandoned as too costly. Instead, *Enterprise* was stripped down to provide parts for building other orbiters.

The first launch

Launch facilities for the shuttle at Cape Canaveral were modified from those built originally for the Apollo program. Shuttles are assembled inside the 525 ft. (160 m) tall vehicle assembly building that once housed Saturn rockets. The completed shuttle is rolled out on its mobile launch platform by crawler transporters to launch pads 39A and 39B, from which astronauts once left for the Moon.

After an initial computer hitch, the very first space shuttle flight was planned for 7 A.M. on Sunday April 12, 1981. The launch began with the ignition of three liquid-propellant engines, which burned for nearly six seconds while computers on the ground examined thousands of separate items aboard the spacecraft. Computers then ordered the large, solid rocket boosters to

fire, and less than one minute after launch, the shuttle had turned to its proper heading for orbit. Two minutes after liftoff, the big boosters stopped burning and were jettisoned into the Atlantic, their descent rate arrested by three parachutes. The boosters would be recovered and towed ashore for use on up to 20 further flights. Meanwhile, *Columbia* moved out across the Atlantic and six minutes later separated from the now-empty liquid tank. *Columbia* reached a height of 84 miles (136 km), at which point thrusters fired to push it into a circular orbit 113 miles (182 km) above Earth.

At the end of the first orbit, the astronauts John W. Young and Robert L. Crippen opened the large cargo bay doors, a vital operation because the radiators used for removing excess heat from *Columbia* were mounted on the inner face of each panel. It could not remain in space for long without the cooling system.

For two days, Young and Crippen checked out *Columbia*'s systems and slept in their flight seats. The cubicles designed into the living quarters below the flight deck were not installed for this maiden flight. Four general-purpose computers for the autopilot reentry assisted the complex landing operation in which the shuttle glided back to Earth, performing a series of S-turns on the way to reduce speed to a level necessary for landing.

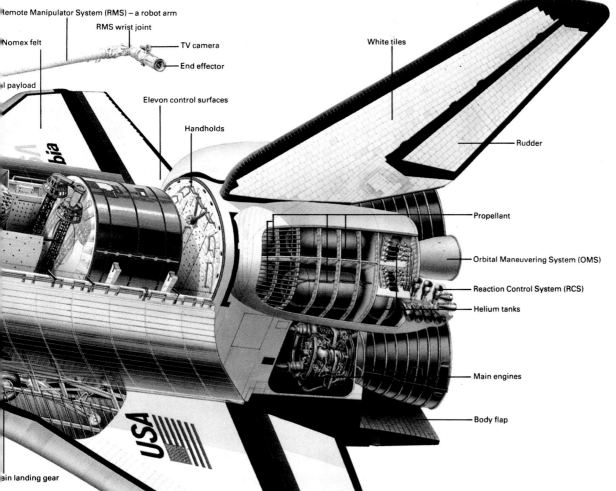

Remote Manipulator System (RMS) – a robot arm

RMS wrist joint

Nomex felt

TV camera

End effector

l payload

Elevon control surfaces

Handholds

White tiles

Rudder

Propellant

Orbital Maneuvering System (OMS)

Reaction Control System (RCS)

Helium tanks

Main engines

Body flap

ain landing gear

◀ A cross section of a space shuttle. The living compartment for the crew takes up less than a quarter of the shuttle's area. A large part of the remaining space is occupied by a cargo bay in which satellites and scientific equipment can be stored.

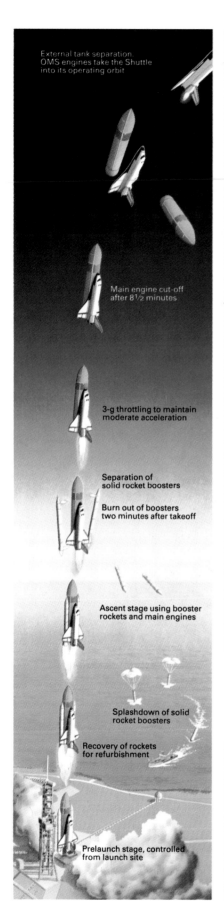

External tank separation. OMS engines take the Shuttle into its operating orbit

Main engine cut-off after 8½ minutes

3-g throttling to maintain moderate acceleration

Separation of solid rocket boosters

Burn out of boosters two minutes after takeoff

Ascent stage using booster rockets and main engines

Splashdown of solid rocket boosters

Recovery of rockets for refurbishment

Prelaunch stage, controlled from launch site

Deorbit burn, using the maneuvering engines to slow the spacecraft

Heat builds up in the atmosphere causing a communications blackout

Maximum heating, with the nose and leading edges reaching 2700°F

Communications restored as the Shuttle slows and turns into a glider

S-turns are performed several times to slow the Shuttle further

Automatic landing phase begins two minutes before touchdown

Final approach with the split rudder acting as an airbrake

Touchdown, one hour after the initial deorbit burn

▲ The launch and landing sequence—the large external fuel tank is the only part that is not recovered and used again. It is jettisoned in low orbit so that it reenters and burns up in Earth's atmosphere. The solid booster rockets, however, are retrieved and may be reused up to 20 times. The space shuttle glides back to Earth and lands safely one hour after its deorbit burn.

Regular operation

The total number of crew members the space shuttle can carry is usually seven. During launch, two crew members sit behind the pilot and commander in the flight deck. The remaining crew members are positioned in the mid-deck area below the flight deck.

The space shuttle can carry several satellites at once in its 60 ft. (18.3 m) long by 15 ft. (4.6 m) wide cargo bay. In orbit, the doors of the cargo bay swing open, and an astronaut on the flight deck uses a remotely controlled arm to pick out the required satellite and release it into space. The same arm can be used to retrieve satellites for inspection and repair. Since the shuttle has a limited altitude, satellites destined for high orbits must have a small additional rocket stage attached to boost them higher. Space probes destined for the Moon and planets must also have powerful upper stages attached to propel them away from Earth after they have been put into orbit by the shuttle. The space shuttle is also used as an orbiting laboratory, taking advantage of conditions impossible on Earth, such as low gravity.

Challenger disaster

Until the shuttle disaster of January 1986, the program had exceeded all expectation. All flights were stopped while NASA tried to understand why *Challenger* exploded shortly after launch, killing all seven astronauts on board. The disaster was the worst to strike the U.S. space program since a fire on a launch pad killed three Apollo astronauts almost twenty years before. The explosion occurred because O-ring seals on the booster rockets failed, allowing hot gases to escape that then burned through the rocket and ruptured the fuel tank causing a massive explosion. Flights were resumed in 1988 after a rigorous investigation resulting in many modifications to the original shuttle design. In 1991, a new shuttle, *Endeavour*, came into service to replace *Challenger* and join the other three existing shuttles, *Columbia*, *Atlantis*, and *Discovery*.

Probes, satellites, and experiments

The space shuttle has been used for many important scientific research projects including the launch of space probes such as *Galileo*, which travelled to Jupiter; *Magellan*, which mapped the surface of Venus using radar; and the Hubble Space Telescope, launched on space shuttle *Discovery* in April 1990 and placed in orbit around Earth, where it is able to study the Universe free from the obstructing effect of Earth's atmosphere. Initial problems with the Hubble telescope's primary lens were rectified by astronauts on space

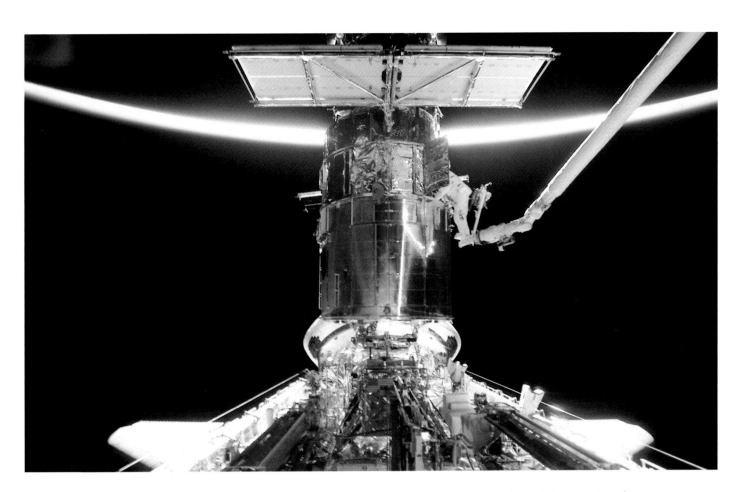

shuttle *Endeavour* during a series of five space walks. The astronauts added correcting mirrors to the telescope that compensated for the spherical aberration caused by faulty manufacture of the primary lens.

Further shuttle missions have also been involved in the servicing and updating of the Hubble Space Telescope as well as the repair and retrieval of other satellites, such as the Solar Maximum Mission, which was repaired while in the shuttle's cargo bay and then redeployed by the shuttle astronauts, and the communications satellites *Westar VI* and *Palapa B-2*, which had failed to reach their required orbit. The shuttle returned these two satellites to Earth where they were checked and refurbished before being relaunched to their correct, higher orbits.

An additional tool developed in 1984 for use on the space shuttle is the Manned Maneuvering Unit (MMU). The MMU is a jet-propelled backpack that enables astronauts to work up to 320 ft. (98 m) from the orbiter, with or without a tether, and which may be used for the maintenance and retrieval of satellites. Twenty-four nitrogen thruster jets provide the propulsion necessary to maneuver the 310 lb. (140 kg) MMU accurately. The most recent versions are more flexible and less bulky than the original MMU, providing astronauts with greater extravehicular movement than was previously possible.

▲ An astronaut working on the Hubble Space Telescope during a 2002 mission to upgrade its optical and operational systems. The ability to anchor satellites to the shuttle's cargo bay has lessened the need for risky space walks by the astronauts and has made it easier for expensive pieces of nonfunctioning equipment to be repaired rather than abandoned.

International Space Station

Most recently the space shuttle has had a primary role in the delivery and construction of parts for the International Space Station (ISS). This is a joint project funded by the United States in conjunction with fifteen other nations: Japan, Canada, Russia, the Netherlands, the United Kingdom, Switzerland, Italy, Belgium, Brazil, Norway, France, Spain, Germany, and Sweden.

The first module of the space station, Russia's *Zarya*, was launched on a Russian Proton rocket in November 1998. This was quickly followed by the first U.S. module, *Unity*, carried into space on space shuttle *Endeavour*. *Unity* was linked to *Zarya* and the next shuttle mission carried supplies for these two units. The third shuttle mission provided equipment to enable the attachment of Russia's *Zvezda* module, which was launched on a Proton rocket in July 2000.

In May 2001, the crew of space shuttle flight STS-100 successfully deployed the Canadarm 2 robotic arm, which will be used in the future construction and maintenance of the ISS. In this way the ISS is gradually being enlarged and is planned to be completed in 2004.

SEE ALSO: Rocket and space propulsion • Satellite, artificial • Space photography • Space probe • Space station • Space suit • Telescope, space

Space Station

Much of the impetus for the initial development of space technology was provided by military and prestige considerations, but space programs have also resulted in considerable scientific and technical advances. One of the most important means by which space technology has enabled the advancement of science is the use of space stations as orbital laboratories in which scientists and engineers experiment under weightless conditions with access to a high vacuum. Using these conditions, scientists attempt to improve human life on Earth by inventing new materials, discovering cures for diseases, and monitoring the health of our planet. In addition, scientists use space stations to further our understanding of the Universe.

Spacecraft

Initially, experiments in space were carried out using crewed spacecraft such as the U.S. Mercury, Gemini, and Apollo and the Soviet Vostok and Soyuz, with the subsequent introduction of orbital stations such as *Skylab* (U.S.A.) and *Salyut*

(U.S.S.R.) providing more space and better living facilities for the crew.

Power was supplied by arrays of solar cells, and stabilization systems kept the stations in the required orientation with attitude jets for position control. The *Skylab* program came to an end in 1974 owing to the planned introduction of the space shuttle, the laboratory itself reentering Earth's atmosphere and burning up in 1979. In contrast, the Soviet *Salyut* program underwent a continued development with a series of stations being launched and used for an ambitious program, including extended flights by resident crews.

The next significant step with crewed orbital laboratories came with the introduction of the U.S. space shuttle, which takes off vertically. Depending on the chosen orbit, the shuttle has a payload of up to 65,000 lbs. (29,500 kg) going into orbit and 32,000 lbs. (14,500 kg) on return. The payload is carried in an enclosed cargo area measuring 15 ft. (4.5 m) in diameter by 60 ft. (18 m) long, and there is space for a crew of three or

▲ An artist's impression of how the International Space Station will look when it is completed in 2004. This multibillion dollar project is being made with the cooperation of 16 different countries and will be the largest structure ever built in space. However, budget constraints may prevent some of its more ambitious projects from being realized.

four additional payload specialists in the pressurized cabin. A particular advantage of the shuttle is that the launch and landing accelerations are comparatively small, pulling a maximum of about 3 *g*, and thus, the payload specialists do not have to be specifically trained.

Spacelab

Applications of the shuttle include the launching of satellites and direct experiments carried in the cargo bay, but one of the most important payloads that the shuttle put into orbit was the *Spacelab* module built by the European Space Agency and used between 1983 and 1997. *Spacelab* was made to fit into the cargo bay and consisted of two main elements—a working area maintained at normal atmospheric pressure to give a shirtsleeve environment and open pallets to carry experimental equipment.

The pressurized module was formed from two segments, each of which was 13.3 ft. (4 m) in diameter and 8.85 ft. (2.7 m) long. The main core module had some working space, including a workbench and also contained life-support and data-processing equipment. If required, more working space could be made available by using the second module.

The experimental equipment was fitted in standard 19 in. (48.3 cm) laboratory racking or mounted on the floor of the module, with connections being available for power supplies and data transmission. Cooling air ducts were built in and liquid cooling systems could also be connected to the equipment. Two windows were fitted to the core unit, one of them made of optical-quality glass to allow observations.

The pallets were used to carry equipment that was to be directly exposed to space. Instruments could be fitted directly to the pallets; power and signal connections were built in. Control of the equipment was from the core module, or in cases where only pallets were being used, the controls could be in the main shuttle cabin. With pallet-only missions, the data-recording and control systems were contained in a special pressurized subsystem. Equipment mounted on the pallets could be adjusted or repaired by crew members wearing space suits.

An indication of the potential offered by this system can be gained from the fact that on the first

▶ An artist's conception of how a future base on Mars might look. Work carried out on the International Space Station may one day lead to humans inhabiting Mars, but there is much to be learned about the planet before this goal can even be attempted.

rounding Earth—the magnetosphere—and investigations of the Sun. Space probes, such as the *Solar and Heliospheric Observatory (SOHO)*, for example, are able to make observations of the Sun and relay the information back to Earth.

Mir

One of the most important space laboratories, the Russian *Mir* space station, began construction in 1986 with the launch of the core module consisting of a 43 ft. (13 m) cylinder with six docking ports. Gradually additional modules were added: the *Kvant 1* in 1987, which was almost as large as the core unit and functioned as an astrophysics laboratory; *Kristal*, which was used for biological and material processing in space and was designed with a docking port for the space shuttle; and the final module, *Priroda*, added in 1996 and used to study Earth. The *Mir* space station was a great success, enabling Russia to perform many important scientific investigations and gain much practical experience in the design and operation of space stations.

During *Mir's* final period of operation, cooperative efforts between the United States and Russia resulted in many shuttle missions to *Mir*, providing experience from which the design and construction of the next important space station developed—the International Space Station.

In the late 1990s, *Mir* began to show its age, and it was finally abandoned in June 2000. In March 2001, *Mir* was brought back to Earth, most of the space station burning up in Earth's atmosphere over the Pacific Ocean.

International Space Station

The International Space (ISS) has had a long development history. In the early 1980s, NASA decided to develop a space station as the next logical progression to the space shuttle. Although the space shuttle is highly flexible and reusable, individual missions can last only 16 days, severely limiting the range of activities possible. On a space station, however, a permanent crew can carry out many long-duration activities, such as experiments that need to be repeated many times or that take a long time to complete. NASA decided that this new space station should be an international project and invited Canada and certain European countries to be involved. In 1984, President Reagan gave the go-ahead for the space station, and in 1988, the participating countries and organizations—which by this time included Canada, the European Space Agency, and Japan—signed an intergovernment agreement, and work began on preliminary designs. The ISS would be a laboratory for space experiments as

flight in November 1983, *Spacelab* carried a total of 71 experiments covering a number of different technical and scientific subjects. They included astronomical observations, studies of the Sun's and Earth's environment, experiments on the behavior of materials under low gravity, biological investigations, and Earth-sensing systems. The advantages of having experimental staff on hand were demonstrated by the fact that several of the experiments malfunctioned and had to be repaired.

Uncrewed laboratories

Although the presence of scientists and engineers is essential for many experiments and the ability to make adjustments and repairs is often valuable, many experiments can be carried out using uncrewed space laboratories. Typical examples include the investigation of the magnetic field sur-

▲ TransHab—a proposed layout for a habitation module that could be added to the International Space Station. From top to bottom, there is a room for exercise, health maintenance, and hygiene, followed by rooms for crew quarters, and on the lower level, a galley and wardroom.

well as providing a platform for future space exploration and satellite repair. By 1993, it had become clear that some of the participating countries were finding it difficult to meet the high funding requirements, and so the schedule was revised to allow more time. In addition, with the end of the cold war, Russia was invited to participate in the ISS, bringing its valuable experience gained from the *Mir* space station to bear on the design and construction of the ISS.

Construction of the ISS

Construction of the ISS began on November 20, 1998, with the delivery of the first module, *Zarya*, which is Russian for "sunrise." This Russian module was launched on an unpiloted Proton rocket and was followed by the first U.S. module, *Unity*, which was delivered by the shuttle *Endeavour* in December 1998. *Unity*, which has six connecting ports, is the first of three nodes that will act as junctions and passageways between work and living units. The first of *Unity*'s six ports was joined to the *Zarya* module using the shuttle's robotic arm, Canadarm. The third mission was also carried out by the shuttle and delivered important hardware and supplies for the two existing modules. During the fourth mission, shuttle astronauts prepared the station for the addition of the next Russian module, *Zvezda*, which was launched on a Proton rocket on July 12, 2000. *Zvezda*, which is Russian for "star," provides control facilities for the ISS as well as living quarters for astronauts, enabling the first permanent crew to be transported to the station in November 2000.

One of the most important additions to the ISS, Canadarm 2, was delivered by shuttle in April 2001. This Canadian-built robotic arm is similar to the robotic arm used on the space shuttle itself, but it is capable of manipulating heavier loads and has added features, such as force movement sensors and full joint rotation. This arm is also capable of moving around the exterior of the space station by moving end over end, thus providing access to almost all parts of the ISS. Canadarm 2 is aiding in the construction of the space station and is a useful tool in maintenance, reducing the necessity for hazardous space walks.

NASA hoped to deliver a crew-retrieval vehicle (CRV) to the ISS in 2003, the X-38, which was going to act as an escape vehicle in case of emergency. The vehicle has, however, been scrapped owing to spiralling costs, as has the planned human habitation unit. Currently a Russian Soyuz module is used as an escape vehicle, but this module can carry only three people, thus limiting the number of crew who can work on the ISS. The future development of the ISS is unclear; budget restrictions may possibly limit the frequency of space shuttle flights and thus the pace of construction.

▶ The cosmonaut Yury Usachev sorting food on board the *Zvezda* module of the International Space Station. There is more room on board the ISS than on the earlier space stations, but all the living areas are multifunctional and are practical rather than comfortable.

The International Space Station (ISS) viewed from space shuttle *Endeavour* in April 2001. Visible at the bottom of the image is the space station robotic arm, Canadarm 2, which is essential to the process of adding other modules and solar panels to the structure.

Science on the ISS

The ISS science program is divided into six main areas: life science, Earth science, space science, microgravity science, space product development, and engineering research and technology. Six of the space shuttle modules will be used exclusively for science experiments, while further experiments will be performed outside the station attached, for example, to the external truss structure. Either the results of the science carried out

▼ The space shuttle *Atlantis* docked to the International Space Station (ISS) during a mission to make the ISS ready for the first permanent crew, which arrived on November 2, 2000.

will have direct benefits to humans, such as in the development of new materials with unusual properties and new drugs to treat illnesses, or the scientific discoveries will enhance fundamental scientific knowledge, such as in furthering our understanding of the dark matter that is thought to constitute much of the Universe.

Life science

The life science experiments on the ISS are carried out under a framework provided by NASA's Human Exploration and Development of Space enterprise (HEDS). The policy of HEDS states that the goals of life science on the ISS are to increase knowledge of nature's processes using the space environment, to explore and settle the Solar System, to achieve routine space travel, and to enrich life on Earth through people living and working in space. In response to these stated goals, two research programs have been established: the biomedical research and countermeasures program for human research and the gravitational biology and ecology program for biological research. One of the problems that these programs hope to address is the effect on health of living long term in space; adverse effects include muscle atrophy, bone loss, and alterations to the immune system. Methods for alleviating these problems will be necessary if astronauts are to explore even our closest neighbor, the planet Mars.

Earth science

Understanding weather patterns and climate change are increasingly important in predicting and preparing for extreme forms of weather, such as hurricanes and tornadoes. The ISS Earth science program is designed to increase our knowledge of weather patterns and will also collect data on changing land use and water and atmospheric quality. The orbit of the ISS covers 75 percent of Earth's surface and 95 percent of its population, enabling a broad spread of data to be obtained. Earth-science instruments will also be used to collect data on atmospheric aerosols and the chemistry of the ozone layer.

Space science

NASA lists four main areas of research for the ISS space science program: the structure and evolution of the Universe, exploration of the Solar System, the Sun–Earth connection, and the astronomical search for origins and planetary systems. To carry out this research, a variety of devices will be employed, including the alpha magnetic spectrometer—a particle detector that will be used to look for the dark matter that is believed to extend throughout the Universe and for antimatter. In our own Solar System, ISS scientists will be able to make observations that will help them understand the ways in which space phenomena, such as Sun spots, have an impact on Earth.

Microgravity

Many of the experiments to be carried out on the ISS will take advantage of the very weak gravitational force, known as microgravity, experienced in the region of the space station's orbit. The gravity at the space station is around only one-millionth of that experienced on Earth, and this condition permits much more accurate experiments for testing fundamental physics theories. In addition, these conditions are useful for scientists studying fluid physics, materials science, biotechnology, and combustion physics, where microgravity and a high vacuum may provide better experimental conditions.

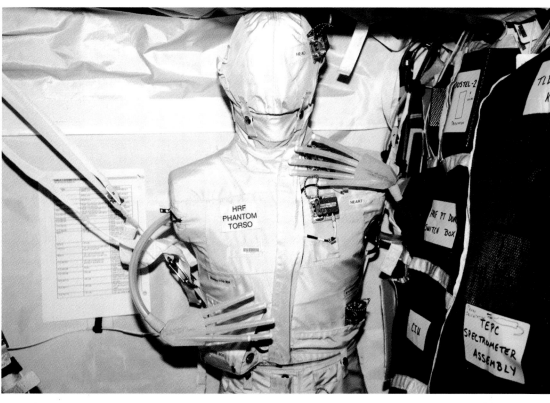

Space product development

One of the most important uses of the ISS is for businesses and academic institutions to develop products that may then be used by industry and ultimately benefit the general public. Until the construction of the ISS, product development in space was severely limited. Now, however, NASA's Space Product Development Office is encouraging industry to take advantage of the unique conditions that the ISS can offer. It is hoped that this program may lead, for example, to the development of new semiconductors, pharmaceuticals, and catalysts used in the petrochemical industry.

Engineering research and technology

Engineering research and technology, or ERT, is divided into three main areas: methods for improving water quality and energy efficiency, development of commercial space communications systems, and new cheaper construction techniques and automated maintenance systems. The result of ERT research will not only improve Earth-based technology but also will provide more efficient and cost-effective techniques for future space travel. The effects on materials of solar radiation, vacuum, and extreme temperatures will be studied on the ISS, and the data gathered will help scientists decide the materials to be used for future space missions.

▲ This dummy, named the phantom torso, is designed to measure the effect of radiation on human internal organs. The data obtained from this torso will be used to devise methods for protecting astronauts from the radiation to which they would be exposed on long-duration space flights.

SEE ALSO: EARTH • ORBIT • ROCKET AND SPACE PROPULSION • SPACE PROBE • SPACE SHUTTLE • SPACE SUIT

Space Suit

◀ Astronauts prepare for the zero gravity in outer space by wearing their space suits underwater. The buoyancy of water provides conditions similar to the weightlessness experienced in space.

The development of the space suit has been a process of building, adding, and reshaping by which astronauts of the shuttle age have become better dressed and more adaptable to the different and demanding tasks currently required of them. The shuttle suit is more than just a protection against the hard vacuum of space or against the heat of the Sun's full glare. It is, as NASA calls it, a self-contained extravehicular mobility unit (EMU) to be used for extravehicular activity (EVA), or space walking.

When NASA's first space suits were used in Project Mercury, the first U.S. manned space-craft, they performed adequately the tasks required of them. There was no room to move around in Mercury, so the astronaut had no real need for flexibility, and it was impossible to leave the craft because there was no hatch. The only reason the astronaut needed a suit was as a backup in case the pressure inside Mercury's cramped cabin failed catastrophically. For that purpose, the one-piece, zip-up, silver suit was adequate.

Each astronaut had to have a suit tailored to fit, but with only seven astronauts in the program this requirement did not cause budget problems. When many more joined the team, however, the cost of tailoring a multimillion dollar suit for each astronaut became prohibitive, so engineers worked to produce a standard suit that could be adapted to anyone. Before their aims could be realized, there remained the need to test in Earth's orbit a suit for all the many EVA operations needed to get ready for the Moon landings, as well as for the lunar flights themselves, which required further advancements in micrometeorite and direct-sunlight protection.

Apollo

The Apollo suit, used for walking and exploring the Moon, was worn over a liquid cooling garment (LCG), which was a one-piece, longsleeved undergarment. It was made from fireproof cloth and carried special plastic tubes through which cooling water would flow, removing excess heat from the surface of the astronaut's body. The suit itself came in several sections. The torso–limb section was made from several different layers of cloth and metallized fabric, each performing different functions. There was a layer to prevent the suit from ballooning when it was pressurized, another layer to prevent stretch, and a third to present a comfortable inner surface next to the LCG. A mechanical system helped move the suit's stiff sections and so eased the load on the astronaut's muscles.

Several connectors were located on the chest: one to bring oxygen in, one to take exhaled carbon dioxide out, one to deliver and remove water in the LCG, one to bring electric leads for communication and biomedical monitoring equipment, and one to take out urine from a small bag in the astronaut's groin. Separated from the torso–limb section, but essential to the Moon-walking astronaut, were pressure gloves, a helmet, and boots. Both of the former were connected to the astronaut by a ring-lock mechanism, which gave a pressure-tight fit. The boots needed a more flexible attachment and were locked by slide fasteners. The astronaut had several visors serving different functions.

None of this equipment was visible, however, because over it all the astronaut wore what NASA called an integrated thermal meteoroid garment (ITMG)—a sort of shaped tent covering everything except a small part of the helmet facing forward. The ITMG was made an integral part of the main suit and comprised 17 separate layers of nylon, beta-cloth, kapton, and beta-marquisette. These materials were all specially designed to make the suit not only flameproof but also a comfortable place to be in while sitting out a fire. The ITMG gave the astronaut that bulky snowman look and provided protection from temperatures as high as 250°F (120°C) in the lunar day and –250°F (–155°C) in a lunar night, from rocks and jagged boulders encountered on the Moon's surface, and from small particles called micrometeoroids streaking through space.

In all, the completed garment weighed around 80 lbs. (36 kg). To this weight would be added another 68 lbs. (31 kg) in the form of a Portable Life Support System (PLSS): a backpack delivering life-giving oxygen, electric power, radio communications, and cooling water to the astronaut. The initial pack allowed Moon excursions to last up to four hours, but improvements to the suit and the backpack extended this period to more than seven hours—a full working day on the Moon.

Space shuttle suit

Although the type of mission flown by NASA's space shuttle is very different from that of an Apollo spacecraft, much of the suit technology developed during the Moon-landing project has been developed for use in shuttle suits. Instead of

▼ The life-support system of a shuttle astronaut carrying out space walks. One main oxygen tank enables the astronaut to work for seven hours, and two secondary tanks can provide a vital 30 minutes of time for the astronaut in an emergency. The sublimator removes water vapor from the suit and cools the temperature to 55°F (13°C).

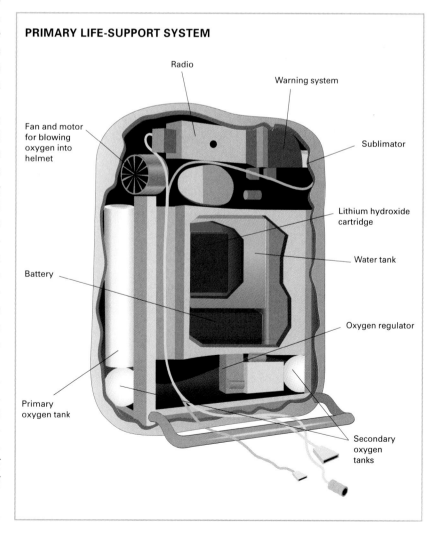

PRIMARY LIFE-SUPPORT SYSTEM

Radio

Warning system

Fan and motor for blowing oxygen into helmet

Sublimator

Lithium hydroxide cartridge

Water tank

Battery

Oxygen regulator

Primary oxygen tank

Secondary oxygen tanks

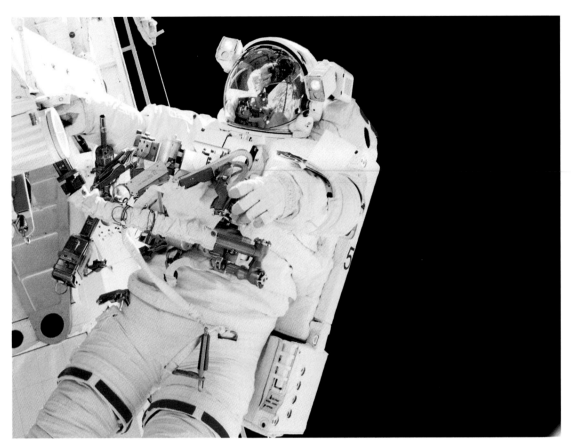

◄ Astronaut Andrew Thomas working in the cargo hold of the space shuttle. He is wearing the Extravehicular Mobility Unit space suit, which incorporates a life-support system in a backpack. Oxygen is blown into the helmet by a fan, and exhaled gases are passed through a lithium hydride scrubber. On the front of the suit is the display and controls module, which lets astronauts control the rate of coolant flow in the suit and the circulation of oxygen, as well as performing diagnostic checks on the state of the life-support system.

making the torso–limb section as a single unit, engineers have built the shuttle suit as a two-piece garment connected at the middle by a large clamp ring. Also, instead of making separate suits for each astronaut (each crew member needing three suits in the case of the Apollo crew), the shuttle suit is assembled according to the available sizes in a standard range of fittings, thus saving both time and money. Each suit is made with a minimum eight-year life expectancy.

Like Apollo suits, the suit has a liquid cooling garment. It also has a small urine container and a drink bag containing 21 ounces of potable water. A biomedical instrumentation subsystem monitors the astronaut's health while in space, and this information is telemetered to the orbiter and to mission control in Houston, Texas. Improvements over the Apollo suit include the use of bearings in the shoulder and arm joints that greatly ease a crew member's movement when bending, leaning, twisting, or crouching.

Balanced to make use of the astronaut's own body mass, the suit is constructed so that the center of gravity of astronaut and suit differs by no more than 4 in. (10 cm), preventing the astronaut from tumbling when pushing against a solid surface.

To move and work outside the shuttle, a PLSS provides oxygen, cooling water, and an emergency pack should the main unit break down. The backpack is bigger than the one used by Moon-walking astronauts and can remove more heat

from the wearer's body. A special control module is attached to the chest by which an astronaut can regulate the flow of oxygen, fix the rate of cooling water, and look for signs of failure, which would require use of the secondary oxygen pack attached to the bottom of the main unit. In all, the suit and backpack weigh around 145 lbs. (66 kg), of which 85 lbs. (38 kg) is the suit alone.

The manned maneuvering unit (MMU), designed to move astronauts around outside the shuttle at the flick of a switch, is housed in the cargo bay and put on only when an astronaut goes outside. The unit consists of a flat pack with supports that protrude from behind on which the astronaut can rest his or her arms and operate small control levers. Twenty-four tiny thrusters, six at each corner, provide jets of nitrogen gas to move the astronaut about. The maneuvering unit weighs around 310 lbs. (140 kg) and is designed to fit snugly around the PLSS.

For use on the International Space Station, the shuttle suit has been updated to include SAFER, a simplified aid for EVA rescue. In the event of becoming adrift, the SAFER, which is attached to the bottom of the PLSS, will permit astronauts to propel themselves back to safety using nitrogen thrusters.

SEE ALSO:	Breathing apparatus • Fiber, synthetic • Oxygen • Protective clothing • Space shuttle • Space station

Space Weapon

◀ The launch vehicles for tests of the hit-to-kill national missile defense are the second and third stages of decommissioned Minuteman II missiles. An exoatmospheric kill vehicle occupies the bulbous shroud atop the missile.

The concept of a space weapon is of a defense system that has the capacity to engage with and destroy hostile objects in the exoatmosphere—that is, beyond the limits of Earth's atmosphere. Existing systems are ground based and can attack only satellites in low Earth orbits; future systems might conceivably center on satellite-borne weapons stations with the capacity to detect and fire on hostile objects at higher altitudes, such as geosynchronous satellites and ballistic missiles.

There are two broad classes of targets at which space weapons might be directed: satellites and ballistic missiles. By far the easier targets are satellites—particularly low-orbiting command,

communications, control, and intelligence (CCCI) satellites in military use. They would be easy to hit because of their stable and predictable orbital paths, yet their destruction would have a devastating impact on the communications and surveillance systems of hostile forces.

In comparison to satellites, intercontinental ballistic missiles (ICBMs) are much more elusive targets. After launch from Earth, ICBMs are designed to escape Earth's atmosphere briefly before falling toward their targets under the pull of gravity, potentially carrying nuclear, chemical, or biological warheads. Given the mode of action and likely warheads of ICBMs, a successful space defense system would have to strike home during

▲ An exoatmospheric kill vehicle in assembly. The infrared/visible sensor it uses to detect its prey is housed in the metal cylinder at the top, and the red-rimmed cones at right and center are acceleration thrusters.

the short period of exoatmospheric flight. Otherwise, destruction of an ICBM could scatter the harmful contents of its warhead in Earth's atmosphere. The task of striking an ICBM during this phase is made even more challenging by its ability to maneuver away from its true ballistic path—the path followed under gravity alone—and by its capacity for splitting into multiple warheads, launching decoys, and jamming the radar detectors set against it.

Satellite targets

In broad terms, military satellites occupy four different categories of orbits: low Earth, elliptical, geosynchronous, and semisynchronous.

Low-Earth orbits. Satellites in low-Earth orbits (LEOs)—between 93 and 1,240 miles (150–2,000 km) above Earth's surface—orbit Earth many times each day. They have detailed views of Earth's surface and can detect weak signals. These characteristics make LEO satellites ideally suited to photoreconnaissance, ocean surveillance, and electronic intelligence—all essential functions in time of war and in preparation for war.

Elliptical orbits. Satellites in elliptical orbits swoop from altitudes of a few hundreds of miles at their nadirs (lowest points) to altitudes around 25,000 miles (40,000 km) at their zeniths (highest points). Satellites in elliptical orbits move slower at higher altitudes, with the result that they can remain visible over a specific arena for up to 8 hours out of 12, making them useful for strategic surveillance of specific regions.

Geosynchronous and semisynchronous orbits. The highest orbits—at altitudes of 22,350 miles (36,000 km)—are occupied by geosynchronous satellites. At that altitude, a satellite stationed over the equator remains above a fixed point on Earth's surface at all times, making it an ideal relay post for civilian and military communications. Semisynchronous satellites orbit at an altitude of 12,500 miles (20,000 km), and they complete one orbit every 12 hours.

Antisatellite weapons

Antisatellite weapons, or ASATs, have been in existence since the late 1960s. In 1968, the Soviet military introduced a coorbital interceptor capable of attacking low-Earth-orbit intelligence satellites. It weighs more than 4,400 lbs. (2,000 kg) and is launched into an orbit similar to that of its target on a modified SS–9 liquid-fueled ICBM. Interception occurs once the antisatellite weapon has completed one or two trips around Earth, at a point where its orbit crosses that of the target. An onboard homing device, which is either an active radar or a passive infrared–visible sensor, generates commands that enable it to close with the target before exploding in a destructive swarm of pellets. The problem with this weapon—as with any other space weapon—is the amount of space debris generated by its deployment and the potential of that debris to ultimately strike friendly satellites or space missions.

The U.S. ASAT system is based on a two-stage rocket small enough to be carried to high altitude by an adapted F-15 fighter. The homing vehicle is fired in the direction of the target and uses eight infrared telescopes that instruct an onboard control processor. The processor has control over small thrusters that maneuver the missile into the path of the target. The homing vehicle itself is small—33 lbs. (15 kg) in weight and 12 in. (30 cm) in diameter. It is not explosive and relies simply on the force of its collision to disable targets. The system was successfully tested during 1984, and two squadrons of specially equipped F-15s have been assigned as launchers for it. In principle, any F-15, including carrier-based aircraft, could be deployed with the weapon, giving the United States the ability to destroy all hostile satellites in low or elliptical orbits within hours.

HEO weapons

In principle, the technology to destroy satellites in high-Earth orbits (HEOs) already exists: the same powerful launch vehicles that routinely deploy satellites in geosynchronous orbit could also send destructive charges to the same altitudes. However, missile launches to satellites at altitudes greater than around 2,000 miles (3,200 km) are expensive and uncertain, and they would not be practical for mass deployment.

One possible approach to the destruction of HEO satellites would be the use of space mines—small satellites carrying an explosive charges that would accompany their potential victims for weeks or months to ensure adequate proximity before being fired by remote command. An alternative would be a laser system that could be based on the ground, in space, or in the air. Because satellites are easy to track over prolonged periods, it would be possible to use a low-powered laser to bore into its target for many minutes until its circuitry was rendered unserviceable.

Defense against ballistic missiles

One of the chief goals of defense researchers is the development of systems that can destroy ballistic missiles in flight. Such a system would constitute an effective defense against nuclear strikes, or indeed against chemical or biological attacks using ballistic missiles as delivery systems.

The two broad classes of ballistic missiles are ICBMs and SLBMs. ICBMs are designed for launch from land-based silos to targets on distant continents, and their projected flight times are typically 25 to 30 minutes. SLBMs (submarine-launched ballistic missiles) are designed for launch at sea, as close as possible to the shore of the target nation. The projected flight times of SLBMs are therefore much shorter than those of ICBMs—typically around 8 minutes.

EXOATMOSPHERIC KILL VEHICLE

The exoatmospheric kill vehicle (EKV) is a key part of the ground-based interceptor of the national missile defense (NMD), an antiballistic missile system currently under development by the U.S. Ballistic Missiles Defense Organization (BMDO). The EKV is designed to knock out its targets by the force of impact alone.

The onboard systems of the EKV include an infrared/visible sensor that detects the target at close range and a computer that calculates its course to impact. Thrusters use a liquid bipropellant to provide the hard acceleration necessary for fatal impact with the target.

The EKV is the payload of a ground-based interceptor that launches it into space. For the purposes of initial tests, the launch vehicle of the interceptor is formed by the second and third stages of retired Minuteman II missiles, although a specially built booster is planned.

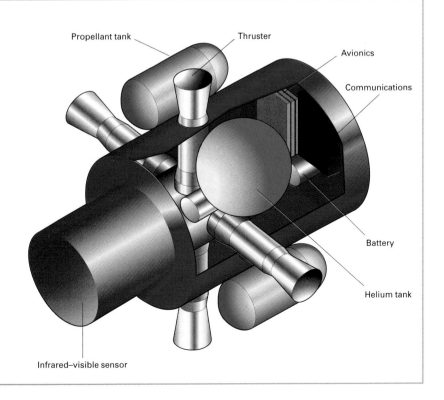

Propellant tank · Thruster · Avionics · Communications · Battery · Helium tank · Infrared–visible sensor

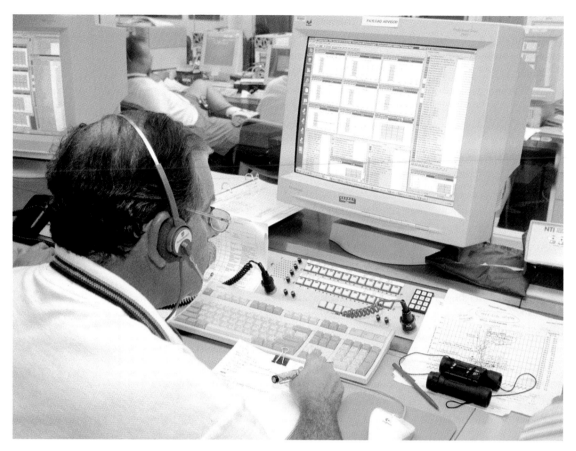

◀ Monitoring the payload during a test launch of a national missile defense system rocket. Scientists are working on a weapon that would physically knock out an enemy missile rather than a warhead that might miss its target and cause unintentional collateral damage to communities on the ground.

Both types of ballistic missiles are at their most vulnerable to detection and attack during the initial boost phase of their flight. That phase begins when the silo doors open, spewing forth hot gases from the missile's first-stage rocket motor. Those gases are clearly visible to any satellite-borne infrared detector that has a view of the silo. As the missile rises, the first-stage booster becomes spent and falls away to let a second stage and usually a third stage take over the boost.

For the present generation of ballistic missiles, this boost phase lasts 3 to 5 minutes, and it is critical for any anti-BM system to lock onto a target ballistic missile during this phase. Once the final booster cuts out, a ballistic missile becomes much less visible to IR sensors. The other means of detecting hostile ballistic missiles is by ground-based early-warning radar stations, which can be confounded by decoy projectiles put out by the ballistic missile during the later stages of its trajectory, adding to the need for early detection.

If an anti-BM system fails to eliminate a target during the boost stage, the only remaining option is to attack during the three remaining phases of the missile's journey. After the booster has lifted the payload clear of the atmosphere and fallen away, the warheads travel on toward their targets on a bus that dispenses them in a 5- to 10-minute bussing phase. Each bus can carry several warheads, as well as a number of decoys, antiradar chaff, and infrared-generating aerosols. As these elements break away from the bus during the bussing phase, the number of targets increases and the targets also become harder to spot, making a successful defense practically impossible.

By the time the bus had dropped its load and the midcourse phase of the attack had begun, the warheads would appear as a threat cloud rather than as individual targets right through the midcourse phase until the terminal phase, when the warheads would reenter the atmosphere only seconds away from the culminating strike. At reentry, the friction of the atmosphere would tear the decoys away from the warhead reentry vehicles, but by then it would be almost too late to target and destroy them.

▼ This control room is the Battle Management/ Command, Control, and Communications (BM/C3) center for the national missile defense (NMD) system. This center receives data from various early-warning systems and will issue launch commands to NMD interceptors if a hostile launch is detected.

Anti-BM weapons systems

Once a ballistic missile has been detected, it must be intercepted in space. Two types of weapons could conceivably do so: orbital weapons that remain permanently stationed in space or "pop-up" missile weapons that are launched when the launch of a hostile ballistic missile is detected. The pop-up system would require launches from submarines stationed as close to the hostile missile silos as possible.

X-ray beams. One of the first anti-BM systems considered by the U.S. military was to use powerful bursts of X rays to destroy their targets. The weapon of such a system was to be carried into space on an interceptor SLBM, where its nuclear warhead would detonate. In a radiation-amplifying process similar to the one that produces laser light, X rays from the explosion would be focused into a beam by a cylindrical array of thin metal fibers fixed around the warhead. Given the intensity of the radiation, this array would survive for only a tiny fraction of a second before disintegrating, and much of the energy of the nuclear explosion would be lost. One of the factors in the decision to abandon this project was doubt that the pulse of directed X rays would be sufficiently strong to knock out a target.

Lasers and particle beams. Another type of weapons system that has been considered for use against ballistic weapons would use high-power beams—typically around 25 MW—to destroy the targets. The beams could be generated by chemical excimer lasers based on hydrogen fluoride or they could be particle beams.

The simplest method of using such weapons would be to have the equipment necessary to generate the beams mounted on a network of low-Earth-orbit satellites. This method would require around six times as many orbiting weapons as are actually needed in a given attack, since LEO satellites spend the majority of their time over the horizon from any given arena and only a small number would be in useful positions when needed. It has been estimated that such a system would require at least 300 satellite-borne weapons to counter a full enemy launch.

As an alternative, the laser beams of such a system could be generated on the ground in home territory and directed toward their targets by a battle station in geosynchronous orbit. This Strategic Defense Initiative (SDI)—popularly known as Star Wars—could conceivably function using banks of 1,000 MW excimer lasers, but a particle beam would be defeated by Earth's atmosphere. On receiving a launch warning, the ground-based lasers would be fired at the geosynchronous battle station mirror; that mirror would then direct the laser beams onto fighting mirrors in low-Earth orbit. The fighting mirrors, which would be able to give an accurate resolution of the target, would redirect the incoming laser beams and concentrate them on the target missiles.

All the components of this weapon system—lasers, sensors, mirrors, and command computers—are technically possible. However the scale and projected cost of the project were considered disproportionate to the threat of a large strike.

National missile defense

Since the end of the Cold War in the late 1980s, the threat of a full-scale nuclear attack launched between superpowers has diminished greatly. Meanwhile, the threat of a small-scale nuclear, biological, or chemical attack launched on a superpower by a smaller "rogue state" has become more significant. In response to the changing threat, the approach to defense against ballistic missiles has modified, the current emphasis being on developing relatively low-cost systems capable of dealing with small-scale missile launches.

In the United States, the Ballistic Missile Defense Organization (BMDO) of the Department of Defense is developing a national missile defense (NMD) system that knocks out its targets simply by colliding with them. This approach—if successful—would reduce costs by obviating the need for the high-technology weapons associated with earlier plans for defense against ballistic missiles.

Detection. The detection system of the NMD comprises various planned and existing elements that detect hostile missiles at different stages of their trajectories. The earliest warning of any

▼ An airborne laser system is one prospect for countering Scud-type ballistic missiles launched from the ground. The lasers would be mounted on Boeing 747-400 aircraft and powered by a chemical reaction, which would overcome the need to generate large quantities of electrical power necessary to hit a target.

launch will be traced by infrared sensors on one of a series of satellites. This role would currently go to the existing defense support program (DSP) satellites but will ultimately be performed by the planned high-altitude space-based infrared system, dubbed SBIRS (High).

Midcourse, the progress of an incoming missile will be tracked by a planned series of infrared sensors on low-altitude satellites—the SBIRS (Low). Until that system is fully operational, its function will be performed by upgrades to the existing early-warning radar stations situated in various locations in the Northern Hemisphere.

Close to the planned interception site, tracking is taken up by a high-definition radar system, called X-band radar (XBR). The high-frequency

◀ The Beale Pave Paws early-warning radar station in California. In such radars, fixed arrays of radio-transmitting elements are made to act as if they were movable by modifying the phases of the signal feeds to the separate elements.

FACT FILE

- *A successful interception of a large-scale strike comprising 5,000 nuclear warheads might cause 20 percent of the incoming missiles to disintegrate without exploding. The debris from such a disintegration would release enough radioactive material to deliver the equivalent of a lethal human dose for every 269 sq. ft. (25 m²) of the Northern Hemisphere.*

- *One projected space weapon considered by the United States is a space-based rail gun. Projectiles would be driven by electromagnetic forces at rates of 60 shots a second and travel 625 miles (1,000 km) at a speed of 19 miles per second (30 km/s).*

- *An airborne laser system could prove a fast and effective method of knocking out missiles, with a fleet of airplanes mounting a 24-hour patrol close to enemy territory. Onboard monitoring systems can detect a rocket booster before it shuts off, with the result that the warhead may even fall back onto the enemy rather than the target.*

- *SDI scientists have calculated that it may be economic to use the minerals and metals available in asteroids to build space weapon equipment. Many of the 1,000 to 2,000 asteroids closest to Earth are rich in iron and nickel, and the energy needed to mine and process those metals in space could be as little as 1 percent of that needed to lift the equivalent materials into space.*

radar and advanced signal processing of XBR will enable it to make precise calculations of the courses of missiles, as well as making it possible to assess the damage potential of its warheads and to discriminate individual closely spaced multiple warheads from decoys and debris.

Command, control, and communications. Data from the various detection systems converge at a center called Battle Management/Command, Control, and Communications (BM/C3). This center issues commands to launch interceptors and provides them with course information on the way to the interception site.

Ground-based interceptor. On command from BM/C3, the interceptor launches on a two-stage payload launch vehicle (PLV) similar to that of an ICBM. The launch command is carried by a weapons support system, or WSS, which also maintains the environment of the interceptor prior to launch. In flight, guidance commands are transmitted via an in-flight interceptor communications system, or IFICS. On approaching the interception site, the PLV releases the exoatmospheric kill vehicle (EKV), which then proceeds under its own propulsion using guidance from a homing system connected to its onboard infrared/visible-wavelength sensors. The force of impact is sufficient to destroy its target.

SEE ALSO: Missile • Satellite, artificial • Space shuttle

Special Effects

The term *special effects* covers many of the techniques used in the production of cinematic illusions. It was introduced by an effects expert, Louis Witts, in 1926 on the Hollywood film *What Price Glory?* Special effects can be divided into two main categories—visual or optical effects and physical or mechanical effects. Visual effects involve mainly photographic processes, and physical effects consist of things such as explosions, automobile crashes, the destruction of buildings, and so on.

History

Trick photography is as old as the cinema itself. In fact, most of the early movies used trick photographic techniques. The cinema, for at least a decade after its beginning in 1895, was considered solely as a novelty, and the moviemakers of that era concentrated on producing motion pictures that were as technically inventive as possible. In doing so, they pioneered many of the techniques that are still in use today. Innovators in the field include Britain's G. A. Smith, who took out a patent for a double-exposure technique in 1897, and Robert William Paul, who, also in 1897, built in London what was probably Europe's first motion picture studio.

The name most associated with early trick movies is that of the Frenchman Georges Méliès, a former stage magician. He was so impressed by the first demonstration of moving pictures projected onto a screen—given by the Lumière brothers in Paris in 1895—that he decided to start making his own movies. He employed many of the techniques used by stage magicians as well as pioneering motion picture techniques such as jump cuts, fast and slow motion, dissolves, fades, double exposure, and multiple exposure. The U.S. pioneer Edwin S. Porter was greatly influenced by Méliès and produced many trick movies for the Edison Company. In 1903 he made *The Great Train Robbery*, one of the first motion pictures to tell a story, and so, ironically, Porter was responsible for bringing the era of the pure trick movie to an end. Trick effects continued to be used in silent movies but only to complement the story, rarely for their own sake. In fact, in the 1920s, movie audiences were resentful whenever they detected any use of special effects, preferring to think that the spectacular action they saw on the screen was all real (and owing to the dangerous risks that stuntmen took in those days, such as actually crashing aircraft into buildings, it often was real). For many years the use of models, dou-

▲ The special effects director of the film *Starship Trooper* works on a model of a spacecraft. Models are often used to represent large structures that would be difficult to re-create at full scale. They can also be replicated easily if the script calls for explosions or collisions.

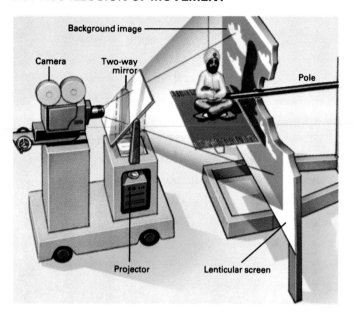

ZOPTICS ILLUSION OF MOVEMENT

Background image

Camera

Two-way mirror

Pole

Projector

Lenticular screen

▲ With front projection, the stationary actor is made to appear to soar by zooming the camera and background projector simultaneously (below)—a technique known as zoptics.

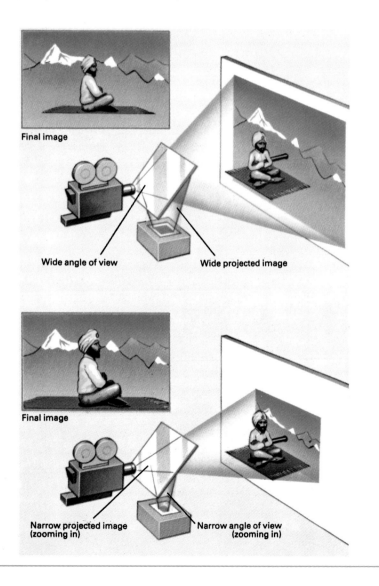

Final image

Wide angle of view

Wide projected image

Final image

Narrow projected image (zooming in)

Narrow angle of view (zooming in)

ble exposures, and so on was considered by audiences to be cheating, and it was not until fantasy and science fiction movies became popular in the 1930s that the blatant use of special effects became acceptable again.

Trick photography

The basic techniques of trick photography make use of the nature of movie film, in which each frame lasts for only a fraction of a second on the screen and the persistence of vision of the human eye gives the impression of continuous movement. In the jump cut, for example, the camera is stopped and some change is made to the scene being photographed—an actor may move out of view, or a fake prop may be substituted for a real one. If well done and if the camera is not moved or the lighting changed, the eye will be fooled into believing that the action is continuous. Dissolves and fades are now carried out in the laboratory, but in the early days, they were carried out in the camera. One scene is faded out by reducing the exposure, the film is wound back, and the second scene is faded in by increasing its exposure from zero—the result is a dissolve.

Fast motion is achieved by running the film through the camera slower than normal, and slow motion is achieved by running it faster. A film shot at 12 frames per second, when projected at 24 frames per second, will be running at twice the shooting speed. True high-speed photography requires specially designed cameras and shutters and gives very slowed down movements.

Other tricks can make use of the fact that a camera can make both near and distant objects appear in sharp focus simply by using a small lens aperture. A model dinosaur placed close to the camera, for example, can appear much larger than a human comparatively far away.

Optical effects

Many of the optical effects used in the making of motion pictures were first invented by still photographers in the 19th century. One such technique is the glass shot, which is a painting on a sheet of glass positioned in front of the camera in such a way that it blends in with the real scene that the camera is photographing. Another early technique is the matte shot, one of the simplest ways of combining two image components on the same frame of film to create the illusion that they are part of the same scene. It entails exposing only a portion of each frame of film, while the unwanted part of the scene is obscured by a card cut to the required shape and placed in front of the camera lens. The card is called the matte. The film is then wound back and a new scene is filmed, this time with the previously exposed portion of each frame obscured by another card—the countermatte. The result is a double exposure. Silent-movie-camera operators had a matte box attached to the front of their cameras. The box contained a number of differently shaped mattes with which they achieved many of the optical effects that are today produced in the film laboratory with an optical printer or a computer.

A variation of the matte shot is one that makes use of a matte painting. After filming a scene with the required portion matted out, the partly exposed film is transferred to another camera heavily weighted to prevent vibration, and positioned in front of a sheet of black glass. An artist then paints onto the glass the desired image component that is to be added to the previously photographed scene (usually matte paintings are of background scenery, such as mountain ranges or city skylines). The painting is then filmed, with the black unpainted section of the glass acting as a countermatte.

A later development of the matte shot is the traveling matte, which is one that moves or changes its shape with each proceeding frame of film, for example when the foreground action is to be shown in movement across a moving background. One way to achieve this effect is to produce each individual matte and countermatte by hand, a process similar to cartoon animation and just as time-consuming. This method was used in the making of *2001: A Space Odyssey*, but a number of quicker and cheaper photographic processes have been introduced, most of which make use of the various light-reacting layers of color film to create automatic mattes. One such process is called the blue-backing system, in which the foreground action is lit with normal white light and is photographed on regular color negative film against a blue background, either a blue-painted backcloth or a translucent blue screen lit from behind. The color and the lighting level of the backing are such that they produce an exposure on only the blue-sensitive layer of the color negative to a density greater than that of any object in the foreground. A series of laboratory printing operations involving black-and-white litho film exposed through color filters is then carried out to produce a foreground matte with an opaque area corresponding exactly to the image of the blue backing recorded on the color negative. From this a countermatte can be made in which the blue backing is shown as clear film with an opaque silhouette of the foreground

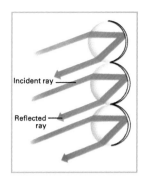

▲ With the front projection method, the background is projected onto a screen consisting of millions of glass beads in the same line of sight as that of the camera. Each bead reflects light in the direction of the projected beam.

▼ A model of a city in Kyoto, Japan, used for filming scenes that would be difficult to achieve using location shots.

action. The two image components are then combined, using the mattes, onto a duplicate negative in an optical printer.

Another method of combining separately filmed foreground and background action is called rear, or back, projection whereby the actors stand in front of a translucent screen onto which background action is projected from behind. The projector and the camera are synchronized—as one frame of the background action is being projected, the shutter of the camera is opening simultaneously. A later variation of this technique is front projection, in which the background is projected onto a particular type of screen in the same line of sight as that of the camera. Using this method, a lightly silvered mirror at 45 degrees placed just in front of the camera lens reflects the image from the projector onto the screen. Because the projector and the camera are in the same line of sight, no shadows are visible around the edges of the actors, and their bodies mask their shadows exactly. The reflective material on the screen consists of millions of tiny glass beads, each of which acts as an optically perfect reflector. This system gives extremely high reflectivity in the direction of the projected beam, so a comparatively low intensity beam can be used.

Miniatures, or models, are traditionally included in the optical effects category. Miniature buildings or whole cities are often used in sequences in which widespread destruction is depicted. War movies often make use of miniature ships and airplanes, which can be up to 50 ft. (15 m) long. One particularly fine example of the use of miniatures is in the 1997 film *Titanic*, where, in the opening section, documentary footage of the sunken wreck is interspersed with footage taken using miniatures. The two types of footage are seamlessly edited together creating the impression that all the footage has been filmed using deep-sea submersibles. *Titanic* also uses a variety of scale models to recreate the dramatic scenes of the ship sinking.

Mechanical effects

Mechanical effects range from making a bullet hole appear in a wall to the blowing up of a whole building. The special effects expert has to be prepared to create whatever effects the scriptwriter includes in the screenplay. Special effects mostly involve scenes of violence and destruction, such as simulated injuries, fires, and explosions. Injuries include bullet, knife, and spear wounds. Bullet hits are achieved by the actor wearing, beneath his or her clothes, a small explosive charge to which is often attached a plastic bag containing artificial blood. When the charge is detonated, either by the actor or by radio control, it blows a

▲ Action movies make considerable use of mechanical special effects, such as car crashes and explosions. In this instance, explosive experts are fixing a charge to the underside of the van to make it tip over and explode.

small hole in the clothing, as well as releasing the blood, creating the illusion that the actor has been shot. Stabbings are simulated by the use of knives made of resin and coated with metallic paint. Artificial blood, contained in the handle, can be squeezed out through small vents in the blade.

In the film *Indiana Jones and the Raiders of the Lost Ark*, the film climaxes with a scene in which the head of the character Belloq explodes, an SS man's face melts to the bone, and another officer's head shrinks. To make these horrific deaths seem real, plaster casts were made of the men's faces in their screaming positions and life masks made. Belloq's exploding head was made of plaster, incorporating a few blood bags, compressed air, a couple of shotgun cartridges, and some primer cord—an explosive flex that requires detonation. The officer's shrinking head was accomplished by means of a vacuum and a series of hand-operated levers inside the model head. To show the melting of the SS man's head, his face and head were built out of successive layers of colored gelatin, which was then melted down in a controlled way. The melting was photographed as a time lapse at less than a frame per second.

Full-scale explosions and fires represent the more spectacular work of the special effects people, who must be fully qualified explosive experts. In Hollywood, they are required to take a state-approved course in explosives and pass an examination. Fire effects can be just as dangerous, especially if they involve the simulation of people burning. The safest method of achieving the lat-ter effect involves the use of a small gas burner that an actor can wear under fireproofed clothing. When the gas is ignited, it appears that a portion of the actor's clothing is alight, but the flames will vanish as soon as the supply of gas is switched off. Another method is for a stunt man or woman to wear protective clothing that has been smeared with alcohol. When ignited, the burning alcohol creates a vapor barrier between the flames and the clothing. For a stunt expert to be completely enveloped in flames, he or she must wear a heavily insulated suit that contains its own air supply.

To create the illusion that buildings are on fire, effects people have developed a portable unit consisting of a motor and a modified pump capable of pumping kerosene from ground level to burners situated up to 100 ft. (30 m) above the unit. A number of burners, placed at open windows and on the roof, can turn a building into a raging inferno when the unit is activated, while the building actually remains untouched. Effects experts prefer to use kerosene for fire scenes because it is cheaper than oil or gasoline and there is less likelihood of any spilled fuel igniting.

Model animation

Model animation is a specialized form of special effects. Like most effects techniques, it dates back to the earliest days of movie production. One of the first motion pictures to feature the process was made in 1897 by the Vitagraph company in the United States. Called *Humpty Dumpty Circus*, it used animated wooden toy animals. In 1907,

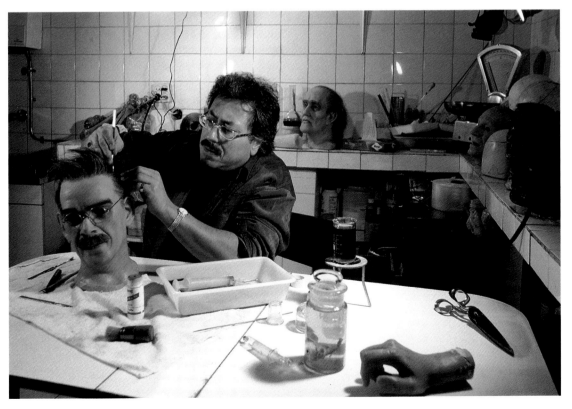

◀ This special effects artist puts the finishing touches to a convincingly realistic head. Such artists are able to create models of human and animal parts that are so like the real thing that the film audience is unable to detect the deception.

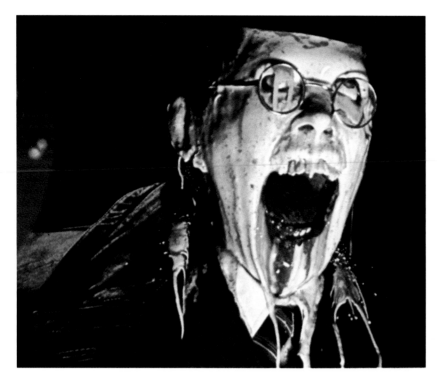

the film pioneer Edwin S. Porter spent 12 hours a day for a week animating seven small teddy bears. The resulting movie, called *The Teddy Bears*, lasted only a few minutes but was a big success at the time. Model animation is achieved through stop-motion photography, which involves positioning the model by hand for each separate frame of film. For one second of movement on the screen, the model must be adjusted and photographed 24 times (film cameras and projectors run at 24 frames per second). The most famous name in the field is that of Willis H. O'Brien, who, in movies such as *The Lost World* and *King Kong*, was the first to combine model animation with live action. This effect is mostly achieved by a system called miniature projection, a smaller version of rear projection. In miniature screen work, a scaled set containing the models is set up in front of the screen, and then a single frame of the live action is projected onto the screen as the models are photographed. The models are then adjusted, the next frame of the live action appears on the screen behind them, and the two image components are again photographed together. When skillfully executed, both models and live action integrate perfectly in the completed film.

Computer-generated images

Techniques for creating computer-generated images (CGI) are increasingly used to produce not only sophisticated animation but also convincing and complex special effects. The film *Gladiator*, for example, has made extensive use of CGI for crowd replication, in which an image of a small number of people is multiplied on computer

▲ At the end of the film *Indiana Jones and the Raiders of the Lost Ark*, the head of SS officer Toht appears to melt. This effect was achieved by first creating a model of Toht's head made up of layers of gelatin and then melting the head in a controlled way.

to create the effect of a large crowd. These crowds were then positioned within an impressive panorama of the coliseum in Rome. Similarly, the film *Titanic* used CGI to create crowds of people on board the ship. Some scenes of people jumping off the ship were also computer generated, avoiding the necessity for a large number of dangerous stunts. During one scene that would have been particularly dangerous for the actors, two stunt people ran along a corridor in the ship followed by a torrent of water. The actors were also filmed running along this corridor without the water, and their heads were then digitally removed and placed on the bodies of the stunt people. In the opening scenes of *Titanic*, the footage of the wreck taken using miniatures was given greater authenticity by the addition of computer-animated fish. Small particles were also added to the water and were made to appear as if they were reflecting the light of the submarines, just as in the documentary footage. These additions enabled the underwater shots to be merged with the documentary footage without the viewer being aware of the difference.

Virtual camera movement

A technique that has become common in films and commercials is that in which an image suddenly appears frozen while the camera seems to move around it. This effect, called Timetrack, was invented by a U.S. cinematographer, Dayton Taylor, and employs a whole series of cameras placed next to each other and surrounding the subject to be filmed. The camera shutters are linked in such a way that their opening and closing can be coordinated to operate at any order and speed required. If the shutters all open and close at the same time, a series of images is provided of the subject at a particular instant. If these images are then run together, as in a conventional film, the viewer has the impression of moving around the subject as if it were frozen in time. This technique was used together with other special effects to create some remarkable scenes in the film *The Matrix*, in which the camera appears to move around the actor, who also appears to be moving in slow motion. In this case, the series of cameras fire sequentially rather than all at the same time. Using Timetrack, it is possible to give the impression of the subject moving forward or backward or being frozen in time, or any combination of these, while at the same time the virtual camera pans smoothly around the subject.

SEE ALSO: ANIMATION • COMPUTER GRAPHICS • EXPLOSIVE • MOVIE CAMERA • MOVIE PRODUCTION • STAGE EFFECT

Spectacles

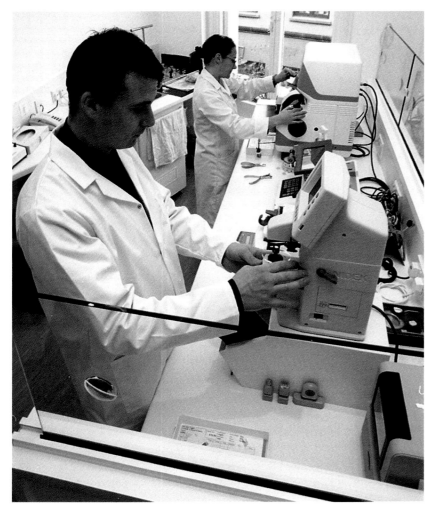

It is not known with certainty who invented spectacles, or glasses, and it was not until the end of the 13th century that any documentary reference to them was found. Roger Bacon, an English monk, and an Italian, Alessandro di Spina, are among the many who claimed to have invented glasses. The first portrait of a man wearing glasses was a 1352 fresco by Tommaso da Modena.

By the 15th century, glassmaking was well established in Europe, and when the printing press was invented, there was an upsurge in demand for spectacles. At first, only convex lenses were made, which would have been useful for hypermetropia (farsightedness) and presbyopia (farsightedness caused by loss of accommodation in the eye) but not myopia (nearsightedness). Glasses with concave lenses to correct myopia were not made until the beginning of the 16th century; Pope Leo X was one of the first to wear them.

Frame materials

The very earliest glasses had lenses mounted in heavy circular frames of copper, lead, or wood. Later, leather, bone, and horn were used, and by the early 17th century, light frames of steel were being manufactured. In the 18th century, tortoise shell joined the list of frame materials, and glasses assumed the basic design we know today.

▲ The wait for a new pair of glasses has been largely eliminated by in-store workshops. Blank lenses can be machined to the correct shape and prescription using computer-controlled tools and fitted to the frames in under an hour.

Modern glasses frames are generally made of metal or plastic. The most commonly used plastics are cellulose acetate and the acrylic resins, which are thermoplastics, that is, they soften on heating and harden again when cooled. Cellulose acetate is not flammable, can be worked easily, and is a fairly long-lasting material.

Cellulose nitrate was once common and, being rigid, kept its shape well, but it was extremely flammable. Acrylic resins such as Plexiglas are not affected by body acids and can be brilliantly colored but are more difficult to manipulate. Optyl, developed in Austria after World War II, is a thermosetting polymer that enables frames to be molded at low unit cost from liquid ingredients.

One of the most popular metal framing materials is rolled gold, which consists of a core made of a base metal, such as brass, covered with a cladding of gold. Stainless steel, anodized aluminum, nickel, silver, and gold-plated and rhodium-plated metals are also used.

Titanium frames are light, thin, flexible, and strong and can be coated to give a variety of attractive effects. Earlier types of rimless glasses were three-piece mounts—a separate bridge and a pair of sides attached at holes drilled in the lenses. These have been largely superseded by brow-bar glasses, which have lenses attached to the brow bar either by screws, spring clips, or nylon string tightened in a groove that runs around the lower edge of the lens.

Cellulose acetate for the frames of glasses is prepared by stacking thin sheets of differently colored cellulose acetate, applying a solvent and a plasticizer, and subjecting the stack to hydraulic pressure to produce a homogeneous mass. This compacted pile of sheets is then turned over on its side and sliced into sheets 0.12 to 0.24 in. (3–6 mm) thick. The direction of the cut is at right angles to the plane of the original sheet, giving rise to the characteristic mottling of the material (often called sliced acetate).

Extruded cellulose acetate is much harder than sliced acetate; it has a longer life and accepts a finer polish. It is made by heating cellulose acetate granules with a plasticizer in a cylinder and forcing the plastic under high pressure through a slot whose dimensions determine the size of the sheet. Color effects are produced by squeezing materials of different colors into the slot.

Frame construction

Frames today are nearly all mass produced, and about 100 separate operations are carried out on each one. The front of plastic frames are made on a routing machine. Slabs of material are bolted to formers, and the eyepiece holes are routed out by small vertical milling tools. Grooves are then cut in the rims to accept the lenses. The bridge is formed by shaping the frame after it has been softened by heating. The sidepieces are produced by injection or compression molding, and the reinforcing wires inserted either during molding or subsequently with heating. Assembly is on a specially designed jig, the metal joints being pinned right through or pressed in under heat.

Metal frames are usually worked by coining, striking, crimping, and bending. These operations cause the metal to become very hard, and to bring it back to a workable condition, it has to be annealed. In this operation, the frames are coated with a protective solution and heated to a high temperature in an electric furnace. The frames are removed, cooled in water, and cleaned. The parts are assembled by electric spot welding, and finally, plastic nose pads and side tips are added. Plating of metal frames is an elaborate, multibath computer-controlled process that gives a variety of finishes, including pastels and primary colors.

Lenses

The glass normally used for lenses is spectacle crown, which has a refractive index (a measure of the ability of an optical material to bend light) of 1.523, although a glass has been developed with a refractive index of 1.70, which is lighter and thinner than crown glass of the same power. For extreme myopia, dense flint glass, with a high refractive index of 1.69, can be coated with a film of magnesium fluoride to remove reflections. For large frames, lenses are often made of acrylic plastics, which are much lighter than glass. Glass and plastics for lenses must be homogeneous, free of striae (linear faults), bubbles, milkiness, or strain. The power of ophthalmic lenses is expressed in diopters—the reciprocal of the focal length in meters.

Lenses are produced in meniscus (one surface convex, the other concave), spherical, or toric form. Toric lenses have surfaces with a different curvature in one plane from that in a plane at right angles; they are used to correct astigmatism, which is caused by uneven curvature of the surface of the eye. Simple spherical lenses are used to correct nearsightedness and farsightedness. Tinted lenses are produced by coloring the glass batch or by vacuum coating the finished lenses with metal oxides. Multilayer antireflection coat-

ing enhances visibility, renders lenses almost invisible, and is advantageous for driving. Photochromatic glass, which darkens or lightens according to the light intensity, is made by including silver halides in the glass composition. Safety glasses for industrial wear are made of laminated glass, toughened glass, or shatter-resistant plastics.

The advantages of plastic lenses, namely lightness and safety, have led to widespread use. Polymethyl methacrylate (Plexiglas) has good optical quality but low resistance to surface abrasion. CR39 (Columbia Resin formula 39) has better resistance to abrasion, but hard surface coatings have been developed to obviate scratching. Such coatings have made the use of polycarbonate, which scratches readily, more practical—it is used in impact-resistant glasses.

Multifocal lenses are commonly used where more than one vision defect has to be corrected. Bifocal lenses have an upper section for distant vision and a smaller, lower section for near vision or reading. There are two types of bifocal lenses, one-piece bifocals and fused bifocals. The former, invented about the beginning of the 20th century, are made by polishing two differently shaped surfaces onto one side of the lens. With fused bifocals, a small spherical indentation is polished onto the outer convex surface of the main lens to accept a small lens that will form the reading section of the finished bifocal. The small lens is placed in position and the assembly heated until the two sections fuse together. To provide the higher power needed for reading, the small reading lens is made of glass with a higher refractive index than the main lens. Varifocal lenses are made so that they blend the distance, middle-vision, and near-vision portions of the lens and dispense with the dividing lines between segments.

◀ Glasses became a fashion accessory when the performer Elton John started commissioning special frames to match his stage outfits. The advent of new materials has led to a wide variety of styles being made available to everyone—even those with perfect eyesight.

SEE ALSO: BINOCULARS • CONTACT LENS • EYE • GLASS • LENS • LIGHT AND OPTICS • OPHTHALMOSCOPE • OPTOMETRY

Spectroscopy

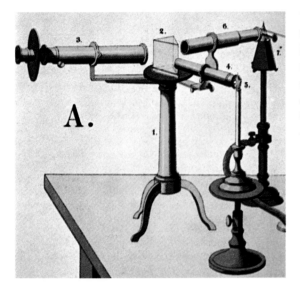

◀ A 19th-century spectroscope viewing a burner spectrum. The nearer telescope contains a scale, illuminated by a candle, which is reflected into the field of view by the prism.

Spectroscopy is the analysis of light, or other forms of radiation, in terms of its spectrum. Its importance lies in the fact that all materials have a characteristic signature of wavelengths in the spectrum. In spectrochemical analysis, for example, the materials present in a given sample can be determined, and in astronomical spectroscopy, many apparently unattainable details of the physical state and chemical makeup of stars, galaxies, and other distant objects can be discovered.

A spectrum is the arrangement of waves in order of their wavelength. Light wavelengths are just part of the entire spectrum of electromagnetic radiation, which ranges from the very long wavelengths of radio to the very short ones of gamma rays. On one side of the visible region is the infrared (longer wavelengths) and on the other is the ultraviolet (shorter). The spectrum can also be thought of in terms of quantum theory, in which a quantum of, say, blue light has greater energy than a quantum of red light.

Early spectroscopy

In his first experiments with a prism, performed around 1661, the English physicist Isaac Newton noticed that, in the spectrum of sunlight, there are a number of fine, dark lines superimposed on the bright rainbow of colors. He thought they were boundaries between colors. At the beginning of the 19th century, the German physicist Joseph von Fraunhofer found that there are a large number of these lines—now known as Fraunhofer lines—and he cataloged hundreds of them. It was two Germans, G.R. Kirchhoff, a physicist, and R.W. Bunsen, a chemist, who discovered that the lines represent characteristic patterns of wavelengths of light absorbed by various chemical elements when heated intensely. With this discovery, they were able to show the presence of several metals in the Sun.

Spectrum theory

After half a century of listing and charting the lines of the spectra of the elements in the laboratory, physicists began not only to realize why some spectra are simple and some complicated but also to recognize the changes in each atom that produced each line. This kind of work is called the theory of spectra, or spectrum theory, so as not to confuse it with spectrochemical analysis. It has led to new knowledge of atoms and isotopes in particular. It depends on the acceptance of the quantum theory, which maintains that energy is not continuous but is always produced in discrete packets called quanta. A spectral line is produced and radiated when an electron moves from one orbital, or energy level, around the atom's nucleus to another nearer the nucleus. A change from a nearer orbit to a farther one, caused by the addition of energy from an external source, results in absorption of the energy and hence an absorption line or possibly fluorescence if the energy is radiated at another wavelength.

In the planetary model of the atom devised by the Danish physicist Niels Bohr, one imagines the electrons as if they were planets orbiting the central nucleus in well-defined orbits. Later work showed up discrepancies in this picture, and today scientists think in terms of an orbital—a region where the electron has the highest probability of being. Nevertheless, the concept of orbits of definite sizes is good enough for descriptive purposes.

Because each element has atoms that are different from every other element by virtue of their different number of nuclear particles, each spectral line is unique to a particular element. For example, an atom of helium has two protons and two neutrons in its nucleus, whereas hydrogen has only one proton. The greater charge on the nucleus resulting from the two protons produces orbitals that are of smaller radius than those of hydrogen. The energy, and hence wavelength, depends in part on the radii of the orbitals involved, so the wavelength of radiation emitted by an electron jumping from the second to the first orbital of helium is shorter than that emitted by an electron jumping between two orbitals of hydrogen. However, larger atoms of heavier elements have orbitals that are much farther out than the lowest ones of hydrogen, so they can produce radiation of longer wavelengths.

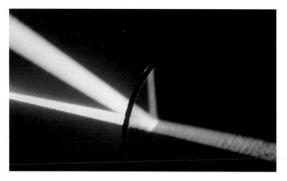

◀ A dichroic filter, used in photography, transmits some colors and reflects the rest. Here, white light entering from the left splits into blue (transmitted) and yellow (reflected).

A gas at low pressure produces its characteristic glowing emission lines by the process just described. In the case of an incandescent solid or very dense gas, the radiation emitted is not in discrete individual lines but is continuous—a continuum of blackbody radiation, giving rise to the complete rainbow of color. In the solar spectrum, this continuum is crossed by dark absorption lines, which are due to cool gases in the Sun's outer atmosphere. Light coming from the Sun may be absorbed by an atom at its characteristic wavelength—the wavelength at which it glows. There is no reason the atom should retain this energy, and it immediately reradiates it at the same frequency, but the chance of it traveling on in its original direction is small. The effect on the observer is that the radiation at that particular frequency has been absorbed, producing a dark line in that part of the spectrum compared with the bright continuum of the overall spectrum.

Spectroscope

In its simplest form, a spectroscope is a device for observing the spectrum of colors produced by a prism or diffraction grating. This technique has led to a wide range of devices, such as the spectrograph, the spectrometer, the spectrophotometer, and the colorimeter.

In spectroscopes and spectrographs, the whole spectrum of light radiation is observed by eye or on a photograph. Spectrometers, on the other hand, usually select one particular small group of wavelengths for measurement by, for example, a photocell—and usually there is some way of scanning this window of wavelengths over a large range. Both emission and absorption spectra are studied. Emission spectra consist of a series of

▼ Absorption curves for a yellow-green photographic light-correction filter (top) and a narrow-cut green contrast filter (bottom) for use with a panchromatic camera film.

bright lights of individual colors, and absorption spectra are seen as black lines where individual colors are missing from the complete spectrum.

Spectroscopes

The design of the elementary spectroscope has changed little since the 18th century. White light passes through a collimator consisting of a slit and a lens that gives a narrow beam of parallel light and is then split up into respective wavelengths by either a prism or a diffraction grating. The resulting spectrum is then examined by means of a small telescope that is focused at the distance of the slit. If the prism or diffraction grating were not there, a sharp image of the slit would show up. When the prism or diffraction grating is in place, the light is refracted or diffracted through an angle that depends on its wavelength. This process produces, not one single image of the slit, but one for each color. The resolution depends on the width of the slit, which can usually be varied.

Often the prism or grating is placed in the center of a small circular table. The collimator and the telescope move around the central axis of the table, and the edge of the table is graduated in degrees so that the angle between the incoming and outgoing beams can be measured accurately. If the dispersion of the spectrum is high, the telescope will have to be moved around to examine various parts of it.

The laboratory version, known as a wavelength spectrometer, has the collimator and telescope fixed at right angles and a constant deviation prism. By rotating the prism, different wavelengths can be sent into the telescope, and the prism's rotating drum can be calibrated directly in wavelengths.

Wavelengths can be measured either in nanometers—billionths of a meter—or in angstroms. Yellow light, for example, has a wavelength of about 570 nm (570×10^{-9} m, or 5,700 angstroms).

Spectrochemical analysis

One early spectroscopist was Norman Lockyer, an amateur astronomer working as a clerk at the War Office in London, England, who went on to become one of the most famous scientists of the 19th century. To study spectra in the

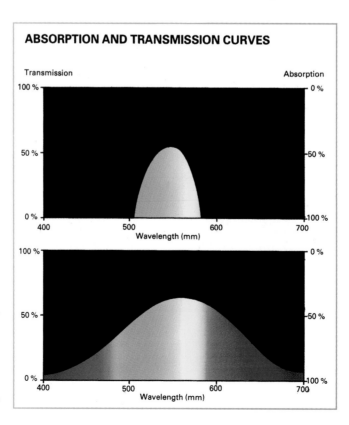

ABSORPTION AND TRANSMISSION CURVES

Transmission — Absorption (top chart): 100 % / 0 %, 50 % / 50 %, 0 % / 100 %; Wavelength (mm): 400, 500, 600, 700

(bottom chart): 100 % / 0 %, 50 % / 50 %, 0 % / 100 %; Wavelength (mm): 400, 500, 600, 700

laboratory, he applied a high current to two poles of metal, producing a glowing spark as in an arc lamp, and photographed the resulting spectrum to give a pattern of lines in which the strongest were also the longest. He was able to measure the intensity of a line by its length, and working on gold alloys from the British Royal Mint, he found an error made by a chemist in one of the standard alloys provided for him to test.

An English physicist, Charles Wheatstone, one of the first electrical engineers, tried to use a spectroscope to prove that the electricity from a battery was the same kind of thing as electricity from a sparking coil. He used a spectroscope to examine the arc from two pieces of each of the metals copper, zinc, lead, and tin and published an approximate spectrum, but he had no way of measuring wavelengths. He forecast that this method might one day be used in analyzing metals; this technique now forms the basis of spectrochemical analysis.

Spectrographs

The first spectrographs involved photographing the spectra and then examining the plates by eye or later on a photographic measuring device such as a densitometer. By replacing the human eye with a photographic plate or film, a permanent record of the spectrum is obtained. The densitometer provides a graph of the spectrum, in which

case the lines observed with the eye—each one, in effect, an image of the slit—are represented as peaks for emission lines or dips for absorption lines on the graph. A photographic spectroscope is known as a spectrograph, and the photographs it takes are strictly called spectrograms—although in practice they are often called spectra. In the 19th century, spectrographs were attached to telescopes to produce stellar spectra, which give information on the physical and chemical makeup of stars. In about 1908, the technique was used in industry for chemical analysis. The sample to be analyzed formed one of a pair of electrodes. An electric current was then passed across the electrodes to form an arc, as in an arc lamp. Laser probes are now used routinely to produce spectrograms.

In the 1930s, the direct spectrometer came into use. It scanned the spectrum directly by means of a photocell, giving a reading on a meter or drawing a graph. During World War II, spectrochemical analysis became one of the main quality-control methods used by suppliers of alloys of aluminum, magnesium, copper, lead, and steel throughout the world. Now equipment has been so far automated that a direct-reading spectrometer will compare the composition of a sample with a standard alloy using a computer to make any comparison or corrections needed for the test. The results are printed out on the

◀ A nuclear magnetic resonance spectrometer has many applications including determining the structure of molecules.

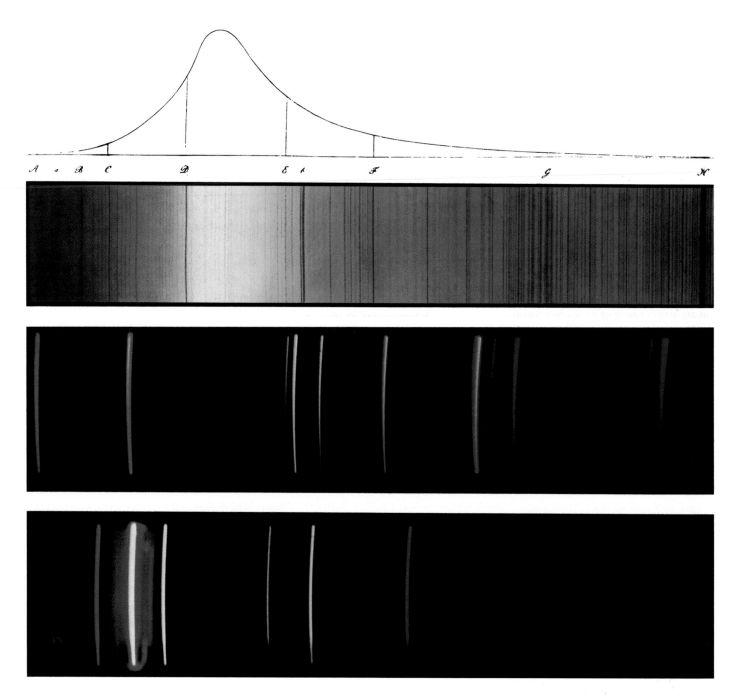

line-printer, and the whole operation can be carried out in five minutes. Thus, in a foundry, a batch of molten metal can be analyzed and the result sent to the foundry controller quickly enough to provide analytical control for each batch of metal without wasting power keeping it hot while awaiting analysis by other methods.

Today spectrographs for spectrochemical analysis do not record the whole spectrum where they have a specific job to do. Instead, the direct-reading technique is employed—a series of photomultiplier tubes or light detectors is set up with each one dedicated to measuring the intensity of a separate spectral line. This method enables the output to be fed directly into a computer or other electronic analyzing system, so facilitating the speed at which the data can be analyzed.

X-ray fluorescence

An equally quick and basic application of spectrochemical analysis is the use of X-ray fluorescence, both in mining and in examining alloys for quality control. In this case, a sample illuminated with X rays fluoresces at certain wavelengths. The sample can be any powdered material or a solid disk of metal. This kind of apparatus, too, has been automated—it can supply up to 20 analytical results for a single sample within ten minutes. For X rays, it is convenient to think of the radiation as particles and to count them with a photomultiplier tube.

For mineral prospecting, portable fluorescence equipment has been made that uses a radioactive isotope instead of a high-voltage generator to provide the power. The radiation from the isotope emerges from a window in the

▲ The absorption lines of the Sun's spectrum (top) with a graph of the light distribution, made with a prism. The emission spectra of helium and sodium are shown in the middle and bottom images, respectively.

machine, which is applied to the surface of the mineral in a mine. Only one element is detected and analyzed at a time, but by using interchangeable filters, the same equipment can be used for several metals. This method differs from the X-ray spectrochemical analyzer in that using an isotope to emit gamma rays is more efficient, in terms of weight of equipment, than using X rays of rather longer wavelength.

X-ray fluorescence analysis is also replacing other spectrochemical methods in museum laboratories, where it has the advantage that specialists can analyze an object without damaging it. The method can be used for such varied specimens as the glaze on pottery, the pigments of an antique painting, and the precious-metal plating on an object made of a cheaper metal.

Forensic laboratories take advantage of this method because for analysis it requires only small samples, such as paint flakes from the clothes of the victim of an automobile accident.

Perhaps the most important applications of spectrochemical analysis are its medical uses in the testing of samples of any liquid in the body, of meat and plants, and of the impurities that pollute Earth's air and water. This application began with

the detection of poisons in the digestive system (whether the poisoning was chronic or sudden), where only a few parts in a million of an element such as lead or mercury may be dangerous. Applications spread to include routine tests of any element normally found in blood serum and other liquids, but gradually spectrophotometry gained prominence over this kind of work from ordinary spectrochemical analysis. In the late 1950s, a widespread outbreak of mercury poisoning in a coastal city of Japan gave rise to an improvement in methods of testing for mercury all over the world.

The nuclear energy industry makes use of spectrochemical analysis at every stage of its processes, from the refining of uranium ore to the testing of the particularly strong steels used in the construction of reactors.

Astronomical spectroscopy

Many advances in spectrum theory were made by studying spectra of stars and nebulas, where matter exists in states impossible to produce in the laboratory. It is true to say that spectroscopy has had as much effect on astrophysics and our knowledge of the Universe as the telescope itself. Spectra are altered by various conditions at their

▼ (1) An electron gains energy (becomes excited) and moves to a higher energy level. Here it is unstable, so it returns to the ground (stable) state, emitting radiation. (2) The absorption and emission frequencies of the Balmer series. (3) A sodium arc excites sodium atoms to produce an emission spectrum. (4) When white light from an arc passes through sodium vapor, sodium atoms produce a continuous spectrum with absorption lines.

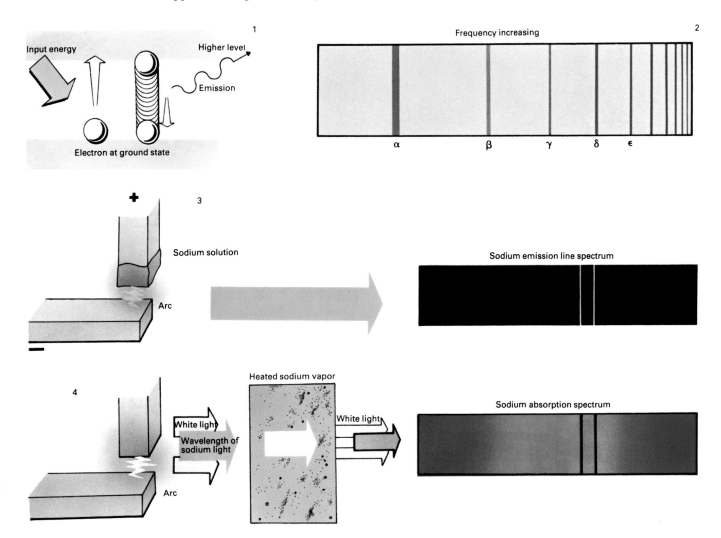

ATOM AND ORBITALS

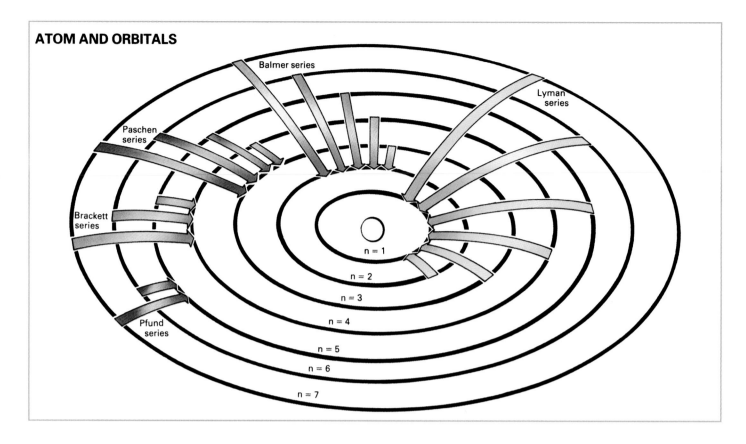

source, such as pressure, temperature, turbulence, magnetic and electric fields, and motion (detected by the Doppler effects), as well as by the chemical compositions of the bodies themselves. It is possible, by looking at more and more distant objects, to determine how the chemical composition of the Universe has changed over its lifetime, because the light left the most distant objects long before Earth was formed.

Absorption systems

Initially, as with emission spectroscopy, work in the field of absorption was limited to the visible region of the spectrum. Early instruments employed a series of colored optical filters to isolate the chosen part of the spectrum in what was called an absorptiometer, or colorimeter. The sample, in liquid form, was placed in a cuvette with transparent parallel faces through which the light was passed before reaching the photocell detector.

A monochromator, often used in spectrophotometers, is a device that isolates specific small groups of wavelengths using either a prism or a diffraction grating. Gratings have the advantage that they spread the spectrum out evenly over the wavelengths, whereas prisms bunch up the wavelengths at the red end. In addition, by giving the grating a reflective coating, it will perform at all wavelengths because all colors are reflected equally well within the limitations of the type of coating and the spacing of the grating lines.

By mechanically rotating the grating or prism, as in the spectroscope, a beam of any chosen color can be isolated. A second slit selects only the wavelengths required. The bandwidth—the range of wavelengths transmitted—can be varied by altering the slit width to pass more light at lower resolution if necessary. The monochromator replaces the filters of the simpler instruments.

Spectrophotometers

Atoms give rise to individual line spectra, whereas molecules or groups of atoms usually produce wider band spectra. These spectra are particularly important in a technique known as spectrophotometry, in which fairly low-quality graphs of spectra are produced by machine.

A photometer is a device that measures light intensity, so a spectrophotometer is the word for a device that measures the distribution of light over a spectrum. An elementary spectrophotometer consists of a monochromator with a light source chosen for the spectral range of interest, a sample compartment, a detector, and a readout system.

The way the recording versions of spectrophotometers work—scanning the spectra and automatically drawing a graph of the absorption—varies with the wavelength being used. When infrared or ultraviolet light is being used, the spectrum of the sample under examination is compared with a reference sample. The emission spectra are detected using either a bolometer or photoelectric cells. If there is no difference

▲ A schematic view of an atom, with the energy bands shown as orbits. Energy is radiated (as electromagnetic waves) when an electron moves from one energy level to another nearer the nucleus.

between the reference and sample at a particular wave number, there will be no output from the detector. If, however, there is a difference, the detector will record an oscillating output, which can be registered by a pen recorder.

In the ultraviolet and visible versions, scattering of light by the system is a great problem, and the samples have to be placed as close to the detector as possible. In this case, the monochromator comes first, and then the beams are split. A common method of recording is to use a glass density wedge in one beam. The wedge is moved up and down to equalize the intensities recorded by the detector. The movement of this wedge is coupled to the pen, which creates a graph of absorption against wavelength.

The visible surface of most stars, including our Sun, emits a continuous spectrum. The color of the emission maximum reveals the star's temperature but not its compostion. Hints of the chemical compostion are gained from the dark lines visible in the spectrum, caused by light absorption by atoms that have escaped from the surface and cooled to a lower temperature.

Infrared scanning spectrometers are widely used in chemical analysis and gas analysis. Nondispersive infrared gas analyzers work at a fixed wavelength and are used for measuring carbon dioxide concentrations and alcohol in breath samples. For many purposes, it is not necessary to vaporize the sample to observe its emission lines. Instead, the molecular absorption bands are studied by means of a spectrophotometer using samples that are liquid or gaseous. Most molecular absorption bands of interest are in the infrared part of the electromagnetic spectrum.

Raman spectroscopy

In Raman spectroscopy, the vibration and detailed bonding of complex molecules are examined by the scattering produced with monochromatic light—light of a single wavelength—such as that produced by a laser. This technique was developed in 1928 by an Indian physicist, Sir Chandrasekhara Venkata Raman, who discovered the phenomenon in which light is absorbed by molecules and then reemitted at higher or lower frequencies, causing the molecules to vibrate or rotate. Elastic collisions between the photons and molecules result in either a gain or loss of energy in the photons, thus producing a distinct spectrum pattern for different molecules.

Microwave spectroscopy

Microwaves are particularly useful for investigating the structure of diatomic molecules—molecules consisting of two atoms. More complex

techniques, involving the substitution of atoms in a molecule with different isotopic species, may also be used to investigate polyatomic molecules, which exhibit much more complex spectra.

There are two types of microwave spectrometer, the Fourier and the Stark-modulated spectrometers, both of which introduce gaseous samples into a vacuum. A microwave signal is passed through the vacuum, causing the sample to change from one quantized rotational state to another, and in the process, the sample absorbs microwaves or emits them at a different frequency. The microwaves then pass into a detector, and the resulting spectrum is recorded. Information from this spectrum can then be used to ascertain the distance between the nuclei and a variety of other properties, such as the magnetic moment of the molecule, the geometric structure, and the distribution of electrons.

One important application of microwave spectroscopy in cosmology has been the discovery of low-level microwave radiation that is identical to the radiation cosmologists predict should remain in the Universe as a consequence of the Big Bang.

▶ The portable borehole logger spectrometer can measure very small concentrations of tin within 30 seconds by X-ray fluorescence, making it useful for on-site analysis.

SEE ALSO: ASTROPHYSICS • ATOMIC STRUCTURE • BODY SCANNER • CHEMISTRY, ANALYTICAL • COSMOLOGY • ELECTROMAGNETIC RADIATION • ELEMENT, CHEMICAL • LIGHT AND OPTICS • MASS SPECTROMETRY • QUANTUM THEORY • TELESCOPE, OPTICAL

Speech and Language

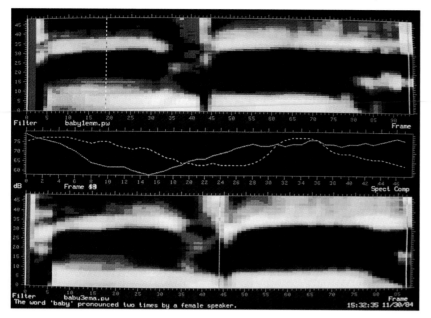

The word 'baby' pronounced two times by a female speaker.

15:32:35 11/30/84

Speech is a learned method of human communication that uses voice, articulation, and language skills. Voice is the sound we produce when air is forced out of the lungs against the vocal cords, which are connected to the larynx (voice box). The vibrations in the air flow produce sound, which is articulated by changing the position of the lips, lower jaw, tongue, soft palate, and teeth. Different sequences of these elementary speech sounds produce words, which vary according to the language that is being spoken. Any particular language consists of using words (spoken or written symbols) in an agreed upon way.

For many years, linguists have tried to reconstruct the origins of language by comparing animal and human methods of communication. In an attempt to understand why and how languages constantly change, with both time and place, linguists have examined the spread of major languages and their diversification into thousands of dialects. More recently, language researchers have documented the private slang of close-knit groups of people. Despite much progress, scientists are not yet agreed on how language arose.

Theories about origins

Prehistoric *Homo sapiens* probably possessed languages similar in structure to those spoken today. Somewhere between 40,000 and 50,000 years ago, primitive culture underwent a profound change, and many people believe that language evolved around this time. Tools became more varied and sophisticated, art appeared on cave walls, and there is some evidence of notational systems engraved on batons and other objects. Skulls of

▲ Computer graphics images of various waveform representations of the voiceprint of the word "baby" as spoken by a female voice and reproduced on a speech synthesizer. From the top, the waveforms show the amplitude, the filtered representation, the energy level, and finally, a spectral representation at the bottom.

that era had brains large enough to cope with language, and teeth, jaw, and a throat structure that would have allowed a wide variation of sounds to be made rapidly.

One theory is that humans simply expanded the communication system they already had. Like many animals, primitive humans probably had a repertoire of calls and cries for different occasions: cries to warn of danger or to frighten off intruders, cries of distress, and mating calls. According to this school of thought, these different warning cries were only a step away from being names for various enemies, and thus early humans started out with a system in which these calls increased in number and eventually became labels for objects and actions.

Other scholars claim that language could not have arisen in this way because humans still retain a primitive call system, observable in babies. Babies' cries can be identified not only by the parents but also by observers who speak another language. This theory suggests that language may be a different, additional system that has grown up alongside a series of inherited calls.

Supporters of this theory point out the parallel with birds. In addition to a simple call system of a few basic signals, such as an alarm call and a call to congregate, many birds have developed songs that differ markedly from each other. In a call system, each call normally conveys a specific message, but in birdsong, a single note has no significance—the song depends on the sequencing of the notes. The same is true of human language. An individual sound, such as *p*, *t*, or *o*, does not usually mean anything by itself. For the most part, sounds become meaningful only when they are combined together, as in *top*, *pot*, or *opt*.

In addition, call systems tend to be genetically inbuilt, unlike either birdsong or human language. A chaffinch reared in a soundproof room away from other chaffinches, for example, never learns to sing normally. Birds may have developed complex songs in order to attract, court, and keep a mate, and it may be this factor that was important in the development of human language.

Even though it is not known how humans first acquired language, it is not just by chance that human children born today learn to speak. Humans are biologically adapted to speech—the human tongue is mobile and muscular, the teeth are relatively even, and the throat and larynx are streamlined. These and other adaptations allow a human being to make a wide range of sounds rapidly, a skill that chimps and gorillas do not have.

There is also evidence that parts of the human brain are set aside for language—certain areas within the left hemisphere seem to be important for understanding and producing speech.

Language creativity

All languages of the world display similar basic characteristics, such as creativity. No natural form of animal communication has this property. Creativity refers to two overlapping aspects of human language. First, it means the ability to say and understand things that might never have been said before, such as "Green caterpillars sometimes eat large holes in pink hats." Second, it means the ability to respond to a given situation in a nonstandardized way. For example, the advances of an amorous lover could be rejected by saying "Keep your hands off," "Don't mess my hair," or simply, "Go away." A female vervet monkey, however, would respond to a similar situation with a stereotypical call, a screeching sound known as the anticopulatory squeal-scream.

The characteristic of creativity has important implications. It means that the acquisition of language is not merely the piecemeal accumulation of a fixed set of messages. Instead, it involves learning underlying principles or rules that enable a speaker to produce and understand an indefinite number of new utterances and reject ill-formed ones, such as "Holes caterpillars hats sometimes green large pink eat." Although every language has its own set of rules, they all use the same type of rules, or universal grammar.

The American linguist Noam Chomsky has theorized that humans possess a kind of language-acquisition device, or "language organ." According to Chomsky's theory, the device is an innate mechanism or cognitive structure that is preprogrammed with the underlying rules of universal grammar. Depending on the language to which a child is exposed, the mechanism will select from the rules those that are appropriate for the language being spoken.

All languages are hierarchically structured in the sense that each sentence consists of a set of basic slots that can be expanded. In the sentence "Lloyd walked home," each slot can be replaced or expanded in numerous ways without altering the basic pattern—as in "The donkey walked slowly up the street" or "The fat, gray donkey walked very slowly up the crowded street."

Not only can humans choose different words, or groups of words, to fill each slot, but they can also shift these slots around without losing track of the meaning—as in "Up the crowded street walked the donkey." Furthermore, they can sometimes omit items and still be understood.

Given that all languages have these structural similarities, why are there so many different ones? Some people have suggested that it would be a good idea to reduce the number of languages or, better still, agree on a single language that would eventually be adopted by the whole world. Esperanto is the best-known attempt to create a universal artificial language. It was invented by a Polish scholar, Ludwig Zamenhof, and first published in 1887. Its supporters claim that it can be learned easily because it has eliminated the irregularities in structure found in existing languages.

Language change

Proponents of Esperanto, or any other similar language, are unlikely to see it adopted worldwide, however. It is difficult to create a language that would be equally easy for everyone, and because Esperanto is based on European languages, it is much easier for, say, a Spaniard to learn than for a Japanese. A more serious problem is that languages are always changing—differences creep in and dialects form.

In language change, the social, linguistic, and psychological causes interact with one another. Human beings tend to form themselves into social groups based on factors such as age, social

▼ Humans are biologically adapted to speech in a way that no other animals are; the human tongue is mobile and muscular, the teeth are relatively even, and the throat and larynx are streamlined. Under the control of the speech centers—believed to be in the left hemisphere of the brain—these and other adaptations, such as the ability to close off the nasal cavity, allow humans to make a wide range of sounds rapidly, something that is impossible for chimpanzees and gorillas, for example. Those animals could not be said to be able to communicate using language; rather, they signal to each other by means of a limited number of basic call signs.

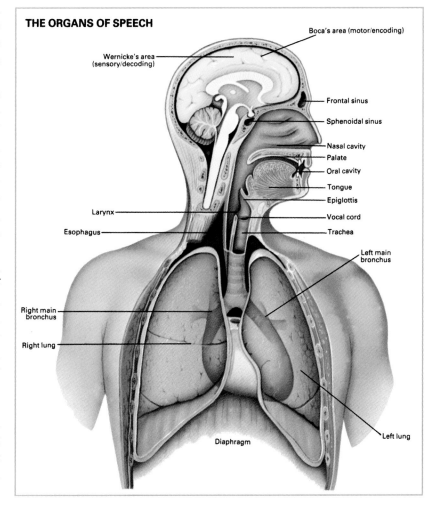

THE ORGANS OF SPEECH

Wernicke's area (sensory/decoding)
Boca's area (motor/encoding)
Frontal sinus
Sphenoidal sinus
Nasal cavity
Palate
Oral cavity
Tongue
Epiglottis
Larynx
Vocal cord
Esophagus
Trachea
Left main bronchus
Right main bronchus
Right lung
Left lung
Diaphragm

class, and occupation, and members of certain social groups often adopt a particular pronunciation in order to distinguish themselves from other social groups. For example, the inhabitants of Martha's Vineyard, an island off the coast of Massachusetts, have adopted the vowel sounds of a group of fishermen as a way of distinguishing themselves from people vacationing on the island. The fishermen were felt to embody old-fashioned virtues such as honesty and the ability to work hard—all regarded as lacking in the visitors.

The private speech of a group is likely to fade away when the group disbands, but surprisingly often, changes spread outside the immediate social group and take hold in the population at large. Such changes often start out as variant forms that exist alongside the standard speech of a community and are at first regarded as substandard. Slang is usually simply the private vocabulary of a small social group that has spread to a wider set of speakers but has not yet been generally accepted. As more people use them, slang words become indistinguishable from the rest of the vocabulary.

Hearing and saying

In the late 20th century, computers were developed that not only could understand the spoken word in order to receive commands and input data from the speaker but also could produce "spoken" words. Almost every computer communicates with its programmer via verbal text—words and phrases—preprogrammed to fit the circumstances. Such a facility is almost infinitely flexible. Data can be retrieved from the computer worded at specific levels of complexity or simplicity,

▼ Teaching a partially deaf child to speak by amplifying the sounds of her own and her teacher's voices. The hearing mechanism plays a key role in the maintenance of speech; it acts as a source of instant feedback by which the brain can monitor the sounds we produce. Speech is so fundamental to human experience that deaf people will have real problems in everyday life unless they are given training to help them overcome the disability.

and even languages can be translated (including idiomatic expressions). So why do we need computers that not only understand the spoken word but also reply in kind?

It makes commercial sense to reduce as much as possible the time taken to input information. Speaking is quicker than typing. In the same way, it may soon become more practical for a computer to have ears than a keyboard.

The industrial applications of this development are obvious. Every machine can be operated, controlled, and monitored by verbal instruction. In addition, information that is input as text can be output as speech, as occurs in the relay of computer-operated telephone weather reports in the United States. Demanding, high-stress occupations, such as flying, could be made simpler if voice-recognition systems allowed pilots to keep their eyes on one set of instruments while executing some other maneuver. It is possible for a computer to be programmed to ask patients medical questions in an impersonal manner so that diagnosis may be speedier and less stressful for the patient. The use of voiced computers is also of great importance to handicapped people. Voice-controlled wheelchairs, for example, already give a degree of independence to the severely disabled.

Speech recognition and synthesis

Some personal computers and PDAs (personal digital assistants) on the market support speech recognition, enabling the user to input data or give commands using speech. Customer service industries have also been quick to see the possibilities of automated speech-recognition technology. Some airlines, for example, have switched to using automated systems that respond to customers' voices in order to relay flight information.

The main problem is to make a computer that will recognize ordinary speech by any user. There have been three main approaches to the design of speech-recognition systems. One system enables the computer to recognize a small amount of words spoken by a broad range of speakers and has proved to be relatively accurate. The second method enables the computer to recognize a large number of words spoken by one person, a reliable system providing the person's speech patterns remain consistent. The third method—which is the least accurate but the most promising for universally converting speech to text—enables the computer to learn an individual's speech patterns and apply them to a large range of words.

Speech can be analyzed by plotting the relative strengths of sound against time and frequency on spectrograms—the darker the mark

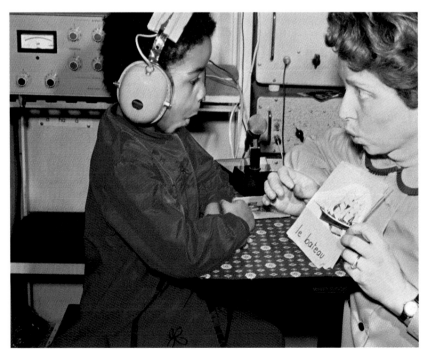

on the spectrogram, the stronger the sound. Unfortunately, they are not easy to interpret. For the moment, though, vocabulary has proved the most problematic factor in all serious research.

Vocabulary storage is caught in a vicious circle—the better a computer can listen to sounds, the more information it has to store and analyze. Just how much information this entails can be judged by the fact that many computers now operating in voice recognition sample an incoming sound at intervals of less than a microsecond. The better the sampling rate, the better the chances of recognizing the sound—and the more accurately the sound can later be reproduced by the computer. The ability of a computer to produce "spoken" words is known as speech synthesis.

In all systems, the vocabulary is reduced to digital form (that is, binary, 1s and 0s) for storage. Once an incoming sound has been analyzed, the computer has the information with which to reproduce the same sound. Sound production is usually carried out by decoding filters in conjunction with an amplifier or via a frequency-to-voltage converter system.

Computers can produce speech either by splicing prerecorded words together or by producing sounds, syllables, or parts of words called phonemes. Phonemes can then be memorized as various combinations that are subsequently reproduced as words. The method of vocabulary storage corresponds to the method of word reproduction—if words are stored as combinations of phonemes, speech will also be constituted of such combinations. Vocabulary corresponds to storage capacity and depends on whether the computer's response is to be mono- or polysyllabic.

To achieve a genuinely human sound, a computer must also be programmed to take into account the noise factor of human speech—the cords, throat, teeth, and tongue—a quality without which the tone generated by a computer sounds metallic. However advanced the computer system may be, the result will always represent a compromise. Real human speech is incredibly flexible in tone and also incorporates body language—one mode of communication that can never be computerized.

Speech synthesis is used today to aid handicapped people to communicate—for example, the development of voice synthesizers that are sensitive to touch or movement or respond to keyboard input. Prospects for the future are bright, but the capabilities of speech synthesis are still too limited for general use.

▲ A voice-recognition device being used to check off weapons in an armory. The number of each gun is called out to the computer, which then checks it off against a database.

SEE ALSO: ARTIFICIAL INTELLIGENCE • HEARING • OTOLARYNGOLOGY • SOUND • VOICE RECOGNITION AND SYNTHESIS

Speedboat

Early powerboats used reciprocating steam engines. Higher speeds became possible after the development of steam turbines—the *Tubinia*, built in England by Charles Parsons, achieved a speed of nearly 35 knots (about 40 mph, or 64 km/h) in 1897. However, they were soon replaced by internal combustion engines.

A gasoline engine was first fixed to a boat by Jean Joseph Lenoir, a Frenchman, as early as 1865, but the true forerunner of the speedboat was built in 1886 by the German engineer Gottlieb Daimler, who equipped it with his engine (also demonstrated in other applications, including the automobile and the motorbike). The engine was of a single-cylinder design with an output of around 1 horsepower (750 W), and the boat was 20 ft. (6 m) long. A speed of 6 mph (10 km/h) was achieved during trials on the Neckar River.

A development of this design—with twin cylinders giving an output of 2 horsepower (1,500 W) at 720 rpm—went into production in 1888 and was installed in a number of boats. Similar boats were built by enthusiasts in other countries—the development of the speedboat had begun. By the early years of the 20th century, organized races were being held, and speeds were beginning to increase. In 1904, the winner of the American Power Boat Association Gold Cup race had a speed of 23.6 mph (38 km/h). Up-to-date racing speedboats are capable of speeds in excess of 100 mph (160 km/h), and the specialized boats used for speed-record attempts are faster.

Wave resistance

The first powerboats were simply rowing or sailing boats with the engine mounted amidships and driving a propeller at the stern. To obtain higher speeds in racing boats, a long and narrow hull shape was adopted, following the design of high-speed naval vessels, such as destroyers. These hulls were of the displacement type, in which the support for the boat is the upward force of the water displaced by the hull.

When a hull of this type moves through the water, it generates bow and stern waves that move with the boat, a series of waves being formed along the length of the hull. The greater the speed of the boat, the longer the waves. As the speed increases, the waves space out and become more pronounced until there is a single wave with peaks at the bow and stern. Attempts to increase the speed further result in the stern wave breaking away from the vessel, reducing the displacement at the stern. The boat adopts a bow-up attitude—it tries to climb up its own bow wave. In some cases, the effect is to draw the stern down, and to avoid this problem, the early designs of speedboats had a squared-off stern. With a pure displacement vessel, the limit-

▲ The *Spirit of Norway* powering its way across the water in the Class I World Offshore 2000 Championship. Speedboat racing is highly competitive: the record speed stands at 318 mph (512 km/h).

ing speed is given by V = 1.4 L, where V is the velocity in knots and L the waterline length of the vessel in feet. In practice, early speedboats were probably not pure displacement vessels, and higher speeds were achieved. As speed increases, however, the forces needed to overcome the wave resistance rise sharply to become the major resistance to motion—at lower speeds, the skin friction is more significant.

To allow higher speeds, a different hull design is required—the planing hull, in which the necessary support is supplied by hydrodynamic forces acting on the bottom of the hull. The concept of the hydroplane was first proposed by an English scientist, William Froude, who produced designs for a planing hull supported on three points in the 1870s. The concept was not developed because there were no suitable engines at the time.

By the beginning of the 20th century, however, gasoline engines with much better power-to-weight ratio were available, and the planing hull became a practical proposition. As soon as planing starts, the length of the wave created increases while its height decreases, and less energy is required to form the wave. In addition, a substantial portion of the hull is no longer in contact with the water, thus reducing the frictional drag. Because of these effects, the boat suddenly speeds up as it starts to plane, and the engine can be throttled back with the speed maintained.

Planing surfaces

The action of a planing surface moving over the water can best be explained by considering the equivalent case of a stationary surface in a moving water stream. As the water contacts the plane, it splits into two streams, the main one passing under the plate and a smaller portion, the spray, being deflected to flow up the plate surface in the opposite direction to the main flow. The region on the plate surface where the two flows separate is the stagnation point, and here the water flow is brought to rest instantaneously.

Analysis of the flow characteristics using Bernoulli's principle shows that the changes in flow velocity create a change in pressure, with the pressure being greatest at the stagnation point and then falling away to the rear of the plate. It is this pressure acting on the plate area that provides the lift, which can be shown to be a function of the water flow deflected in the forward direction.

In the case of a practical hull shape, analysis of the flow characteristics is much more complex—with the deflected spray also moving sideway on the hull—but the basic principle is the same. With a high-speed vessel, the deflected spray can be clearly seen emerging to either side of the hull.

To an observer, the spray appears to be deflected sideway or even back along the hull, but this apparent direction is a combination of the actual spray movement forward from the hull and the forward velocity of the boat.

Hull forms

The earliest planing designs were simply flat-bottomed boats that skimmed across the water surface. Further development gave the stepped hull, in which the bottom surface of the hull was formed into one or more steps. As the boat started to plane and lifted out of the water, the stepped-back areas came clear of the water so that the boat was carried on a series of contact areas just before the steps. This design had the effect of reducing the surface drag and allowing higher speeds with a given engine power. With most planing hulls, there is a marked transition between the relatively flat planing bottom and the sides of the hull—with the angle of the transition being the chine. Hard chine hulls have a marked chine angle.

Flat and slightly rounded hulls have good planing characteristics with small wetted areas but tend to lack stability under adverse conditions. Improved performance under such conditions is obtained by giving the fore end of the hull a sharp V-shape, thus reducing the effects of wave impacts, while the rear portion of the hull retains the flat planing profile. A development of this concept is the deep V planing hull in which the V

▼ A catamaran made of fiber-reinforced plastic, which can be accurately made into curved hull forms. The hull is made from two separate sections molded together to provide strength and streamlining. It has shallow contact with the water for improved speed and maneuverability. Controls for the engine (set high above the surface of the water) and rudder functions are by direct cable link (seen along the outside of the boat). Water spray on a windshield causes poor visibility, so the windshield is eliminated. The absence of a windshield also decreases wind resistance.

extends for the length of the hull, with the bottom having a number of spray rails running lengthwise. These spray rails provide stability by deflecting the movement of the spray across the hull to turn it down. As the boat's speed increases and the boat rides higher in the water, successively lower pairs of spray rails come into action.

Multihulls

Increased stability can be achieved by the use of multiple hulls joined together above the waterline. A common arrangement is the catamaran with two hulls. Others are trimarans with three hulls, and outrigger designs with a main hull and one or more smaller floats, or sponsons. In many cases, the hulls and the connecting link form a tunnel that generates aerodynamic lift that acts with the planing lift. An early example of this type was the sea sled developed in the United States by Albert Hickman. It had an inverted V tunnel sloping down from the front of the boat to disappear at the stern. A development of this design has the tunnel open at the stern to allow a through airflow, the lift produced being mainly of the ground-effect type.

The aerodynamic lift can be a disadvantage if it causes the front of the boat to lift, and in the picklefork arrangement, the link between the two hulls starts some way back along the hulls. Another solution to the problem is to use airfoils to lift the tail, and the thrust from the engine can be angled to trim the attitude of the boat. Multihull designs are widely used for circuit-racing craft and speed-record attempts, but the deep V hull is generally regarded as stronger and more suitable for the high stresses encountered in offshore racing.

Power plants

It was the development of internal combustion engines (offering high power-to-weight ratios) that made the modern speedboat practicable, and they remain the dominant power source. Engines can be divided into two broad classes—inboard and outboard—according to the way they are fixed to the boat. As the name suggests, outboard engines are designed to be mounted on the outside of the hull, normally at the stern. They are integrated units with the engine and propeller connected by a vertical drive shaft, and can be pivoted on their mounting for steering.

Inboard engines are carried within the boat hull. They drive the propeller or propellers either through shafts that penetrate the hull or through inboard/outboard drives. With direct drives, the engine has to be placed well forward in the boat to give a suitable angle for the drive shaft. To achieve a better weight distribution with the engine farther aft, a V-drive transmission may be installed.

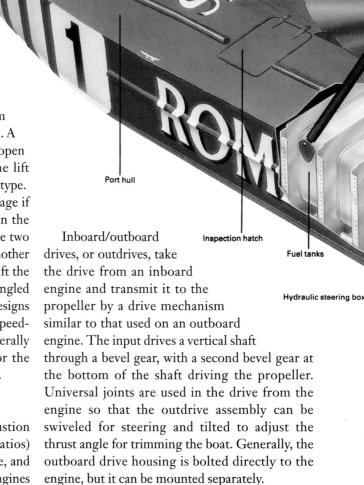

Inboard/outboard drives, or outdrives, take the drive from an inboard engine and transmit it to the propeller by a drive mechanism similar to that used on an outboard engine. The input drives a vertical shaft through a bevel gear, with a second bevel gear at the bottom of the shaft driving the propeller. Universal joints are used in the drive from the engine so that the outdrive assembly can be swiveled for steering and tilted to adjust the thrust angle for trimming the boat. Generally, the outboard drive housing is bolted directly to the engine, but it can be mounted separately.

The propellers used for high-speed engines have to be specially designed to handle the high powers and difficult working conditions involved. One favored design is the supercavitating propeller that induces cavitation at the blade surfaces and allows high-thrust loads to be achieved.

Another approach is the surface-piercing propeller that runs with its centerline on the water surface and only the lower blades in the water. This propeller imposes high loads on the blades but can give high efficiency. It is used in prop-riding hydroplanes, where the lifting effect of the blade helps to keep the stern up out of the water.

For some applications, a water-jet drive may be used. Water is drawn in near the front of the boat and pumped out to the rear as a high-velocity jet. Where the aim is to achieve the highest-possible speeds, the drive is normally provided by an aircraft type of jet engine giving a direct thrust.

Construction

Large speedboats may be made from welded steel, aluminum, or plywood. The most common form of construction for smaller craft is fiber-reinforced resin that allows the ready reproduction of complex shapes by the use of molds. Glass fiber is the material normally used, but for highest strength and low weight, other reinforcements such as carbon fiber and Kevlar are employed. High standards of construction are called for—at high speed, water is effectively solid. With inshore racing craft, increased safety is achieved by the use of protective capsules for the driver, which separate from the rest of the boat in the event of a crash.

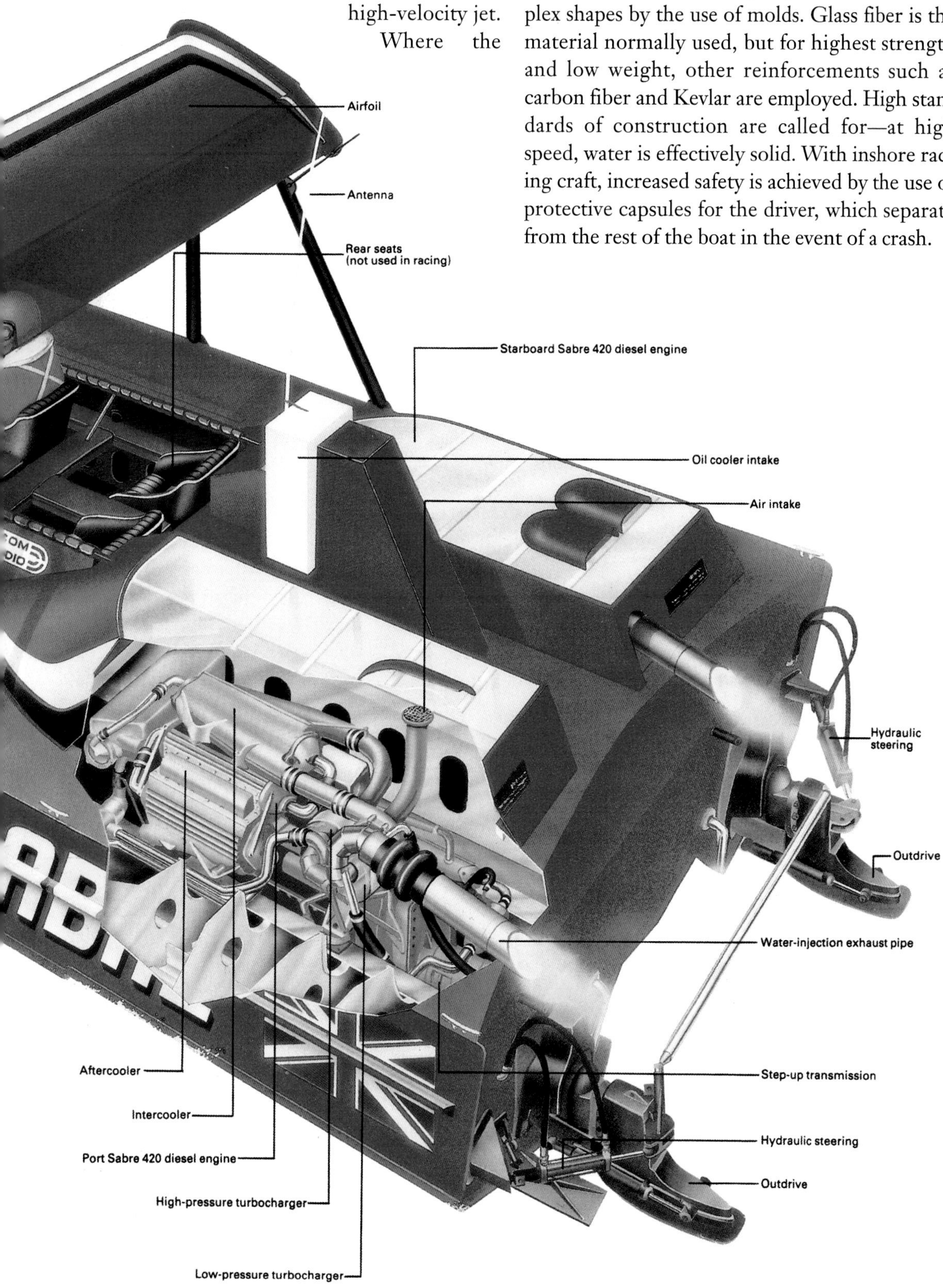

◀ The Romans Sabre Class II catamaran has aluminum hulls and two turbocharged lightweight engines. Catamarans and other multihulled speedboats are more stable at high speeds and so are used for racing.

Airfoil

Antenna

Rear seats
(not used in racing)

Starboard Sabre 420 diesel engine

Oil cooler intake

Air intake

Hydraulic steering

Outdrive

Water-injection exhaust pipe

Aftercooler

Intercooler

Port Sabre 420 diesel engine

High-pressure turbocharger

Low-pressure turbocharger

Step-up transmission

Hydraulic steering

Outdrive

◀ A V8 3.5 liter outboard speedboat engine, which, in 1981, set new standards of performance.

Speed records

The most extreme types of speedboat are those intended for water-speed-record attempts. Generally, the boats used for record attempts embody the limit of available knowledge—and have frequent failures and many fatal accidents. The first speed records were set by racing boats, and the period up to the late 1930s saw successive records set by American and British drivers in stepped hydroplanes powered by aircraft engines. For example, *Miss America X* (built by Commodore Garfield Wood) had four V12 Packard engines with an output of 6,400 horsepower (4,800 kW) in a 38 ft. (11.6 m) hull and achieved 124.91 mph (201.02 km/h) in 1932. A different approach was adopted for Donald Campbell's *Bluebird*, which used a single Rolls Royce engine of 2,150 horsepower (1,600 kW) but had a better power-to-weight ratio. Campbell regained the record for Britain, eventually raising it to 130.94 mph (210.72 km/h) in 1938.

Stepped hydroplanes were reaching the limit of their development, with successive records showing an increase of only a few miles per hour. The solution was the three pointer developed by Adolf Apel in the United States. His design had a concave hull with two floats (sponsons) in the sides of the forward section. These sponsons gave the necessary buoyancy, acting as the forward planing points, with the third point being a wedge at the stern so that the rest of the hull was lifted clear of the water at speed. A new *Bluebird* designed to these principles allowed Campbell to raise his record to 141.7 mph (228.04 km/h) in 1939.

The first successful attempt with a jet boat was made by Campbell, with a series of runs from 1955 to 1964 giving his final record at 276.31 mph (444.66 km/h). Subsequent attempts by various drivers resulted in even higher speeds. The 300 mph (480 km/h) barrier was broken by the Australian Ken Warby, who achieved 317.60 mph (511.13 km/h) in 1978 and remains unbeaten.

FACT FILE

- In 1921, the new world water-speed record was set by Miss America II, a 32 ft. (9.7 m) hydroplane powered by four V12 aero-engines. Twin immersed propellers drove the record-breaking craft at 80.57 mph (129.66 km/h).

- In the 1930s, the famous Russian composer Rachmaninov, who lived on the shores of Lake Lucerne in Switzerland, used to compete with the lake's passenger steamers in a four-cylinder motorboat.

- At the end of World War II, Japan was preparing a large number of kamikaze speedboats powered by automobile engines, each carrying 4,000 lbs. (1,800 kg) of TNT. More than 6,000 of the suicide boats were built for the Okinawa campaign, but they were discovered and destroyed by the U.S. Patrol Torpedo Boats before they could go into action.

- In the James Bond movie Live and Let Die, a stuntman, Jerry Comeaux, made a record 110 ft. (33 m) ramp jump in a Glastron GT-150 speedboat powered by a 135-horsepower (100 kW) Evinrude Starflite engine. His takeoff speed was 56 mph (90 km/h).

▶ A monohull Scarab speedboat powered by 1,250 brake horsepower units based on Chevrolet auto engines.

SEE ALSO: BOAT BUILDING • HYDRODYNAMICS • MARINE PROPULSION • OUTBOARD MOTOR

Speedometer and Tachometer

A speedometer is a device found on automobile dashboards that indicates the road speed of the vehicle. Almost without exception, a speedometer is combined with an odometer, which indicates the total distance that the car has traveled. A trip facility is commonly offered, which shows the distance traveled on a particular journey.

Two kinds of speedometers are fitted to automobiles—mechanical and electronic. Mechanical speedometers are analog devices, usually showing speed by moving a needle or colored bar against a scale, whereas electronic speedometers may have analog or digital displays. Usually, LEDs (light-emitting diodes) or LCDs, (liquid crystal displays) are used.

Speedometers

The most common type of speedometer display uses a pointer on a circular or arc scale. Another type is the straight-line speedometer, which has a colored helix printed on a tube. As the tube rotates, a section of the helix appears to advance along the scale. Instrument displays may be lit from around the edge and have fluorescent markings to make them easy to read in the dark, or they may be back lit. The best of these designs have even lighting and high legibility.

Mechanical speedometers have changed little since their inception in the 1920s. The speedometer is driven from a point on the vehicle transmission that is rotating at a speed directly proportional to the vehicle's road speed—there is often a special point on the transmission tail shaft. Drive to the speedometer is transmitted by means of a flexible shaft of multistrand wire rotating inside a flexible tube. This assembly is called the flexible drive or, more commonly, the speedometer cable.

The flexible drive is connected to the main spindle of the speedometer, which carries a magnet. Close to the magnet and pivoted on the same axis is an aluminum disk, or cup, called the drag cup. The drag cup, in turn, is connected to the speed indicator, which may be a needle, a pointer, or a moving colored bar.

On the opposite side of the cup from the magnet is a steel stator. When the vehicle moves, the magnet is rotated—the steel stator rotates under the influence of the magnetic field. Eddy currents (with the associated magnetic field) are set up in the aluminum drag cup, causing it to try to follow the rotation of the magnet.

Some electronic speedometers rely on conventional flexible drives to transmit speed infor-

mation between the transmission and the dashboard. Once at the dashboard, a microprocessor is used to count the rotations of the drive. If some kind of analog display is being used, the output from the microprocessor is used to control a small electric motor that drives the indicator. Fully electronic displays use the output to drive a digital readout or, sometimes, an analog display.

Odometer

The odometer is simply a counting device that acts as a distance recorder. Analog odometers consist of a number of adjacent drums, each with numbers 0 to 9 printed around them. The drums are positioned behind a window in the speedometer so that only one number on each drum is visible. Each drum has a transfer pinion with two sets of teeth that engage in the internal gearing of the drums. The internal gearing of each drum also has two sets of teeth. On one side there are 20

▲ The tachometer on this Honda 750 motorcycle is fitted to the right of the speedometer, with rubber mountings protecting the delicate mechanisms of both instruments from vibrations.

▼ Left: a speed and distance meter. The counting device is the odometer, or mileage counter; the numbers show through a slot in the dial. Right: a mechanical speedometer on a high-performance Moto Guzzi Le Mans Mark III motorcycle.

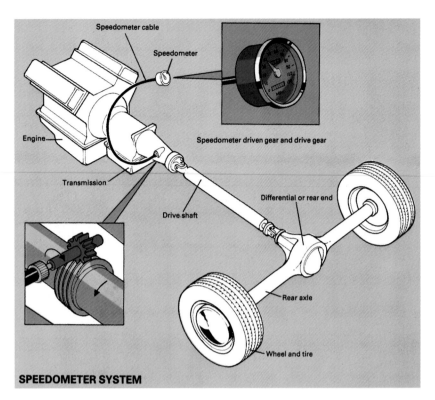

SPEEDOMETER SYSTEM

teeth, but on the other there are just two knock-over teeth. Each time a counter comes up to the 9 position, a knockover tooth engages with the transfer pinion to the right and turns that drum for one-tenth of a revolution before disengaging. The effect is for the counter to advance one digit. Electronic odometers may be motor-driven versions of the traditional types or digital displays driven by a microprocessor that keeps count of the incoming pulses.

Tachometer

The tachometer, or revolution indicator, is an instrument for measuring engine speed and is calibrated to indicate the number of revolutions the engine crankshaft makes in any one minute. The number of revolutions as a vehicle is shifted through the gears is an indication of engine performance. The tachometer is useful to racing car drivers, drivers of large commercial vehicles with many gear ratios, and drivers of ordinary cars who want to get the best out of their engines.

The coil-ignition, or original impulse, tachometer, now obsolete, is triggered by the current pulses produced in the low-tension circuit by the contact breaker, which is operated by a cam on the distributor drive. The change of current in the low-tension (LT) side of the coil generates the high-tension (HT) voltage supplied through the distributor to the spark plugs. On any internal combustion engine, this pulsing is directly proportional to engine speed and is therefore suitable for triggering the tachometer. It is done by the transformer principle of primary and secondary

▲ The speedometer is linked to the transmission by a flexible cable so that forward movement of the rear wheels will register a reading even if the engine is switched off. Any rearward movement does not register a reading, because the gear mechanism in the meter is disengaged. Inset, top right: the dial, as it appears on the instrument panel. Inset, bottom left: the linkage drive at the transmission end.

coils, the primary loop being formed from the LT lead and the secondary by a fine wire bobbin. The coil senses the induction pulse, which is amplified and fed to the triggering circuit designed into the circuit board. The circuitry interprets the frequency of the pulses as a voltage, which is fed to a moving-coil voltmeter—the indicating dial of the instrument, which is calibrated in revolutions per minute rather than in volts.

With the advent of transistorized and capacitor-discharge ignition systems, the LT current was reduced to a few milliamps. This reduction changed the pulse shape, making it ineffective for a current-triggered tachometer, and led to a different circuit design that measures the voltage pulse at the contact breaker terminal on the coil. The voltage-triggered tachometer is now generally used by vehicle manufacturers in preference to the current type.

The induction tachometer was developed for use on diesel engines, which do not have electric ignition systems. The induction tachometer, therefore, senses rotational or peripheral speed by means of a magnetic perception head. When a ferrous object moves in close proximity past the sensor, there is a variation of the reluctance in the sensor's magnetic circuit. The resultant electromotive force (pulses generated in the perception head coil) is then transmitted via the two terminals on the sensor to the tachometer head. The instrument is also connected to the vehicle's 12- or 24-volt DC (direct current) supply. The number of ferrous lobes permitted to pass the sensor per revolution varies depending on the ratio of the takeoff shaft to the crankshaft.

The self-generating tachometer was supplied to certain manufacturers for original equipment and has since been superseded. The installation used a generator that was connected directly to the instrument. The generator was mechanically driven from a suitable ratio takeoff, producing an alternating current (AC) voltage proportional to the speed of rotation of the generator shaft. By rectifying this voltage, a direct relationship between voltage and engine speed was obtained on the tachometer scale.

The high-tension tachometer, designed for marine engines, operates off the HT plug leads. It is connected to a 12-volt supply and senses the HT voltage via a screened trigger cable that is twisted around each plug lead, thus enabling the tachometer to operate with different types of ignition systems.

SEE ALSO: AUTOMOBILE • CAM • DIGITAL DISPLAY • ELECTRONICS • TRANSFORMER • TRANSMISSION, AUTOMOBILE

Sphygmomanometer

A sphygmomanometer is an instrument used with a stethoscope to measure blood pressure. The word is derived from the Greek *sphygmos* (pulse) and manometer, an instrument used for measuring the pressure of a gas. The first practical sphygmomanometer was invented in 1896 by Scipione Riva Rocci, an Italian physician. This early design used a column of mercury for the manometer—a system still used today. Physicians at this time, however, used their fingers to detect blood flow, producing relatively inaccurate results. The technique of listening with a stethoscope for changes in blood flow—introduced in 1905 by a Russian physician, Nikolai Korotkoff—proved to be much more accurate and led to a greater understanding of blood-pressure-related illnesses.

The sphygmomanometer consists of an inflatable rubber bag enclosed in a cuff made of a firm unyielding material. Connected to the bag are two tubes—one is attached to a hollow rubber ball that pumps air into the bag, and the other connects to a manometer, which registers the pressure in millimeters of mercury. The cuff must be long enough to be wrapped around the arm of a patient. It used to be about 3 ft. (0.90 m) long, but because materials currently used allow the surfaces of the cuff to adhere to each other, it can now be shorter by about one-half. Cuffs used today are also much broader than those used on early models and consequently provide more accurate pressure measurements.

Manometers

Manometers are commonly U-shaped tubes filled with a liquid such as mercury. By leaving one end of the tube open to the air and connecting the other to the system being measured, it is possible to measure the pressure differential. Two types of pressure-recording systems are in general use in sphygmomanometers, the mercury gravity manometer and the aneroid manometer. The first consists of a glass column containing a volume of mercury at its base fixed to a calibrated scale. The second uses a sealed metal chamber, called the bellows, that expands with the application of pressure, and a gear sector transmits the movement to the indicator needle on a gauge.

Blood pressure

Blood pressure is the pressure that blood exerts against the walls of the arteries. Two measures are recorded—the first is the systolic (when the heart contracts, pushing blood out and around the body via the arteries), and the other is the diastolic

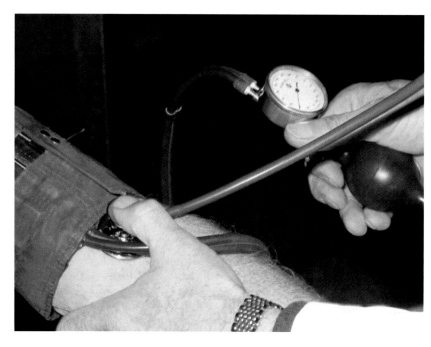

▲ A sphygmomanometer used to measure arterial blood pressure. The cuff is inflated around the upper arm and the pressure is then read off a scale that gives the systolic and diastolic measurements.

(when the heart dilates, allowing blood to reenter). The systolic is the maximal arterial pressure, the diastolic the minimal.

To measure blood pressure, the deflated cuff is wrapped around an arm—with the rubber bag on the inside. The cuff—which must be the correct width for the arm—is placed above the antecubital space where the brachial artery has been palpated. A stethoscope is placed over the palpable artery, and air is pumped into the bag until the reading on the gauge is about 30 mm above the point at which the pulse disappears. The inflated bag acts as a tourniquet, cutting off the blood supply. No sound will be heard through the stethoscope at this stage, so very slowly, air is released from the cuff.

When pulse beats are heard, the measurement on the manometer is noted. This is the systolic pressure. Deflation of the bag continues slowly until the pulse beat disappears again—the measurement recorded now is the diastolic pressure. The blood pressure is recorded as the systolic pressure over the diastolic pressure. The upper normal limit is usually taken to be 140 mm of mercury for systolic and 90 for diastolic.

There are more accurate and sophisticated methods of measuring blood pressure (such as inserting a fine tube into an artery), but with a sphygmomanometer, the pressure can be measured easily with no discomfort to the patient.

SEE ALSO: BAROMETER • BLOOD • GAS LAWS • HEART PACEMAKER • MANOMETER • PRESSURE

Spinning

Spinning is a process in which fibers, such as cotton, wool, or polyester, are assembled into a thin ribbon that is twisted to make a continuous thread called a yarn. The earliest recorded invention for spinning a yarn is the spindle whorl. This simple device is a wooden stick, pushed partly through the center of a wooden disk. When held vertically by a short length of seed yarn, the spindle rotates freely and enables twisting of small amounts of fibers attached by hand onto the free end of the seed yarn, so increasing the yarn length.

Early methods

The spindle whorl dates back to around 200 B.C.E. It was used for spinning wool in Babylon, Greece, and Rome, cotton in India, and flax in Egypt. Its uses continued to provide the only method of spinning in Europe until 1300 C.E., when it was superseded by the hand spinning wheel. This device consists of a large wheel turned by hand to rotate a wooden spindle fixed in a simple bearing. When the opposite hand, holding the fiber to be twisted,

is moved toward the wheel, the spinning action changes from twisting to winding up the length of yarn formed. Until 1770, the spinning wheel provided yarns for weaving on hand looms. Spinning and weaving were part of a cottage industry.

It was the early developments in weaving that led to the demise of the hand spinning wheel. In 1773, an Englishman, John Kay, invented the flying shuttle, an automatic means of propulsion for putting yarns in the weft during weaving. This shuttle speeded up the weaving process and increased the demand for a faster method of spinning. The result was a series of inventions during the latter part of the 18th century, which—together with the introduction of the steam engine by James Watt in 1782—ended the cottage-based spinning process and gave birth to the spinning-mill era of the Industrial Revolution.

One of the more significant developments in spinning methods (which have always kept pace with improvements in weaving methods) is ring spinning. It was invented in the United States around 1830 and is still the most used method worldwide. The ring spinning of cotton, wool, and synthetic fibers falls into two categories. Short-staple spinning involves cotton and synthetic fibers of similar length. Long-staple spinning pertains to wool and synthetics of similar lengths.

Short-staple spinning

As raw material, fiber is purchased in bales weighing up to a ton. If a handful of cotton is taken from a bale and looked at closely, it will be seen to have embedded among the fibers dirt particles, sand, small pieces of leaf, and pieces of cotton seed. Before the fibers can be spun into yarn, these impurities must be removed. The opening and cleaning machines perform this function. Bales are broken down into small clumps, or tufts, of fibers weighing only a few ounces—and it is during the process of breaking down or opening the fiber mass that the impurities are removed.

On passing through several cleaning machines, the fiber tufts are fed to carding machines. A typical one, the short-staple card—also called the cotton card—consists of three main cast-iron cylinders, each having a continuous saw-tooth metal band wound around its curved surface to give a covering of projecting sharp points. The first roller—the taker-in, or licker-in—breaks the tufts into smaller sizes, which are transferred by a stripping action onto the second cylinder—the main cylinder, or swift. Above the main cylinder, approximately 100 rectangular plates, or flats, are fitted closely to the sharp points on the cylinder surface. The flats are also covered with sharp points angled to oppose

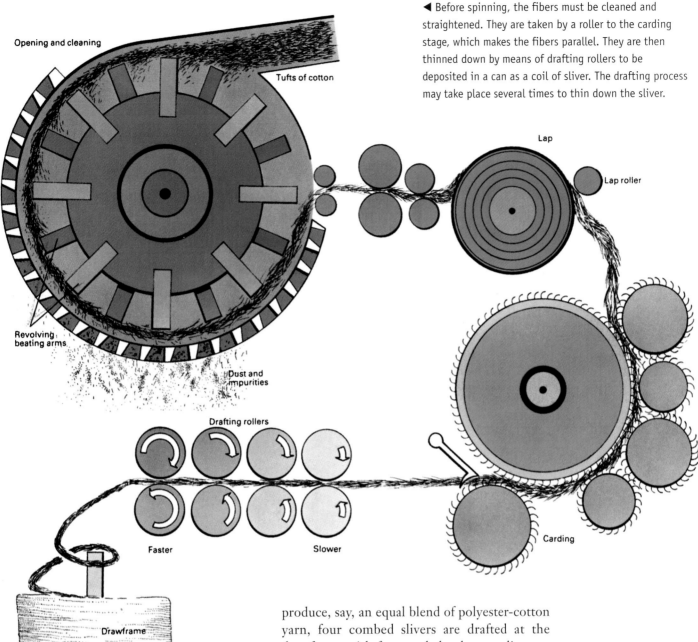

Opening and cleaning

Tufts of cotton

Revolving beating arms

Dust and impurities

Drafting rollers

Faster

Slower

Drawframe

Lap

Lap roller

Carding

◀ Before spinning, the fibers must be cleaned and straightened. They are taken by a roller to the carding stage, which makes the fibers parallel. They are then thinned down by means of drafting rollers to be deposited in a can as a coil of sliver. The drafting process may take place several times to thin down the sliver.

those on the main cylinder. When the tufts on the main cylinder enter the flats, a carding action occurs, and the opposing points of the flats and main cylinder comb out the fibers. The carded fibers are removed by the third cylinder, the doffer, which is stripped of the fibers to form the card web. This is lightly compressed into an untwisted rope, the card sliver, and coiled into a tall can, called the sliver can.

Combing takes place after carding—its function is to remove short fibers. The longer the fibers, the stronger and more uniform the yarn. Yarns made from combed sliver are called combed ring-spun yarns. In short-staple spinning, only high-quality cottons (Egyptian quality) are combed. Synthetic fibers are not combed. To produce, say, an equal blend of polyester-cotton yarn, four combed slivers are drafted at the drawframe with four carded polyester slivers—blending by doubling.

Drafting and twisting

In the ring-spinning mill, drafting (thinning out) takes three separate operations—the drawframe, the roving frame, and the ring frame. In the drawframe, three or four pairs of rotating rollers are positioned in line so that the distance between successive pairs is slightly longer than the fiber length to prevent fibers from breaking during drafting. Each pair of rollers rotates faster than the one behind. The card slivers fed to the back rollers are drafted by stretching between the rollers, with the amount of stretch equal to the size of draft.

The drawn sliver now has to be highly drafted to produce a thin ribbon of fibers, which when twisted, gives a yarn of the required count. Because the draft needed is large (around 100), drafting is done in a minimum of two operations.

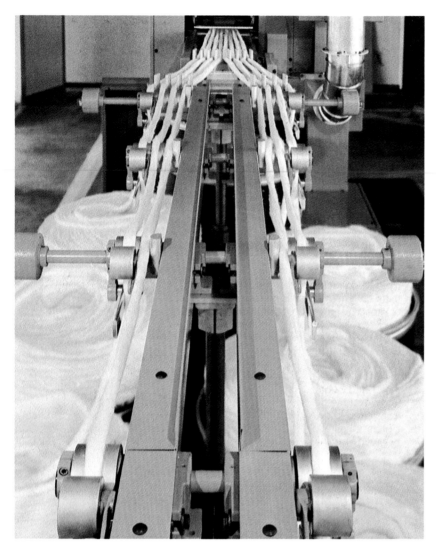

When wool fibers are put through the combing operation, the resultant yarn is called worsted yarn, and the process worsted spinning. With no combing, the process is known as semiworsted spinning, and the yarn semiworsted yarn. Unlike short-staple spinning, two or more worsted or semiworsted yarns are usually plied before being used in weaving or knitting. Such yarns are used in woven fabrics for coats and men's suits and in knitted garments for outer wear.

New spinning methods

Until the early 1970s, ring spinning was the only commercially viable high-speed method of yarn production. However, since then a number of new methods have replaced ring spinning in certain areas of yarn manufacture. Ring spinning is labor intensive, produces small yarn packages, and requires a large factory. Rotor, friction drum, and hollow-spindle wrap spinning are three important methods that overcome these disadvantages.

In rotor spinning it is sliver—not roving—that is fed to the machine. The sliver is drafted by a fast-rotating (700 rpm) pin-covered roller, the opening roller, which removes individual fibers from the sliver. The fibers are then sucked off the opening roller down a tapered tube. The yarn is formed by a fast-rotating rotor and then wound onto a bobbin. Large yarn packages can be made, because there is no ring surrounding the bobbin to limit the amount of yarn that can be wound up.

Friction drum spinning also uses a sliver feed. However, the fibers are deposited to form a drafted ribbon between two rotating perforated drums. Suction through the holes in the drums holds and compacts the ribbon as it is twisted into a yarn. Twisting is achieved by frictional rolling of the ribbon between the drums. The production rate is up to 656 ft. per minute (200 m/min), ten times faster than ring spinning.

Hollow-spindle wrap spinning uses a roller-drafting system designed to produce a thin ribbon from a sliver feed. The ribbon is passed through a rotating hollow spindle. Mounted on the spindle is a tube called a pirn. A fine continuous filament of either nylon or polyester is prewound onto the pirn. This filament is pulled through the hollow spindle with the drafted ribbon. As the spindle rotates, the filament is wrapped around the drafted ribbon and forms the yarn. In this method, wrapping with a filament replaces the insertion of twist to produce a yarn—and production of up to 328 ft. per minute (100 m/min) can be achieved.

In the roving process, a draft of five is used to thin the drawframe sliver. The "roving" now becomes too weak to handle without receiving a small amount of twist, approximately three-quarters of turn to one turn per inch (tpi). Too much twist will hinder the final drafting at the spinning stage on the ring frame. Here a draft of up to 20 can be used. As the drafted material leaves the front rollers, it is highly twisted (up to 40 tpi) to convert it into a yarn. The formed yarn is wound onto the bobbin, passing under a C-shaped metal clip (traveler), which is loosely clipped onto a fixed ring around the bobbin. The bobbin is mounted on a driven spindle, which rotates it, causing the yarn to pull the traveler around the ring. Each full circle puts one turn of twist into the drafted material.

Long-staple spinning

The sequence of operations for spinning wool is similar to that for cotton, but some of the machines use different principles. In opening and cleaning, the wool fibers are scoured by passing through a series of baths in which a soapy liquid is used to remove the dirt and grease. After rinsing in further baths, the wool is dried in ovens.

▲ A roll-feed table used for sliver off-take, when it is drawn over rollers and collected onto spools. The process is repeated taking the cotton from the spools (shown here) over a pair of draw-off rolls. The sliver is monitored by raisable contact rolls, and the machine stops automatically if the thread breaks. The yarn is twisted into shape by frictional rolling between drums. As it is pulled from the drums, new fibers are deposited and twisted onto its end. The finished yarn can then be woven into cloth.

 SEE ALSO: COTTON • FIBER, NATURAL • FIBER, SYNTHETIC • HOSIERY AND KNITWARE MANUFACTURE • LOOM • TEXTILE

Spirit

Fermentation is a process whereby sugar is transformed into alcohol by the action of yeast. One of the most familiar fermented liquids is wine, which is made when the natural yeast in grape skins acts on the natural sugar in the juice. Beer is produced by introducing yeast into a sweetened liquid obtained from a cereal, usually barley. Spirits are made by distilling fermented liquids. Alcohol is more volatile than water, so it distills more readily, and spirits therefore contain more alcohol than the original fermented liquid.

The origins of distillation are not certain. Claims are made for its introduction to the Indian subcontinent 2,000 years ago, possibly from China. It has been practiced in Europe only for about half that time, at first for making medicinal preparations and later in the production of perfumes from flower essences. Commercial distillation is not much more than 400 years old. There are two common types of alcohol: ethanol, which occurs in alcoholic drinks, and methanol (also called industrial, or wood, alcohol), which is poisonous and comes from a range of sources.

Distillation is mainly carried out by two forms of still. The best known is the pot still, or alembic, which is like a large kettle, nearly always of copper and tinned on the inside. To this is attached a condenser, which cools the spirit-containing vapor and restores it to liquid form. There are various styles of pot stills and a great range of sizes—the particular design depends both on the spirit being distilled and on local traditions and regulations. The other type of still is the patent, or Coffey, still, and the process of distilling with

this still is known, accurately, as continuous distillation. The patent still employs steam to separate the spirit from the alcoholic wash with which it is charged. The system was invented in Scotland by Robert Stein in 1826 and perfected five years later by an Irishman, Aeneas Coffey.

Continuous distillation is used for producing spirits in very great quantities, and the spirit from a patent still is usually very strong, almost flavorless, and highly refined. The spirit from a pot still is less strong and carries with it flavor characteristics from the alcoholic wash from which it has been distilled. Such flavors are essential for the production of fine spirits with natural and distinctive taste, such as good whiskey or brandy. However, spirit from the pot still also retains some unwanted ingredients called congeners, which partly disappear when the spirit is matured in traditional wooden casks.

Whiskey

Whiskey is produced all over the world; the best known is Scotch whisky. The art of distilling was likely brought to Scotland from northern Ireland by missionary monks, and the first such distillates would have had medical uses. Whisky is first recorded in Scottish history in 1494. By 1500, it was drunk at the court in Edinburgh, and in 1505, the king gave it official recognition by placing its control in the capital in the hands of the Royal College of Surgeons. The word *whisky* is derived from the Gaelic *uisge beatha*, which means "water of life." The "e" in *whiskey* is a fairly recent addition in Ireland and the United States.

▲ Taking a sample of bourbon sour mash from the fermentation vat in the Wild Turkey distillery in Lynchburg, Tennessee. By law, bourbon must be made from a mash containing at least 51 percent corn.

After a turbulent history, Scotch whisky settled down to legal existence and growth with the introduction of the patent still, and blending was introduced about 1860. Blending meant that the pungent pot-distilled malt whiskies, mostly associated with the Highlands, were mixed with the much lighter grain whiskies produced by patent distillation. This new type was more to the taste of the English, and within a fairly short time, Scotch whisky had conquered not just the British market but also that of the whole civilized world.

Malt whisky is made wholly from malted barley. Malting is the process of steeping barley in water. When the barley has started to sprout, it is dried, and peat smoke is allowed to permeate the drying barley. The barley is then dressed and ground and more water is added, and from the resulting mash, a sweetish liquid (wort) is drawn off and cooled. The wort is run into huge vats where it begins to ferment after yeast has been added, making a sort of beer (wash). From this alcoholic wash (about 10 percent alcohol), which carries the essential characteristics of Scottish water and peat, malt whisky is distilled.

There are two distillations. The first produces a weakish and rather rough spirit called low wines. This liquid is charged into a second pot still, and the result is Scotch malt whisky. Before it becomes lawfully Scotch whisky, however, it must be matured in wood for a minimum of three years. It is usually matured for much longer: a period of 8 to 10 years is common.

Grain whiskey is produced by continuous distillation from corn to which some malted barley has been added. It is rarely matured for more than three years. Blended Scotch whisky, by far the most popular type, is a mixture of malt and grain whiskies. A good blend will contain about 30 individual malts, whose character will depend on the distillery of origin, although at least one famous brand contains more than 60 different malts. There is no regulation as to the quantities of grain in a blend, but a fine brand will contain about equal proportions of malts and grain. Some whiskies are recasked after blending for further maturing in wood, a method that ensures that the whiskies in the blend are thoroughly married. Eventually, the blended whiskey will be diluted with purified water to the strength demanded by its intended market. If a Scotch whisky carries an age, it is the length of time spent in the cask in the case of a straight malt whiskey or, in the case of a blend, the age of the youngest constituent whiskey.

There are a great number of legally defined American whiskies, but internationally, the only important one is bourbon, protected from 1964

▼ To make malt whiskey, malt is first made from barley and water. The sprouted grains are then processed into a mash from which wort is separated. Fermentation and double distillation of the wort yields whiskey.

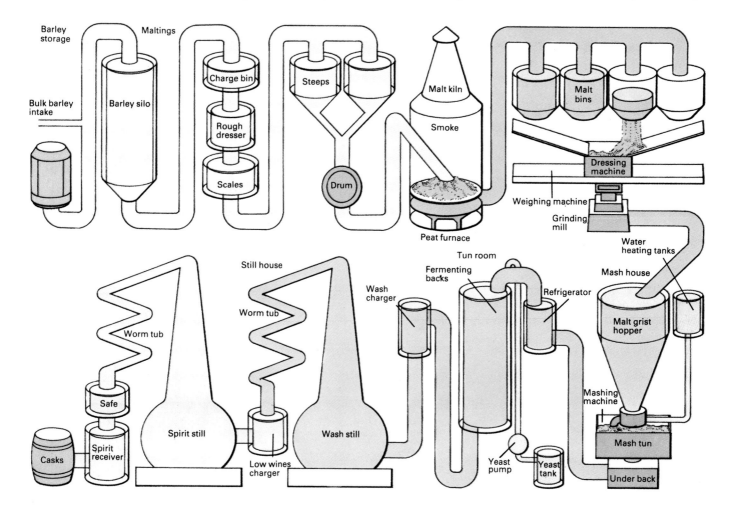

◄ Pot stills in a gin distillery. Gin is made by redistilling a purified spirit to which flavorings, particularly juniper, have been added.

by an act of Congress. Many aspects of its production are controlled by law; for example, it must be produced from a mash containing at least 51 percent corn, and it must be matured in new casks to ensure that the resulting spirit will have the characteristic strong flavor of bourbon. Its home is Kentucky, but it is produced in several other states of the United States.

Canadian whiskey is a lighter spirit than bourbon but lacks the character of Scotch. Corn is the principal grain in the mash, but some wheat and malted barley are also used.

Irish whiskey is unique in having a proportion of oats in the mash in addition to wheat, rye, and barley, of which half is malted. It is mainly a pot-still product and is distilled three times and matured for a minimum of seven years.

Brandy

Brandy is defined as a distillate from wine or wine by-products. It is made in all wine-producing countries, but some such distillates are of extremely poor quality. It is important to differentiate between grape brandy and distillates such as cognac. Grape brandy, whether French or from any other country, may be distilled from any sort of wine, probably by continuous distillation, and sometimes has a little good pot-still brandy added to give it some character. There is, unfortunately, very little legal significance in words and initials that appear on brandy labels.

The leading brandy of repute is cognac, a closely controlled product coming only from special areas in southwestern France and centering on the towns of Cognac and Jarnac. It is produced under strict regulations. Double distillation is employed, as it is for Scotch whisky, though the stills are much smaller. The special wine of the district, from which cognac is distilled, is not matured and is distinctly acid. Like all distillations, the spirit is colorless when it leaves the stills. It is matured in Limousin oak casks.

By an elaborate topping-up process, average age is built up. A proportion of each distillation is matured, unblended, for as many as 50 years, when it will improve no more. It is then placed in big bottles, and a little is added to the brand's oldest blends, giving extra distinction. No cognac matured in France carries a date. Vintage cognac is a brandy sent to Britain a year after the vintage from which it was distilled and matured in England. A bottle of vintage cognac should carry the date of the vintage and the date of bottling, for it is the time it spends in cask that counts—no spirit improves in the bottle.

The other good-quality French brandy is the highly flavored Armagnac, produced slightly farther south. Production is only about a quarter that of cognac, and it is much less well known.

The color of a spirit has nothing to do with its taste or quality. Although spirits will pick up varying amounts of color from cask maturing—quite a lot in the case of old malt whiskey but much less for cognac—commercially, color adjustment is required to retain a brand's standard. It does not affect the flavor in any way.

Gin

The production of gin began in Holland, where it first appeared as a medicinal preparation about 1550. Dutch gin is markedly different from the best-known type, London Dry (the name now denotes a type of gin rather than its place of origin). In 19th-century England, gin was produced in great quantities and was sold very cheaply. It has become a universally respected spirit and the prime constituent of many people's favorite mixed drinks. The international reputation of London's gin started with the introduction in the late 19th century of unsweetened gin, which marked the separation of what was to become known as London Dry from its Dutch precursor.

In Britain and the United States, gin is produced from a purified grain spirit by redistilling it in a pot still in the presence of various botanical extracts, the most important being essence of juniper, from which gin derives its name. Other botanical flavorings include coriander, licorice, orris root, cardamom, anise, fennel, bitter almonds, and lemon peel—precisely which ingredients are used and in what proportion depends on the particular brand of gin.

Rum

To be so named, rum must be distilled from the by-product of the production of cane sugar in a cane-sugar-producing country. The rum market in the United States, for example, is almost wholly supplied by Puerto Rico. Though a few special rums are distilled in pot stills, nearly all commercial rums are from patent stills. When water is added to molasses (the residue of cane-sugar production), natural yeasts start a speedy fermentation. From the resultant alcoholic wash, an extremely clean spirit, often called cane spirit, is distilled. To make dark rum other than extra quality grades, a concentrate of rum flavoring and flavorless coloring matter are added to the white distillate. The color, white or dark, does not affect the potency of the drink.

Vodka

Vodka is the national drink of Russia and Poland. Literally translated, the word means "little water". It can be made from a variety of sources, including potatoes, wheat, rye, and sugar beet or a mixture of these. After distillation, the spirit is purified by filtration through charcoal, diluted with water, and then bottled without undergoing any aging. Vodka made in this way is only very slightly flavored and is designed to be drunk ice cold, but in its homelands, numerous flavors are infused into the drink—for example, in Poland, zubrowka is made by flavoring vodka with a type of grass of the same name.

▲ Two of the condensers in the Wild Turkey distillery. After liquor from the fermented mash has been processed in the column continuous still, the vapor passes into the condenser. The resulting liquid flows into the pot still, or doubler, from where it is passed into another condenser. The liquor, now ready for maturing, is decanted into specially made barrels, which have been burned on the inside. Over the eight-year maturation period, the charcoal surface of the inside of the barrel serves to filter out any impurities and to enhance the flavor of the bourbon.

Liqueurs

A liqueur is a spirit that has been sweetened and flavored with herbs or fruits or a mixture of both. There are countless liqueurs made throughout the world—in some countries, almost every village has its own distinctive liqueur. Most liqueurs are made by flavoring a spirit base—for example, cognac—with an infusion of the flavoring material, although sometimes the flavoring is added before distillation. Although the recipes of most liqueurs is a closely guarded secret, many have a single predominant flavor, for example, green Chartreuse (licorice), yellow Chartreuse (anise), Cointreau (orange), crème de menthe (mint), curaçao (orange), Grand Marnier (orange), Irish Mist (honey), Kahlua (cocoa-coffee), kümmel (caraway), amaretto (almonds), ouzo (anise), sabra (chocolate), Midori (melon), Tia Maria (coffee), and triple sec (orange).

All drinks mentioned above are spirits of one sort or another, but the list is by no means complete. Virtually wherever there is some vegetable matter that will ferment, there will be a distilled spirit derived from it. Other well-known spirits include the cactus-based tequila of Mexico; slivovitz, the plum brandy made in Eastern Europe; and kirsch, made from cherries.

SEE ALSO: ALCOHOL • BEER AND BREWING • DISTILLATION AND SUBLIMATION • SUGAR REFINING • WINEMAKING

Sports Equipment

The origins of some games are lost in the past (golf, for instance, appears to have originated in the 15th century), but others were developed over a short period more recently. Because of basic differences among games, equipment varies considerably in shape, size, and constitution, and manufacturing methods differ accordingly. The adoption of new materials and manufacturing techniques is limited by the rules governing the games, which are often designed to preserve traditional aspects. For instance, the resilience of golf balls made in the United States is strictly limited, and such a rule is likely worldwide.

Wood and leather, as natural materials, have been used for many years for golf, tennis, cricket equipment, and so on, but newer materials such as high-strength alloys, rubber, plastics, and carbon fiber are superseding them in many sports.

Tennis balls

Tennis (properly, lawn tennis) was developed from real, or royal, tennis, a game dating back to the 14th century. Lawn tennis was perfected in the 1870s and was played with a ball made of rubber that bounced much better than the cloth-stuffed ball used for real tennis. Covering the rubber with felt improved its wearing qualities. The felt seams were joined by stitching, which was replaced by rubber cement in the 1920s.

The manufacturing method consists of first mixing rubber with special ingredients (clay for reinforcement, and sulfur and accelerators for vulcanization) in an internal mixer, which consists of a pair of intermeshing rotors within a chamber. The rotors continuously shear the rubber-powder mixture until it is homogeneously blended. The mixture, or compound, which has a puttylike consistency, is then forced by hydraulic pressure through the circular die of an extruder to produce a continuous rod, which is chopped into identical pieces, or plugs, by a high-speed rotating knife. Each plug is then placed into a cavity of a multi-cavity forming mold that squeezes it into a hollow hemisphere—one-half of a tennis ball.

Heat is applied so that the rubber becomes vulcanized—that is, converted from a puttylike material to an elastic material. Two hemispheres are joined together with rubber cement to form a core (rubber ball). The core may be pressurized with air or gas to 10 to 12 psi (0.7–0.8 bar) above atmospheric pressure. Alternatively, the core may be the pressureless type, in which case the bouncing qualities are obtained solely from the rubber of the core, which must be thicker and specially

◀ As leisure time increases, so does the demand for new and exciting sports. Sailboarding is one sport that has grown in popularity over the last twenty years.

compounded for the purpose. Most balls are pressurized because they are generally preferred by good players. The usual method is to include a chemical inflation pellet of sodium nitrite and ammonium chloride when the two hemispheres are glued together. When heat is applied, the pellet decomposes, releasing nitrogen.

The felt, or melton, with which a tennis ball is covered, is a high-quality cloth of wool and nylon. The weft (transverse) yarns are made from a wool and nylon mixture, and this mixture is woven into the cotton warp (longitudinal) yarns, so that the weft appears predominantly on one side of the cloth. This surface is subject to a teasing, or raising, operation to produce a hairy surface that is then consolidated by fulling—a process in which the natural felting properties of the wool are exploited by working the cloth in a soap solution to produce the necessary surface texture.

The melton is coated with rubber solution on its reverse side and is then cut into dumbbell shapes, two of which are used together to cover the surface of the core. The dumbbell covers are

◄ This machine turns the center of a golf ball—made of liquid in a rubber envelope—while the rubber thread is stretched around it. The golf ball is finished with a thermoplastic cover that sets dimples into the surface for better flight.

applied by hand, and the degree of stretching is carefully controlled, so an exact fit is obtained. Rubber cement applied to the edges of the dumbbells becomes vulcanized in a further molding operation, in which the ball is heated in spherical molds. A steaming operation raises the nap, and the ball is tested for deformation under load, so that balls are matched before they are packaged. The International Tennis Federation specification states that the ball must be yellow or white, between 2.5 and 2.6 in. (6.35–6.5 cm) in diameter, and between 2 and 2.06 oz. (56.7–58.4 g) in weight. The ball must bounce between 53 and 58 in. (132–145 cm) when it is dropped from a height of 100 in. (250 cm) onto a concrete base. Different degrees of bounce are used for different surfaces—a ball for a hard clay court requires less bounce than a ball to be used on a grass court.

Golf balls

Golf balls were originally made of wood; in the 17th century, these balls were superseded by balls made by stuffing boiled feathers into a hand-stitched leather case using a wooden tool and then a stuffing iron to cram them through a hole left in the leather. From 1850, they were made from solid gutta percha (a rubberlike substance made from the milky sap, or latex, of various South American and South Pacific trees), until the rubber-cored ball was developed in about 1900 and rapidly accepted—especially after it was used by the winner of the Open Championship in 1902.

The rules of golf lay down only the maximum weight and minimum size for a golf ball—1.62 oz. (46 g) and 1.62 in. (41 mm) in diameter in Britain and elsewhere except the North American conti-

nent, where the minimum size is 1.68 in. (42 mm) and a maximum resilience is specified.

A golf ball consists of three main components —a center (usually liquid or resilient rubber), around which are windings of highly elastic rubber thread, and a cover to protect the thread and to incorporate the dimple pattern.

A significant amount of the mass of the ball is concentrated in its center, which must allow the windings to distort readily when the ball is struck by the club so that the subsequent rapid recovery of the highly tensioned thread creates a high ball velocity. However, because the center must also absorb a minimum amount of energy at the point of ball–club contact, a liquid center has been used in premium balls for many years.

One way of making a liquid center is by mixing fine clay into water and glycerine. The mixture is then measured into hemispherical cavities in rubber molds. Because of the thixotropic nature of the mixture (its tendency to become thinner when stirred or shaken but to have a high viscosity when undisturbed), the rubber molds can be brought together vertically so that spheres of paste are produced. The molds are refrigerated to freeze the paste spheres, and they are then removed, coated with rubber, and subjected to a hot molding operation to vulcanize the rubber coating. The result is a small, heavy, deformable sphere of liquid inside a rubber envelope.

Rubber thread is produced by mixing rubber with special ingredients to obtain a highly elastic sheet after vulcanization—this process is carried out by winding the sheet onto large drums, which are put into steam-heated chambers. The sheet is then passed between multiknife cutters to produce rubber thread about 0.06 to 0.02 in. (1.5–0.5 mm) in diameter. The golf ball core is made by stretching the rubber thread to about 900 percent and winding it onto the center by means of a core-winding machine.

The material that forms the cover of the ball is a thermoplastic material that is made into hemispherical shells on an injection molding machine in which the hot plastic material is forced under pressure into cold molds. Two shells are placed around each core, and the assemblies are inserted into precision dies in a compression-molding press, which molds the cover material onto the cores under the action of heat and pressure. The dimple pattern is molded into the surface of the ball by the profiled surface of the die.

The molds are cooled and the balls extracted and accurately trimmed. Prepaint treatment follows, and the balls are spray painted on machines adapted for painting spherical objects. The balls are matched for compression (that is, deformation under load), the low-compression (or high-deformation) balls being segregated as lower grade. The balls are then identified by a stamping process and coated with polyurethane lacquer.

The dimple pattern molded into the ball surface has a very important function—the size and shape of the dimples are critical. The golf club is designed to produce a backspin to the ball at contact—causing it to spin about a horizontal axis so that the top of the ball is moving against the direction in which the ball is traveling. The air flow over the top of the ball is therefore speeded up, and that below the ball is retarded, producing a local reduction of air pressure immediately above the ball and an increase in the air pressure immediately below it, resulting in an upward force, or lift.

The dimple pattern controls the degree of lift achieved by the ball by influencing the interaction between the ball's surface and the air flow, and it also affects the drag experienced by the ball in moving through the air. The distance the ball travels through the air is therefore directly dependent on the dimple pattern.

After World War 1, the Royal and Ancient Club in Britain set out a rule, known as the "1–62 formula". This rule states that a golf ball should have a maximum weight of 1.62 oz. (45.93 g) and a minimum diameter of 1.62 in. (41 mm). The larger sized American ball, introduced in 1932, weighs 1.62 oz. and has a diameter of 1.68 in (42 mm). The American ball had replaced the small British ball entirely by 1980.

Tennis rackets

Tennis rackets first became subject to a specification in 1981, after an International Tennis Federation (ITF) study of the "spaghetti," or double-strung racket, which was introduced in 1977 and gave considerable topspin to the ball. The ITF subsequently made a rule: "A racket shall consist of a frame, which may be of any material, weight, size, or shape and stringing. The stringing must be uniform and smooth and may be of any material. The strings must be alternately interlaced or bonded where they cross. The distance between the main and/or cross strings shall not be less than one-quarter of an inch nor more than one-half inch. If there are attachments they must be used only to prevent wear and tear and must not alter the flight of the ball." In 1979 the ITF had limited racket length for professional players

▼ A craftsman uses a spokeshave to shape the blade of a cricket bat, which is made from willow.

to 29 in. (72 cm) and racket width to 12.5 in. (31.2 cm). These rules were subsequently extended to nonprofessional players.

Until the 1920s, racket frames were made by bending single sawed sticks of ash to the familiar racket shape after they had been softened by steaming. Subsequently, similar types of frame were produced by steam bending several thinner sticks and gluing them together to produce a plied frame. In the 1930s and 1940s, a process was developed for producing frames from even thinner sticks, or veneers, that could be bent cold. Strength was improved by adopting urea formaldehyde glues—the basis of the laminated frame.

Modern tennis rackets are made from steel and aluminum alloys and from composite metal, glass fiber, and carbon fiber constructions. They are more expensive than wooden ones but provide greater power and ball control.

Wooden squash and badminton rackets are manufactured in a way similar to wooden tennis rackets but often incorporate a steel shaft for improved lightness and strength. Newer materials, similar to those used for tennis rackets, have also largely superseded wood in these sports.

The manufacture of wooden rackets is a minor art form. Various woods are used in each frame. The basic strength of the frame is provided by ash and beech, but the throat, or wedge, area is usually sycamore or mahogany. Lightweight obeche is used as a spacer in the handle area, and hickory may be used to give strength and wear resistance to

▶ Cycling is a hugely popular sport for all ages. Changes in frame shapes and materials have led to machines that can tackle a variety of terrains but that are extremely light and easy to pedal.

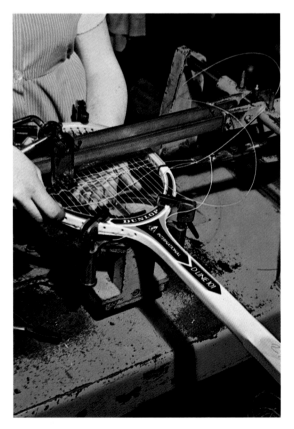

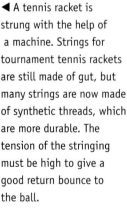

◀ A tennis racket is strung with the help of a machine. Strings for tournament tennis rackets are still made of gut, but many strings are now made of synthetic threads, which are more durable. The tension of the stringing must be high to give a good return bounce to the ball.

the outside of the frame. Sometimes, a wood such as walnut is used for its decorative appearance.

The sticks, or veneers, are obtained from specially selected logs by sawing, slicing, or peeling. Peeling is more efficient in yield of wood. In this operation, the log is steamed for a considerable time and is then rotated about its axis while a continuous veneer of wood is pared away by a knife blade that contacts the log along its whole length. The veneer is cut into strips parallel to the grain and they are bent to form the basic keyhole contour of the frame so that the grain of the wood achieves the greatest strength and rigidity.

Shaped pieces for the throat and handle are specially profiled, and all the components are coated on mating surfaces with urea formaldehyde glue. They are then assembled into a bending jig, and the characteristic racket shape is produced by the application of hydraulic pressure, which bends and consolidates the component parts around a former. Clamps are attached, so the formed bend may be removed from the jig and passed through ovens to cure the adhesive.

Up to three racket frames can be cut longitudinally from one bend. Handle pieces are then glued on (together with reinforcement in the shoulder area), after which the frame is subjected to a succession of shaping and sanding operations. Stringing holes are produced on a multi-spindle drilling machine, but subsequent countersinking and grooving operations are carried out largely by hand. The application of transfers, painting, and lacquering completes the process of manufacture.

Racket strings can be made from natural gut (produced from the intestines of sheep). Although such strings are preferred for top-class tennis, because they allow more precise ball control, strings made from nylon filaments by a spinning or braiding process are more popular because of lower cost and improved durability. Typical stringing tensions are 55 to 60 lbs. (25–27 kg) for a tennis racket, 35 to 40 lbs. (16–18 kg) for a squash racket, and 25 to 30 lbs. (11–14 kg) for a badminton racket.

Golf clubs

Golf clubs are subject to certain specifications regarding their constitution, which are designed to preserve the character of the game; certain other aspects, such as face markings and grip shapes, are also closely specified.

The rules allow the golfer to use a set of not more than 14 clubs—these clubs would typically consist of four woods, nine irons, and a putter. Clubs vary in weight (which is mainly determined by the head), length (which is determined by the shaft) and loft, which is the angle the face of the club makes with the vertical in the address position. Clubs get shorter, heavier, and more lofted as they increase in their numbered sequence.

The heads of wooden clubs, which were once largely made from persimmon, are today made from laminated blocks of maple shaped so that the alignment of the laminations changes to maximize the directional strength in the hosel area where the shaft is inserted. The heads are turned on a copy lathe to produce the rough shape characteristic of a golf wood, and areas are routed out on the hitting surface (face) and base (sole) to allow the fitting of a plastic face piece and metal soleplate, respectively. The weight of the wooden head is adjusted by adding lead to a hole drilled in the sole before the baseplate is screwed into position. The wood surface is sanded and painted after carefully shaping the club face.

Iron heads were originally hand forged— now they are either drop forged or cast by an investment casting process. In this process, the metal is poured into a ceramic mold, which is often made from a wax master (lost-wax process). Mild steel is normally used for forged heads, and stainless steels are common in castings. Castings have the

◀ Most sports need special equipment, and baseball is no exception. Shown here are a first baseman's glove, protective helmets, bats— which are usually made of ash wood—and a baseball.

advantage that they can be produced to closer tolerances than forgings and allow more design freedom for weight distribution and intricate detail. Additionally, the hole for shaft attachment may be cast rather than drilled. The heads are finished by grinding and polishing to produce the correct weight as well as a high surface finish.

In the early days, shafts were made of split ash, and later of hickory. Tubular metal shafts date from the 1890s but were not exploited until the early 1920s—although they gained acceptance in

◀ The amount of equipment needed for the sport of body building depends upon the level at which it is being practiced. Professionals require many different types of weights, as well as other types of special equipment, but at the most basic level, all that is needed is a set of dumbbells.

the United States, they were not authorized for golf in Britain until 1929. Shafts are now produced from steel alloy (manganese and boron) in tapered form by a step-tapering process in which a metal tube is forced through dies of progressively smaller diameter over a reducing length of the shaft to produce the characteristic stepped-taper effect. By this means, the appropriate distribution of flex is obtained, and the smaller diameter of the shaft where it is attached to the head has a thickened wall for improved strength. Different overall stiffness can also be produced by changing the wall thickness of the original tube.

The shafts are cut to the appropriate length and glued or riveted to the head. Leather or rub-

◄ To protect themselves from their opponent's foil, fencers must wear a wire mesh mask, a jacket and pants of tough material, and a glove. In tournaments, a fencer is connected to a machine that electrically registers when an opponent's foil makes contact with his or her body.

FACT FILE

■ Athletes and fitness buffs are using personal pulse meters, a recent hi-tech addition to sports equipment. Worn as a wristwatch, strapped to the chest, or attached to workout apparatus, the pulse meter can be preset to upper and lower limit levels, and a warning tone sounds if the limits are broken. The instrument is also used after exercise to measure the heartbeat recovery rate, which indicates the level of fitness.

■ New giant-sized punchballs can be used by two boxers simultaneously. The punchball is marked with target areas, and point-scoring punches are counted by an inbuilt electric meter. This machine can eventually declare the winner of a bout without the boxers touching each other.

■ Clay-pigeon shooting is being revolutionized by a laser system that allows the targets to be used repeatedly without damage. Adapted shotguns emit a light beam with the same speed and range as a 12-bore shotgun. A hit illuminates the light-reflecting material on the target, and a light-source receiver marks up scores on a digital display board.

■ For minimum wind resistance in speed events, as well as for warmth, skiing and skating competitors are wearing specially developed skin suits. Made from laminated polyurethane, nylon, and foam resin layers, the suits are tested in wind tunnels for aerodynamic efficiency.

ber grips are then fitted, and the balance, or swing, weight of the club, about 6 in. (15 cm) from the top of the grip, is measured so that sets of matched clubs can be made up.

Baseball

A standard baseball has a cork and rubber center with a layer of woollen yarn wound around it. The ball is finished with a layer of horsehide, stitched into place. The ball weights between 5 and 5.25 oz. (about 150 g) and measures 9 to 9.5 in. (about 23 cm) in diameter. A baseball bat is made from a single piece of hardwood machined smooth and hand finished. The bat is round in section and not more than 2.75 in. (7 cm) in diameter at its thickest. The rules require that the bat must be less than 3.5 ft. (1.07 m) long.

Protective gear is worn by the players on the field. The catcher wears a mask, chest protector, shin guards, and a thickly padded leather glove that has a solid face except for a cleft between thumb and index finger. The first baseman wears a glove that is thinner and more flexible, has a solid expanse for the four fingers, with webbing between the thumb and index finger. The remaining fielders wear padded finger gloves with leather straps connecting thumb and index finger.

SEE ALSO: Aqualung • Bicycle • Diving suit • Hang glider • Protective clothing • Sailboard • Sports medicine

Sports Medicine

Sports medicine is a wide-ranging discipline. Sports physicians are involved in the treatment, coaching, and counseling of athletes, and in the rehabilitation of athletes who have undergone surgery or suffered illness. One recent development has been the supervision of disabled athletes, whose participation in all branches of sports has increased dramatically over the past 20 years or so. Another development affecting the population as a whole has been the increased emphasis on keeping healthy through exercise.

Most serious athletes today regularly visit a human performance laboratory. Here, electrical monitors and gas-exchange systems can be attached to the athlete's body while he or she works out, for example, on a treadmill or cycle ergometer. These monitor the performance of the athlete's heart, lungs, and biochemistry. Underlying disorders can be detected by measuring such parameters as the blood plasma's acidity and the levels of blood lactate, urea, and hormones as well as hemoglobin concentration.

Benefits and dangers of exercise

Sports physicians advise patients who are undertaking exercise. Regular exercise can slow down the development of some illnesses, such as arteriosclerosis, and alleviate the effects of others, such as chronic bronchitis, diabetes, and hyper-

tension. It can also counteract some of the age-related changes in the body. However, elderly people and patients with any medical condition should train only under medical supervision. For example, diabetic athletes need to avoid exercise if they have not eaten for several hours, since their blood sugar level could fall dangerously during exercise. Glucose-rich food or drink should always be available for them.

Healthy eating can greatly enhance performance. A properly balanced food intake limits fatigue, both in training and during competition. Athletes, for instance, are made aware of the importance of eating large amounts of carbohydrates before endurance events, such as a marathon. Consuming adequate antioxidant nutrients, such as vitamins E and C and beta-carotene, is also important to fight free-radical damage caused by vigorous exercise.

A sports physician will pay special attention to the food eaten by younger athletes. Adolescents are growing and developing rapidly, and they require most nutrients, especially calcium, in much greater amounts in relation to body size. Female athletes might need to include iron-rich food in their diet; several studies have shown that up to 80 per-

▼ The Drug Testing Center at the Barcelona Olympics in July, 1992 played an important role in the Games. Athletes are banned from using a wide range of drugs that could have an effect on their performance. Even ordinary cold remedies have to be checked for compliance before they can be used.

◄ Testing an athlete's fitness on a VO₂Max machine, which measures the amount of oxygen used in a given period. The doctor measures her pulse rate as she walks on a treadmill.

cent of female runners may be anemic or suffer from iron deficiency.

Because human beings vary greatly in their physique, some sports are far more suited to one person than to another. Sophisticated anthropometric instruments are now available to measure very accurately such variables as height, weight, girth, muscle size, body fat, and bone mass. Using the data obtained, coaches can choose the training to suit the individual.

Sports psychologists help by training athletes in emotional control, self-esteem, and interpersonal skills. Because people with different temperaments do not react in the same manner to stress, athletes are given questionnaires so that the most suitable counseling can be given. Sports psychologists can therefore help athletes enjoy training, display the appropriate amounts of aggression and concentration, and cope adequately with failure—and with success.

"Staleness," or overtraining, is a recognized cause of reduced achievement, particularly in elite athletes. It shows up as a leveling off or even a falling off in performance because of a failure to tolerate or adapt to the training load. A physician can prevent this situation by carefully controlling the stress imposed by exercise and by varying the training to limit fatigue.

Until the 1970s, very few girls and women took part in vigorous competitive sports or even in regular exercise programs. As the number of female athletes grew, it soon became clear that vigorous sport could lead to a variety of reproductive disorders. For example, hormonal imbalance can cause a delay in puberty for up to three years as well as irregularities in the menstrual cycle. In some instances, the disturbances are severe enough to cause infertility and bone loss. Menstrual disorders may afflict as many as 50 percent of endurance runners, but in most instances, simply exercising less will return the menstrual cycle to normal.

Drug testing

In 1988 at the Seoul Olympics Ben Johnson, a Canadian, ran the fastest 100 meters ever seen. However, it was the steroid Stanolozol that had enabled him to perform this feat. In an effort to detect such abuse, the International Amateur Athletics Federation introduced widespread out-of-competition drug testing in 1990.

As the number of athletes testing positive for drugs has risen, there has been a decline in performance levels compared with those achieved in the early 1980s. This decline may indicate that earlier standards owed something to drug abuse, which is now being detected and deterred.

Polycarbonate helmet

High-density foam neck collar

Plastic and high-density foam shoulder pad

Plastic and high-density foam chest pad

High-density foam kidney and back protector

High-density foam hip pad

High-density foam thigh pad

Leather glove

54cm
28.5cm
425gm

Hard plastic protective cup

High-density foam knee pad

Hard plastic and high-density foam shin pad

US footballer's padding

◀ Football players have led the way in using protective clothing to avoid injury to their bodies. Careful warm-up exercises also help to reduce the risk of pulled muscles and torn ligaments.

The banned substances include stimulants, such as caffeine in concentrated form, and analgesics, such as codeine. Even a few cups of strong coffee before an event may put an athlete over the limit. It is therefore essential for athletes to consult a physician familiar with the substances on the International Olympic Committee (IOC) banned list before accepting a prescription.

During the 2000 Sydney Olympics, the IOC introduced blood testing for banned substances in addition to urine tests. China dropped 40 athletes and officials from its team, including seven rowers who tested positive for erythropoietin (EPO), a performance-enhancing drug. However, it is thought that thousands of athletes continue to use the banned but undetectable human growth hormone (HGH), which enhances performance but can also lead to heart defects.

◀ Computers can help analyze the movement of an athlete—here a discus thrower—to improve performance and avoid medical problems.

SEE ALSO: DRUG AND ALCOHOL TESTING • HORMONE • METABOLISM • MUSCLE • SPORTS EQUIPMENT

Spray Gun

A spray gun is an air-driven device for applying a coating to the surface of an object without physical contact between the application tool and the surface. Spray guns usually apply liquids—notably paints, varnishes, and pesticides—but certain types deliver fine powder coatings.

Development of the atomizer

The development of the spray gun can be traced back to an atomizer devised by Dr. DeVilbiss, a medical practitioner of Toledo, Ohio. In the early 1800s, DeVilbiss was searching for a superior means of delivering liquid medications to the oral and nasal passages of his patients—at that time, swabbing was the usual technique.

The atomizer DeVilbiss developed introduced liquid from a container through a nozzle into a stream of moving air created by squeezing a flexible bulb. The passage of air over the nozzle created a partial vacuum that drew the liquid into the air as a mist of tiny droplets carried in the airstream. The device proved effective in delivering medications and was soon put to use for other purposes, such as spraying perfume.

The use of continuous supplies of compressed air broadened the applications of atomizers and led to the development of the modern spray gun. Spray guns are used mostly in the application of surface coatings (paints and varnishes), and paint-spraying guns will be the main focus here. Nevertheless, the principles that apply for paint spraying apply for spraying other materials.

Modern spray guns

Spray guns are so-called because of their passing resemblance to handguns: a spray gun has a hand grip, a trigger for controlling the spraying operation, and a nozzle in place of the barrel. A spray gun is powered by compressed air and usually a pressurized liquid. The liquid and compressed air are directed separately through channels in the spray gun, meeting only at the spray head.

Fluid supply. Fluid enters a spray gun through a fluid inlet directly behind the spray head. Its further progress is controlled by a needle valve (fluid needle), which consists of a cylindrical barrel and a needle-shaped rod. The barrel of the valve tapers sharply at one end—the fluid tip—forming a tight seal around the sharp end of the needle as long as the valve is held closed by a spring.

During spraying, the valve is held open by the trigger. Fluid can then flow through the gap between the needle and the barrel opening, forming a fine stream as it enters the spray head. The

▲ Spraying the underside of a vehicle chassis with anticorrosion primer. The protective clothing and mask are indicative of the hazard of spray paint if inhaled or absorbed through skin. Tasks such as this are now performed by robots in many factories.

rate of fluid flow through the fluid tip is determined by the viscosity of the liquid, the size of the opening, and the distance through which the needle retracts when the trigger is pulled. This last factor is controlled by an adjustable screw.

Air supply. Compressed air is delivered by a hose attached to the bottom of the handle. From there, it passes to a valve in the gun body that controls its flow. The valve opens when the trigger is pulled, admitting air to a baffle ring that distributes it around the spray head.

Air then passes through holes in the baffle ring into a dome-shaped cavity called the air cap. The fluid tip is located at the center of the dome cap, and the streams of air from the baffle ring break the issuing stream of fluid into tiny droplets as they converge. The mixture of air and fluid droplets then rushes through an orifice in the front end of the air cap, forming the spray.

As the trigger is pulled at the start of paint spraying, the air flow starts first, followed by paint flow as the trigger is pulled further. This sequence ensures that the paint is always atomized and prevents slugs of liquid paint from being projected at the workpiece and spoiling the finish.

Air-cap horns. Air-cap horns are two jets that direct air from opposing sides at the conical spray that issues from the air cap. This mechanism is desirable for paint spraying, because the sweeping motion of a paint sprayer using a conical spray would leave a band that was densely covered near the center but more sparsely covered at the edges. An excess of coating would then have to be applied to ensure that all parts of the surface were coated, thus increasing costs and promoting sagging—the formation of run marks that can occur in thickly applied paint on vertical surfaces.

The amount by which the spray is flattened can be altered to suit the work in hand by means of a spreader-width adjustment valve mounted at the rear of the gun body. The valve alters the setting of an opening inside the gun, regulating the flow of air through a second series of holes in the baffle ring to the air-cap horns.

Variations

The amount or volume of air used by a spray gun is determined by the size and design of the air cap. The flow of air is measured in terms of cubic feet (or cubic meters) per minute.

Two types of air caps are available. One is the suction-feed cap, which is designed so that air passing through the air cap creates a partial vacuum in front of the fluid tip by the venturi effect, which allows atmospheric pressure to force paint up to the spray gun from the container beneath it.

The other type of air cap, the pressure-feed cap, is not designed to create a vacuum in front of the tip, and these caps are used in fast production where the fluid is fed to the spray gun under pressure. In some cases, the pressure is created by the effect of gravity on liquid in a container mounted on top of the spray gun. For high-volume applications, however, the liquid is best supplied to the spray gun from a pressurized container.

Another variable in paint spraying is the formulation of the paint itself. Easy passage through the gun and good atomization are promoted by low viscosity, while sagging of the applied coating is avoided by high viscosity. A compromise is achieved by manipulation of the solvent blend: a large proportion of highly volatile solvent ensures that most of the solvent evaporates at the atomization stage and in the spray, so the paint is much thicker by the time it hits the surface.

Electrostatic spraying

One disadvantage of conventional paint spraying is the amount of overspray—paint that overshoots the workpiece. Electrostatic spraying provides one means of reducing overspray by using the attraction between negative and positive electrical charges. In many industrial painting processes, such as the application of primer paint to car bodies, the spray head is maintained at a high positive voltage, so the spray particles acquire positive charges. The workpiece must be a conductor and grounded so that negatively charged electrons can rush into it and collect on its surface in response to the positive charges.

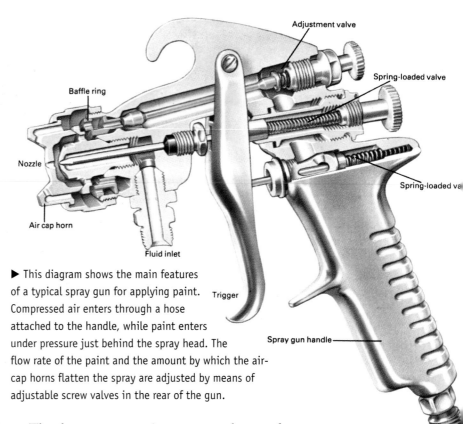

This diagram shows the main features of a typical spray gun for applying paint. Compressed air enters through a hose attached to the handle, while paint enters under pressure just behind the spray head. The flow rate of the paint and the amount by which the air-cap horns flatten the spray are adjusted by means of adjustable screw valves in the rear of the gun.

The charges attract paint to uncoated parts of the workpiece, including crevices and parts of the surface that are not in the direct line of fire of the gun. Furthermore, since most spray coatings are insulators, further paint is not attracted to parts of the surface that have already been coated.

Other advances

Manual paint spraying is inherently risky, since the solvents used in conventional spray paints are highly flammable and harmful if inhaled. For this reason, industries where paint spraying is routine tend to use robots to manipulate spray guns. This trend has been led by the automotive industry.

The solvents released by conventional spray paint are harmful to the environment. This issue is being addressed by increased use of water-based sprays and solvent-free powder coatings.

This small, general-purpose spray kit uses an electrical compressor (right) to supply high-pressure air to its spray gun. The paint is held in the container attached below the spray head.

SEE ALSO: AEROSOL • AIR • COMPRESSOR AND PUMP • CORROSION PREVENTION • PAINT • POWDER COATING • VENTURI EFFECT

Spring

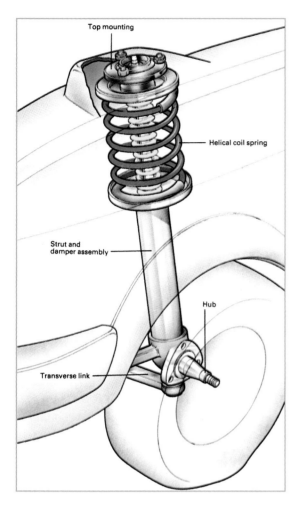

◀ The MacPherson strut, an economical spring design that comprises a telescopic strut, an integral shock absorber, and a helical coil spring.

Springs are mechanical devices that can absorb and store energy using the elastic properties of the material of which they are made. Elasticity is the mechanical property that enables a material to be deformed by an applied load and to recover its shape with removal of the load. The elastic modulus, or Young's modulus, of the material is obtained by dividing the applied stress by the resulting strain in the material; the formula may be expressed as

$$Y = \sigma/\varepsilon$$

where the Greek letter σ (sigma) represents stress, measured as the force per unit area, and the Greek letter ε (epsilon) represents strain, measured as the change in length of the material divided by the original length. According to Hooke's law, stress and strain are proportional to one another, producing the equation

$$F = kx$$

where F is the applied force, k is a constant, and x is the displacement of the material.

At the elastic limit, however, the relationship breaks down, and further stress results in permanent deformation of the material. Both fluids and solids have elastic properties that can be used to give a spring action.

Fluids

Fluids—gases and liquids—have no shape of their own but adopt the shape of their container. Liquids are virtually incompressible, but gases will adopt not only the shape but also the size of their container, by expansion or compression, and are useful materials for absorbing shock or storing energy. Shock absorbers used in the suspension systems of motor vehicles are usually only damping devices for the coil or leaf springs in the system, but some suspension designs use the compression and expansion of an enclosed volume of a suitable gas, such as air. An additional spring effect may be obtained by the expansion and contraction of the container.

Solids

The diversity of elastic properties among materials can be illustrated by comparing rubber and lead. A slug of rubber will, under pressure, expand to fill a limited space and will recover its original shape when the load is removed. A slug of lead, on the other hand, will spread out under pressure to occupy a limited space but will remain in its deformed state when the load is removed. It can absorb energy but cannot store it—it has no elasticity and is of no use as a spring material.

Between these two extremes are metals such as copper, phosphor bronze, and steel, which are each elastic to a certain limit. These metals are used as springs by varying elastically the geometry of the design of the spring.

Spiral springs

Spiral springs are the most common. They are flat or cylindrical (helical) in shape or some variation of these two shapes, such as conical (tapering cylindrical) or volute (nonflat spiral). The force required to produce one unit of deflection is called the stiffness. The spring rate is the ratio of applied load to deflection.

Flat spiral springs may be used to store mechanical energy and before the introduction of electric clocks and watches were frequently used to power these devices.

A close-coiled helical spring has the coils wound so tightly that they are in contact with each other in the unloaded state of the spring.

This type of spring is used as an extension spring, that is, it stores energy when it is stretched out. Extension springs may be used for such purposes as automatic door closers and balances. More familiar is the open-coiled spring, used as a compression spring. An example would be the spring in a car seat or in a mattress or the spring used in the recoil mechanism of a gun.

Leaf springs

Leaf springs are often used in automobiles, railway cars, and other vehicles. They are made up of a number of strips of spring-quality steel of varying lengths stacked together so that the shortest length (leaf) is nearest the source of the load. Leaf springs are supported at the ends and carry a central load (semielliptic or simply supported) or are supported at one end and carry a load at the other (quarter-elliptic or cantilever type). The strips are free to slide over one another in service and act as a laminated beam. Each leaf is given an initial curvature, and the load required to straighten a leaf spring is called the proof load. It is also called the maximum design load, because it causes the spring to bottom—or reach its maximum permissible deformation in service.

Other types of springs

In the disk spring, the spring material is formed into a shallow dish, with the spring effect being given by the flattening of the disk. A number of such springs can be arranged in series, with different effective rates being achieved by opposing or nesting the dishes. Torsion bars consist of a long bar anchored at one end and subjected to a twisting action by a load applied to a crank arm at the free end.

Hydraulic springs, consisting of a fluid-filled cylinder and a piston, may be used in situations where high loads are used. The movement in this spring results from the small compression of the fluid combined with the expansion of the cylinder.

Manufacture

Coil springs are wound around a mandrel, or former. For making small numbers of special-purpose springs, a lathe may be used. The mandrel is inserted in the chuck, one jaw of the chuck is loosened, the bent end of the spring wire is inserted, and the jaw is tightened again. The lead screw of the lathe is engaged according to the number of coils needed per inch of the finished spring, and the tool post of the lathe is used to guide the wire onto the mandrel.

For mass production of springs, special-purpose machinery has been developed in which the spring wire is pulled off a reel by means of

▲ A lightweight restoring spring. Springs are made in a wide variety of shapes and sizes to suit the load they are to bear.

rollers and fed into the machine. The wire passes over a stationary mandrel and strikes a deflector plate; doing so makes it curl itself around the mandrel. At a predetermined point in the machine cycle, the wire feed stops to allow the end of the spring to be cut off.

Design

The choice of the type of spring and the material it is made of depends upon working space, working temperatures, corrosion resistance, load frequency, and required spring life, as well as the size of the load and the required movement. Various mathematical formulas are used to arrive at the appropriate design.

For most situations, springs that are made of ordinary carbon steels of the hard-drawn and oil-hardening type are satisfactory. Proper heat treatment and tempering are necessary to remove internal stresses after cold working in the coiling operation. For high-temperature and high-stress requirements, high-nickel alloy steel may be used—a stainless steel or nonferrous alloy is used if corrosion resistance is necessary. Copper-base alloys are expensive but are used for their electric properties and corrosion resistance in electric components and at sub-zero temperatures. Phosphor bronze is often used for contact fingers in switches on account of its low arcing properties. Some special nickel-base spring alloys have been developed to have a constant modulus of elasticity over a wide temperature range and can be used in precision instruments where accuracy of movement will be maintained despite fluctuations of temperature.

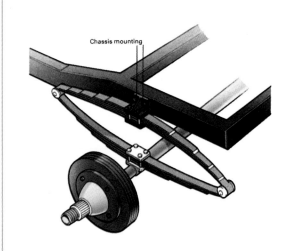

FULL ELLIPTIC SPRING

Full elliptic springs consist of two halves set in mirror symmetry. The two halves are each made of leaf springs, which consist of curved strips of spring-quality steel of varying lengths placed over each other in such as way that the shortest is positioned next to the load.

Chassis mounting

SEE ALSO: CLOCK • ELASTICITY • IRON AND STEEL • METAL • SUSPENSION SYSTEM

Stabilizer, Ship

Stabilizers are designed to reduce the rolling of a ship in order to prevent cargo from shifting and causing a list. They also reduce problems caused by the ship's motion for the catering services and increase passenger comfort on ferries and liners. A steady motion is necessary for accurate gunfire on a warship, and stabilizers are fitted to many naval vessels to control the angle of roll. Various types of stabilizer have been tried with varying degrees of success, including bilge keels, oscillating weights, and gyroscopes, but most modern vessels use antiroll tank systems or stabilizer fins.

Antiroll tanks

Frahm antiroll tanks, which have been successfully since the beginning of the 20th century, provide stabilization when the ship is moving or at rest. They are usually fitted near to amidships, either in between deck space or lower down in the vessel above the double bottom. They consist of a wing tank on both sides of the ship; the tanks are connected by a cross tank and are about half-filled with water or oil. The arrangement is like a U-tube, but the cross-sectional area of the uprights (the tanks) is significantly greater than that of the connecting horizontal section.

When the ship rolls, the liquid flows from one side tank to the other, giving a momentum that resists the roll. The tank dimensions are designed to suit the ship. An air connection is provided between the tops of the tanks to allow the fluid to flow without causing a pressure lock. Air valves on this connection allow control of the fluid flow to suit the roll conditions, and for maximum stabilization, the fluid oscillations are adjusted to be 90 degrees out of phase with the ship's movement.

In activated antirolling tanks, a high-capacity, low-pressure air compressor supplies air to the upper part of the tanks, and by varying the pressure in each tank, water can be moved from one side of the ship to the other to give a stabilizing effect. A gyroscope is used to stop and start the compressor and to operate the tank air valves as it senses the ship's motion.

▼ Cutaway section of a nonretractable fin stabilizer showing the fin and inboard actuating mechanism. Most of today's ships either use stabilizer fins such as this or are equipped with antiroll tanks, which are located near to amidships.

Flume stabilization is similar in principle but uses a flume tank placed transversely across the ship. It comprises two side compartments and a center compartment, which contain water. The motion of the fluid from one side of the vessel to the other is controlled by a restriction called a flume. Liquid depth is constant in the center compartment during the transfer process. The tanks are carefully designed to tune the liquid frequency to the natural period of roll of the vessel and to maintain the 90-degree phase relationship necessary for stabilization. The flume prevents the liquid movement from coming into phase with the ship's movement and causing a disastrous increase in the rolling.

Stabilizer fins

Stabilizer fins project from the hull and produce a turning moment on the ship to oppose any rolling motion. As the ship moves through the water, the flow over the protruding fins, port and starboard, is deflected according to the angle of the fin, producing either an upward or a downward stabilizing force. As the ship rolls, the fin on the ascending side of the vessel will generate a downward force, and the fin on the other side will produce an upward force. The magnitude of these forces depends on the angle through which the fins are rotated from the horizontal position and the speed of the water over the fin surface.

The angle of rotation of the fins is set by a gyroscopic control system that senses the roll of the ship and adjusts the fins accordingly by means of hydraulic rotary motors. Fin stabilization is very effective when the ship is moving at optimum working speed but less so at lower speeds. For critical applications—such as in warships—several sets of fins may be fitted. The fins can be fixed or arranged to rotate back into a recess in the hull of the ship when not required.

Gyroscopic stabilizers

A gyroscope can reduce the average angle of roll by about 50 percent but is bulky and expensive. A German inventor

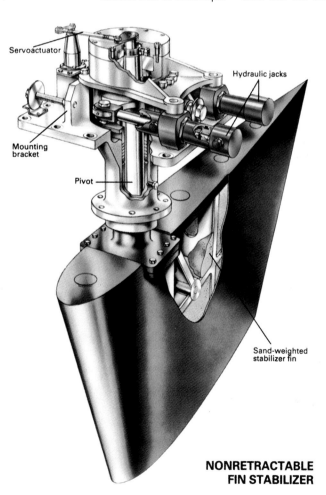

Servoactuator

Hydraulic jacks

Mounting bracket

Pivot

Sand-weighted stabilizer fin

NONRETRACTABLE FIN STABILIZER

TANK STABILIZER WITH AIR CONTROL

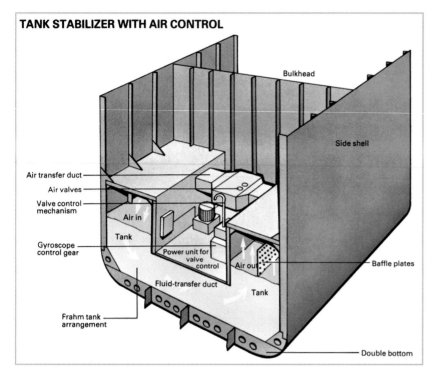

Bulkhead

Side shell

Air transfer duct
Air valves
Valve control mechanism
Air in
Tank
Gyroscope control gear
Power unit for valve control
Air out
Baffle plates
Fluid-transfer duct
Tank
Frahm tank arrangement
Double bottom

motion of the ship. The pilot gyroscope operates electric contacts that power the precession motor in the required direction.

Oscillating weights

The system of oscillating weights involves moving weights from one side of a vessel to the other to counteract the rolling motion. The phase of the weight movement must lag 90 degrees behind the rolling motion of the vessel (the two movements must always be out of step), and so the timing of the operation is critical. One experimental method moved a truck on curved rails so that its weight produced a stabilizing force on the ship. Oscillating-weights systems are no longer used, partly because they are noisy and partly because control in irregular waves is difficult.

Bilge keels

Bilge keels are longitudinal fins attached to the hull along both sides of the ship, extending for about one-third of the length of the vessel. They are riveted or welded to the shell where it curves to form the bilge at the bottom of the ship. The keels offer minimum resistance to the forward motion. They are connected to the hull in such a way so that they will break off without damaging the shell if they strike an obstruction.

Bilge keels resist motion in the rolling direction by impeding the fluid flow around the hull and work better when the ship is moving rather than when it is stationary. They are effective at damping out the angle of roll and tend to increase the period of roll—the time taken to roll from one side of the ship to the other and back again.

named Schlick was the first to use this system. Later, about 1913, stabilizers invented by an American scientist and inventor, Elmer A. Sperry, were introduced in the United States. The Schlick gyroscope was installed with the spin axis vertical and the support-frame axis horizontal. When the vessel rolls, the gyroscope frame swings in its bearings in a fore-and-aft direction. This motion is called precession and is a function of the gyroscopic action. A roll to starboard causes the top of the gyroscope frame to move aft if unresisted at the bearings. The opposite motion occurs for a roll to port. The rolling of the ship causes precession of the gyroscope. If precessional motion is resisted by applying brakes to the bearings of the support frame, a stabilizing effect is set up in opposition to the rolling of the ship.

Brake control of the Schlick type of stabilizer is difficult to achieve, but the Sperry stabilizers were arranged with a precession motor meshed with a vertical ring gear to precess the gyroscope in a direction opposite the rolling motion of the ship. Control of the precession motor is achieved by a small pilot gyroscope that is sensitive to the transverse

▲ An activated tank stabilizer with air control. The principle of operation is that water in the lower part of the tank flows from one side to the other to compensate for wave motion. The water distribution between the two sides of the tank is determined by gyroscopically controlled air valves.

◄ A stabilizer fin being mounted to a large Japanese ferry. The fin is made of steel castings and fabrications with an outer epoxy resin coating. The motion of the fin through the water generates upward or downward forces, according to the angle of attack, to counteract the rolling motion of the ship. The angle of the fin is altered automatically by a hydraulic motor controlled by a gyroscope.

SEE ALSO: BOAT BUILDING • GYROSCOPE • HYDRODYNAMICS • SAILING • SHIP • SUBMARINE • SUBMERSIBLE

Stage Effect

The term *stage effect* encompasses all the visual and audio devices used to support an actor's performance in a theater or to enhance the atmosphere of a musical performance. This article will concentrate mainly on the visual effects, such as scenery, lighting, projection, and pyrotechnics.

Scenic effects

Scenic effects reached their peak in the late 19th century, when the vogue for melodramas called for the extensive use of moving set components. Revolving stages and elevators would be used in the portrayal on stage of such events as full-scale horse races and train crashes, for example.

Elevators, turntables, and castored wagon platforms that slide complete scenes from storage at the side of the stage are common in big opera houses, particularly in Germany. However, such devices are used mainly to move scenery behind the curtain during intermissions rather than to create effects before the audience.

Big musicals on Broadway and in London's West End use small castored trucks, often motorized, to move elements of scenery in conjunction with turntables and lighting to produce scene changes that can have a magical quality.

Two of the oldest traditional scenic effects—trapdoors and scrims—are still in use today. Trapdoors are now mainly confined to certain types of comedy shows and classic plays, where they allow characters to appear magically through the floor. A small square hatch in the stage slides open, and the actor rises on an elevator. Although most of these elevators are still the original type—that is, they have a counterweighted mechanism—they are seldom used today at the speed that formerly propelled acrobats high into the air for a spectacular entrance. Such feats would be performed using a star trap—a section of floor with hinged flaps that opened upward as the performer rose on the elevator and then fell back to conceal the opening as soon as the actor had burst through.

Other older types of trapdoors include the ghost glide, which allowed an apparition to rise slowly from below while gliding across the full width of the stage. The grave trap and the cauldron trap, placed center stage, took their names from their use in 19th-century productions of Shakespeare's plays *Hamlet* and *Macbeth*, respectively. Vampire traps, or vamps, were springed openings in scenery that allowed actors to appear to pass through solid walls.

▲ Pyrotechnics and stage lighting in use at a rock concert. The stage is bathed in a reddish light, while the vocalist is picked out by two crossed spotlights. In the background, bright flames rise from pyrotechnic powder burning in flash pots.

▲ A traditional ghost illusion used an angled sheet of glass in front of the stage. The ghost image would be made to appear on the glass screen by projecting bright light onto an actor out of the audience's sight below the stage. The audience would perceive the image to be some distance behind the screen, where a fellow performer could safely run it through with a sword.

Scrims remain the best way of making a vision appear and disappear. A scrim is a fine sheet of cloth on which a scene is painted. Illuminated from the front, the painted scene appears solid. When the light is faded from the front and the stage behind is illuminated, the scrim becomes translucent and reveals the stage.

Lighting effects

In the early 20th century, directors who wished to stage realistic events were wise if they moved to the evolving field of cinematography, whose photographic trickery could produce much more convincing dramatic effects than could be achieved on stage. Those who remained in theater took a different approach by suggesting an environment rather than portraying it in detail. Much of this type of scene setting is done by the use of lighting effects; thus, a flickering red lighting effect suggests a hellish underworld, for example.

The most basic function of lighting is to make the players on a stage clearly visible to the members of the audience. It is done principally with highly focused spotlights, directed at the stage from above the audience, that are manually steered to follow performers around the stage. Spotlighting has the effect of concentrating the attention of the audience on the main action.

The general stage lighting is provided by overhead lamps that wash large areas of the stage in light. Different shades of light, obtained by placing colored gels in front of lamps, are used to create specific effects; also, separate parts of the stage may be lit in different colors to emphasize

their separation. There may be many hundreds of lighting changes in any given play, and these changes are rehearsed by the director and lighting engineer before the start of a run of performances. Once the director has chosen a given lighting condition, the engineer programs it into the lighting desk computer. The same condition can then be called up using a preset button when the appropriate cue arises in the stage action.

Another form of lighting, frequently used in televised quiz shows and rock concerts, is the moving pin spot. As the name suggests, pin spots are narrow beams of light that are meant to appear as such, rather than to illuminate specific objects. The luminescence of such beams is greatly enhanced when used with a smoke machine. Rows or rings of such lamps may be mounted on rigs above the stage and audience, and the beams sweep up and down or scan from side to side in synchronization.

Other forms of lighting include lasers, stroboscopes, and black light. Lasers tend to be projected from behind the audience onto a screen or ceiling. The laser beam is made to scan by playing it onto a movable mirror. The movements of the mirror can be programmed to spell words, to trace images, or simply to form fans or tunnels of light. As with pin spots, laser lighting effects become much more effective when used with smoke effects.

Stroboscopes are xenon flash lamps connected to circuitry that provides regular pulses of current, resulting in rapid sequences of flashes. Stroboscopic lighting creates the impression of slow motion and can disorientate the audience.

Black light is ultraviolet light generated by fluorescent tubes from which dangerous frequencies have been filtered. Black light is invisible to the human eye, but it can make fluorescent dyes and paints glow intense colors. It is used to illuminate fluorescent scenery and costumes.

Projection

A useful way of avoiding heavy set movements for scenery changes is to project scenery onto a screen behind the players. Where there is a sufficient depth of the stage, back projection is used. In other cases, images are front projected from above the stage. This effect requires slides with images that are distorted so that they produce an undistorted image when projected at an acute angle.

Types of projector include standard carousel projectors and circular-slide projectors, in which a slide rotates in the projector beam with its axis offset from the projector lens. Images are projected onto a large backdrop by using a number of paired projectors, with each pair covering a separate part of the backdrop screen. Scene changes are effected by fading all pairs from one machine to its partner; the carousel in the unlit projector then advances to be ready for the next change.

In addition to the slide projection of static images (or looped images in the case of wheel projectors), moving images are sometimes used as backdrops. Moving images are achieved by cinematic or video projection or even by having a high-definition video screen at the back of the stage.

Natural phenomena

Some stage directions call for the portrayal of natural phenomena, such as weather conditions. A number of techniques are used, and many are borrowed from theater for the dramatization of rock concerts and other musical performances.

Mist, fog, and smoke. Low-lying mist is produced by dropping dry ice (solid carbon dioxide) into hot water. The resultant vapor clouds are heavier than air, so they form a rolling blanket that drifts over the stage floor. Artificial smoke is produced by vaporizing an oil-based liquid using heat from an electrical element. The resulting fumes are then propelled by carbon dioxide gas.

Rain and snow. Rain and snow may be reproduced by dropping effects materials from a slotted bag suspended above the stage. Snow may be reproduced by flakes of white fire-resistant material, while clear plastic particles represent rain.

Snow and rain effects can be projected onto the backdrop using several circular slides with carefully graded soft and hard focusings superimposed to produce realistic images. The sound of rain or sleet reinforces the visual effect and is usually a recording of dry peas falling on metal.

Rain on windows can be reproduced by running water down glass panes into troughs and recirculating the water using an electrical pump. A similar setup using a large pump and a suitably "rocky" plastic channel can reproduce a waterfall.

Sky effects. Various sky effects can be reproduced using circular slides of cloud images, sometimes in conjunction with a static slide of a skyline. Stars can be portrayed by tiny low-voltage lamps embedded in the backdrop or by using the tips of small bundles of optical fibers fed with light from a single spot lamp behind the set.

Storm effects. Perhaps the most difficult meteorological effect to portray convincingly is lightning. Xenon-filled electronic flash tubes, similar to those used in photography, are the basis of most systems, although their recharge time makes sequences of rapid flashes difficult. The illusion of an electrical storm is improved by the use of recorded sound effects, which are made either by shaking a large metal thunder sheet or by beating a large-circumference thunder drum. An older thunder effect used cannon balls in a timber thunder-run high above the stage.

Pyrotechnic effects

Pyrotechnics covers a wide variety of materials and devices intended to produce flashes, flames, or smoke or combinations of all three. Pyrotechnics are a favorite tool of the stage managers of rock concerts, and flashes and clouds of colored smoke are standard fare in traditional British pantomimes, particularly when genies and other fantastic characters suddenly appear on stage through trap doors. Apart from providing a startling visual effect, the associated smoke conceals the workings of the trap door.

One class of pyrotechnic material includes flash paper, strips and cords made of nitrocellulose. These materials are shipped wet with water to avoid accidental ignition and then dried before use. Ignited by a spark wheel or an electrical glow plug, flash paper burns with a bright orange flame and produces neither ash nor smoke. Colored flash paper can be fashioned into articles such as magic wands, and sheets of flash paper can be used to cover a doorway that opens with a flash when a character enters the stage.

Other forms of pyrotechnics include powders, liquids, and gels that burn with a flash or a sustained flame when ignited in an appropriate flameproof pot. Some of these products generate large amounts of dense smoke that can be colored or made to sparkle by the use of additives. Others produce loud booming noises when ignited.

▼ This production of the musical *Mutiny* used a mockup of the *Bounty* as its set. The set could be made to rock using hydraulics in a pit under the stage, and the whole ship split in two for between-deck scenes.

SEE ALSO: FIREWORK AND FLARE • HYDRAULICS • LASER AND MASER • SOUND EFFECTS AND SAMPLING • SPECIAL EFFECTS

Stained Glass

All colored glass is stained. The staining is done by including metal oxides or other chemical compounds in the glass manufacture. Throughout the medieval period, the art of creating stained-glass windows was known simply as glazing.

Colors in glass are produced by the absorption of certain wavelengths of incident light by ions in solution in the glass (chromium ions produce green colors, cobalt ions and manganese ions give purple) or by submicroscopic particles precipitated from the glass melt at certain critical temperatures (copper or cadmium selenide are used for ruby). Larger particles, either having a color themselves, such as the excessive amount of chromium or copper compounds in aventurine glasses, or colorless, as in opals also produce color.

History

The earliest existing complete windows are those in the clerestory of Augsburg Cathedral in Germany, built about 1065 C.E. They are attributed to the monks of Tegernee. The technical completeness of these windows suggests that the art had originated much earlier and, being Italo-Byzantine in style, had evolved from the Greek tradition. Another early example, in Le Mans Cathedral in France, shows similar Byzantine influence. In England, the earliest-known glass (12th century) is reputedly in York Minster and is part of a panel depicting a seated king in a Jesse tree window; this panel is similar to panels in St. Denis and Chartres Cathedrals, both in France. Some of the best examples of complete ranges of windows in the early Gothic style of the 12th and 13th centuries are in the cathedrals at Chartres and Canterbury in England.

The discovery of silver stain (silver oxide) in the early 14th century, combined with the greater use of white, led to the general lightening of windows. By the 15th century, however, stained glass began to go into an artistic decline that persisted throughout the next two centuries.

In the 17th century, the ability of glass painters to convey naturalistic effects was increased by the use of enamels, which produced translucent colors when fired, thus avoiding the need to use separate areas of colored glass. The windows in New College Chapel in Oxford, England, painted to the cartoons (preliminary designs) of Sir Joshua Reynolds, are typical.

In the 19th century, the revival of interest in the art of the Middle Ages, particularly by the Pre-Raphaelites, produced windows that had some of the clarity of color and design of early glass. These examples led to the many fine interpretations in 20th-century stained glass seen in the designs of the French artists Fernand Léger at Audincourt and Henri Matisse at Vence, both in

France, and in the windows at Coventry Cathedral in England. The rediscovery of making hand-blown, or muff, glass in the latter half of the 19th century contributed to this revival by making available a better quality of glass, called antique.

Stained glass is both a decorative and a functional medium, and modern architects and designers are using it more in their designs. In addition to being used for windows, stained glass is appearing in hotels, restaurants, bars, private houses, and office blocks in the form of domes, skylights, screens, and murals.

The development of a technique for laminating stained-glass panels has aided the acceptance of stained glass for such applications, particularly in public buildings. Laminated panels are stronger, more resistant to impact and breakage, and safer, so they can be used in applications for which modern building regulations would have made traditional stained glass inappropriate.

Design and cutting

A stained-glass window is composed of variously shaped and colored pieces of glass, with painted detail in line and shading, that are assembled in leads to form glazed panels.

Unlike the fine-art painter, the stained-glass artist has to consider a design strictly in relation to a given site, with precise measurements and structure, so that the completed work fits the window shape and is resistant to adverse weather conditions. The original design is usually made to scale, like an architectural drawing, and includes the arrangement of the leading and the supporting bars. From this design, a full-sized cartoon is made, either enlarged by hand on sheets of paper or by the use of photographic enlargement from the original.

When the cartoon is correct in all its details, a cut line is made by laying detail paper over the cartoon and tracing through the leading pattern—this is the diagram from which the glass will be cut, and its lines are thickened by pencil or ink to the width of the heart of the leads. The shapes of the glass are determined by the necessity to break down the images into the chosen colors (usually, it is impossible to merge from one color to another) and the restriction on the size of glass that can be fixed safely.

▼ A diagram is painted on the plate-glass screen to indicate the lead positions so that the cut glass will be put into its correct position.

The cut line is laid over a plate-glass table illuminated from underneath (called a light box), which enables the black lines of the cut line to show through. The selected glass is arranged over the diagram and cut to the inside edge of the thick line, while the contingent piece is cut to the other side of the line—this allows a narrow gap to be taken up by the heart of the lead.

Cutting is done today with a hardened steel glass cutter drawn firmly over the glass. It makes a scored line of sufficient depth to initiate a fracture with reasonable accuracy. After the cut is made, the glass is fractured either by sharply bending the two sides at opposing angles, if straight, or by tapping the underside of the cut with the back of the glass cutter if curved. The ragged edge of the glass is usually ground down with a grozing iron, a special pair of pliers. When all the glass is cut and laid out on the cut line, it should fit the outside shape exactly, with spaces for the lead hearts.

Painting

Techniques for painting the glass differ from one studio to another. Essentially, though, iron oxides are ground into a smooth paste with water and gum arabic, and suitably diluted and applied to the glass with special long-haired brushes called tracers that can make broad or fine lines. These traced lines are usually fired into the glass before the application of shading—called matting. Matting is effected by laying a thin wash of paint on the shadowed parts and graduating the tones by softening the wash with a badger-hair brush, pushing the paint from light to dark and sometimes stippling to give a varied texture.

To fuse the paint or enamels to the glass, the glass is fired in a kiln. The pieces of glass are laid on a bed of plaster in metal trays warmed in a preheating chamber and placed in the firing chamber, or muffle. As soon as the glass has reached the correct temperature, about 1148°F (619°C), the surface shows an eggshell gloss, and the glass must be removed and placed in the warmest of the cooling racks beneath the firing chamber. It is then brought down progressively until, at the lowest rack, it is cool enough to remove. This process is repeated until all the trays are fired. The glass may be fired a second time if

the lines of matts need strengthening. When silver stain is to be used for additional coloring, a further firing is necessary but at a lower temperature—about 968 to 1022°F (519–550°C).

Areas of color may also be produced by aciding, which makes complicated details, such as those in heraldic work, much easier to design. Some colored glasses are made by casing, or flashing, the basic white glass with a colored film (usually red or blue, because these colors tend to be very dark if used throughout a glass) by dipping the molten glass bubble in a crucible of the required color and blowing again until the coating of color is thinned out over the whole surface. After masking out the parts to be retained as color, the artist can remove areas of the colored film by etching them away with hydrofluoric acid.

Leading

During cutting and painting, the glass is put on glass screens for checking; the pieces are placed in their correct positions with the aid of diagrams of the leading drawn on the backs of the screens. When the painting and firing are completed, the glass is taken down and laid out ready for glazing.

The leads, or calmes, are fabricated from a lead strip passed through a lead mill that forms them into the characteristic H section. They are milled in several sizes from $\frac{1}{8}$ in. (3 mm)—called string leads—to wide border leads $\frac{5}{8}$ in. (15 mm) wide. Leading up begins by placing border leads against battens fixed to the glazing bench at right angles. The glass is introduced progressively from the corner formed by the right angle until the panel is completed. Each piece of glass is surrounded by a lead cut to the appropriate size so that junctions of leads butt into each other to form a neat joint.

When the leading is completed on the panel, each joint is rubbed with tallow to act as a flux and soldered. The procedure is repeated on the other side of the panel. The panels are then made weatherproof by cementing them with a liquid form of putty. The cement is made of equal parts

▲ Craftsmen making stained-glass windows using techniques that have remained fundamentally unchanged for centuries. Above left: painting fine detail onto the glass. Above: inserting sections of colored glass into the lead outlines.

of plaster of Paris and whiting mixed with equal parts of boiled oil and turpentine—lamp black and a little red lead are also added. The cement is rubbed into the leads on both sides with scrubbing brushes and then dried off by sprinkling plaster of Paris over the panel and scrubbing until all the unwanted cement is removed.

Fixing

Fixing generally begins from the base, so in a multipanel window, the sections are made so that the top border lead of the first section will fit into the border lead of the next panel. The panels are worked into the stone grooves of the window frames, and the saddle bars are fixed at set intervals—usually about 12 in. (30 cm) apart—so that the window is supported throughout its height.

Finally, the window is pointed up with mortar inside and out to fill the grooves and obtain a smooth joint against the border leads of the glass. If the stained glass is fixed into metal or wooden frames, putty glazing is used. The panels are placed into the rebate, and after puttying, the retaining beads are screwed back.

Technical developments

The art of glazing remained virtually unaltered until the late 20th century. Slab glass, or *dalles de verre*, as it is called in France, is molded glass in 1 in. (2.5 cm) thick slabs in brilliant colors. Because these slabs cannot be fired or fixed into leads, a form of mosaic design has developed that uses glass shapes and black bonding cement.

Glass mosaic, or glass appliqué, is made possible by the availability of epoxy resin. Here, the normal antique glass is cut to the design and stuck down on plate glass with the clear resin. This adhesion has a chemical rather than a mechanical action, so the panel of glass must be kept flat and left to cure for at least a day before grouting. Grouting is the rubbing in of a compound of fine sand and black coloring mixed with a plasticizer, which fills in little cracks of light between the pieces of glass.

Experiments with industrial products such as resins have led to the production of artifacts that may be free standing—glass sculptures. Fused glass is produced by the fusing together of colored glasses at the melting temperature in prearranged shapes and bonded together as decoration panels or sculptures. A kiln operating at a greater temperature than the usual glass-firing kiln is necessary for this process.

SEE ALSO: G LASS • L EAD • L IGHT AND OPTICS

Stalactite and Stalagmite

Cave features that result from mineral deposition are referred to as decorations and come in many shapes and sizes. There are straws, columns, curtains, the descriptively named caved popcorn, and twisting helictites, among others. As a general rule, the decorations that hang from cave ceilings are called stalactites, and those that rise from the floor are stalagmites. The decorated caves occur only in ice and in water-soluble rock—gypsum and limestone. Because gypsum is comparatively rare, most of the best-known cave decorations are in limestone.

Formation of limestone caves

The size and appearance of limestone cave decorations depend on a number of factors that are unique to each cave. The principal determinant is the amount of carbon dioxide in the water that reaches the interior surfaces of the cave. As rainwater falls and travels downward through the earth, it absorbs carbon dioxide from the surface soil. This carbon dioxide gives it the ability to dissolve and hold more limestone in each drop. The richer the water is in carbon dioxide, the more limestone will be held suspended in it as it works its way through the limestone layers beneath the surface soil and eventually emerges on the cave ceiling.

When a drop of this water reaches the roof of a cave or underground passage, it hangs there charged with its extra-large load of dissolved limestone. However, the air in caves is normally deficient in carbon dioxide, so the gas in the drop of water begins to diffuse out of it and into the cave's atmosphere. Without the carbon dioxide, the water is no longer chemically capable of holding so rich a solution of calcium carbonate (limestone), so it deposits a drop of this salt on the ceiling as the mineral calcite (crystalline calcium carbonate). The drop of water is eventually pushed from its position by the next drop of water running down from above, and it lands on the cave floor where it deposits some of its remaining calcium carbonate.

Over time, this continued dripping into caverns can build up great quantities of calcite on either the ceiling or the floor or both. The size and shape of these calcite deposits depend on the type of limestone, the rate of water flow, and the composition of air in the cave chamber. If a drop of water is very quickly pushed off the ceiling by its successor, it does not have time to deposit much calcite there but retains a lot to leave on the floor. As a result, there is a more rapid growth of the stalagmite than of the stalactite—although the stalagmite will not be very slender.

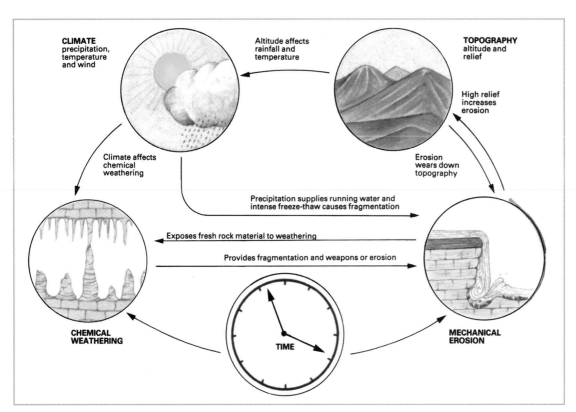

CLIMATE
precipitation,
temperature
and wind

Altitude affects
rainfall and
temperature

TOPOGRAPHY
altitude and
relief

High relief
increases
erosion

Climate affects
chemical
weathering

Erosion
wears down
topography

Precipitation supplies running water and
intense freeze-thaw causes fragmentation

Exposes fresh rock material to weathering

Provides fragmentation and weapons or erosion

CHEMICAL
WEATHERING

TIME

MECHANICAL
EROSION

◀ The main factors that control weathering and erosion are closely interrelated and occur over long periods. The chemical composition, hardness, and structure of rocks are also important—caves found in soft limestone are formed by erosion.

Color, form, and texture

The range of dripstone formations is endless because the sum of the factors governing their growth is so variable. There may even be seasonal variations that affect their appearance. The famous 105 ft. (32 m) tall stalagmites of the Virgin Forest in the Aven Armand cavern in southwest France look like slender piles of tumblers stacked within each other because of some regular variation that occurs between the rate of flow and the cave atmosphere.

Apart from differences in form, there are also differences in color and texture of stalactites and stalagmites. Calcite is remarkable among minerals for the great number of crystal shapes it can produce. Surface film water on the walls of air-rich caves sometimes grows into delicate crystals of aragonite. Aragonite is still calcium carbonate and therefore chemically identical but with a different atomic structure. There can also occasionally be lumps of gypsum in a limestone bed, and they may deposit their own crystals of hydrated calcium sulfate as decorations in a limestone cave.

Stalactites and stalagmites often meet to form complete columns of rock. These features take a long time to grow—it often takes 1,000 years for them to grow just 2.5 in. (6 cm). They can be white (the color of pure calcium carbonate), but impurities often produce a range of colors.

Limestone caves also contain many other formations that are made of deposits of calcium carbonate. For example, water that drips through a long crack in the roof of a cave may deposit a wavy sheet of rock called a curtain. Water flowing down the wall of a cave or over the floor deposits layers of calcium carbonate called flowstones. Some of them resemble frozen cascades of water. Examples include Frozen Niagara in Kentucky's Mammoth Caves, and another is the Frozen Waterfall in Carlsbad Caverns in New Mexico.

◀ Stalagmites are formed on the floor of the cave when water drips and deposits calcium carbonate, which gradually forms a spike. Over thousands of years the stalactites and stalagmites grow toward each other to form columns.

SEE ALSO: EROSION • GEOCHEMISTRY • GEOGRAPHY • GEOLOGY • WATER

Starter Motor

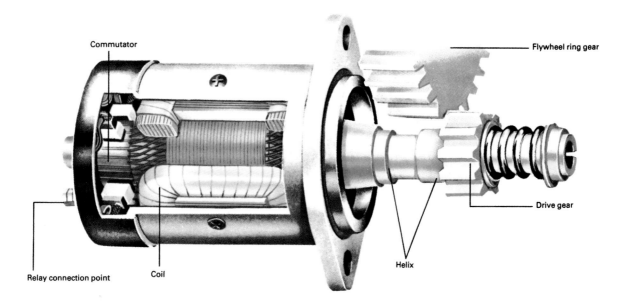

Commutator

Flywheel ring gear

Drive gear

Helix

Relay connection point

Coil

A starter motor is a machine for rotating the crankshaft of an engine from rest to a speed at which the engine will operate on its own. The starter motors used for internal combustion engines are usually battery-operated, direct-current electric motors, ranging in power from 0.5 horsepower (375 W) for motorcycle engines up to 15 horsepower (11.25 kW) for very large diesel engines.

The motors used are series-wound and short-time rated—that is, the windings of the rotor and stator are electrically connected in series, and the motor is designed to produce a high power output for a short time without exceeding a specified temperature. The series-winding characteristics give the starter the initial torque (turning force) it requires to overcome the static inertia and friction of the engine and to accelerate it up to speed in the shortest possible time to avoid too heavy a drain on the battery.

The starter is a dead weight while the engine is running, and so it must be as light and small as possible. To achieve this state, starters are short-time rated at two or three minutes—if a starter motor were required to deliver its maximum power over longer periods, it would have to be bigger and heavier to avoid overheating.

The starter requires a heavy current to operate it. This current is approximately 150 amps on a medium-sized automobile and 1,000 amps on big commercial vehicles. The switching of this current is accomplished by means of a relay or solenoid operating a set of electric contacts.

Engagement with the engine is made through a pair of gears, the ratio of which is about 12 to 1, the larger gear being that on the engine. The smaller gear, known as the pinion, is positioned on the shaft of the starter, and the larger one is mounted on the housing of the clutch of the engine and is known as the ring gear. There are two methods by which this larger gear is engaged, the inertia method and the widely used pre-engaged method.

The inertia starter uses the rapid acceleration of the starter armature, acting on the inertia of the pinion, to create a force that drives the pinion up a helix on the shaft of the starter and hence into mesh with the ring gear. When the engine is running and the starter is switched off, the pinion is driven back down the helix and out of mesh with the ring gear.

The preengaged starter is widely used on both gasoline and diesel engines. The relay that operates the starter is replaced by a solenoid mounted on the starter, which is used to move the pinion up to and into mesh with the ring gear before switching on the current to the starter motor. To ensure entry when the teeth of the pinion and the teeth of the ring gear are not perfectly in line, some means of indexing the pinion gear (rotating it so that it is correctly aligned with the ring gear) must be provided. One such method is to arrange for the solenoid to compress a spring before it switches on the motor so that upon switching on, the pinion is rotated and the spring forces it into mesh. The starter can now be held in mesh even after the engine is running, and to prevent damage to the starter, an over-running device is attached to the pinion.

▲ The inertia starter consists of a gear that is driven up a helix when the motor is switched on and into mesh with the flywheel ring gear.

SEE ALSO: AUTOMOBILE • GEAR • INTERNAL COMBUSTION ENGINE • SOLENOID

Static Mechanics

Statics is a branch of science that considers the forces acting on an object when it is at rest relative to its surroundings. It is one of the two major aspects of mechanics, the other being dynamics, which considers moving objects.

Statics is really a particular case of dynamics, and the laws relating to the action of forces on moving objects are valid for the particular case of bodies at rest. Historically, however, statics developed as a science long before dynamics on the basis of laws independent of the idea of motion. The earliest systematic studies to lay the foundation of statics were made by the Greek mathematician Archimedes in the third century B.C.E.

▲ These fishing-net floats display Archimedes' principle of hydrostatics. That is, a body submerged in a fluid is acted on by an upward force that is equal to the amount of liquid that the body displaces. The floats remain on the surface because their density is less than the density of water.

The principles of statics can be extended to hydrostatics, the study of fluids and of objects immersed in fluids.

Principles of statics

A force may be considered as a physical influence, a push or a pull, that when applied to an object tends to cause motion. The effect produced depends on the force magnitude and on the direction in which it is applied. Force is thus termed a vector quantity, in contrast to quantities such as mass or temperature, which have only magnitude and are termed scalar quantities.

When vectors act along the same line, the combined effect can be found by adding their magnitudes (when they act in the same direction) or by subtracting them when they are oppositely directed. The combined effect of a number of applied forces is termed the resultant of the system. The resultant of forces acting in different, nonparallel directions may be found by application of the parallelogram law, which states that if two forces acting at a point are represented by the adjacent sides of a parallelogram, then the resultant is represented by the diagonal of that parallelogram. For a large number of such forces, the resultant may be found by repeatedly applying the parallelogram law to the forces, two at a time.

For the body to be in equilibrium—stationary relative to its surroundings—the resultant of the forces acting must be zero. If there are two forces acting, then they must exactly oppose each other in direction and be of equal magnitude. In the case that combined forces do not produce equilibrium, the additional force required is referred to as the equilibrant. Three nonparallel forces acting on a body to produce an equilibrium state must have lines of action that all pass through a common point. Under such circumstances, the vectors representing the three forces form a triangle in which the force directions follow each other around the sides of the triangle. This rule is widely applied in statics and is known as the Triangle of Forces theorem—the length and direction of each side of the triangle is proportional to the magnitude and the direction, of each force.

This principle can be extended to systems in which any number of nonparallel forces act at a point on an object. It is found that the vector representation of these forces results in a closed polygon (a many-sided figure) when the forces are in equilibrium. The force directions follow each other around this polygon, as in the case of the triangle.

When forces act at a point on an object, they tend to produce movement of the point. When, however, forces act on a body without meeting at a point, there is a tendency for the body to rotate as well as move along a straight line. The rotating effect of a force about any point is termed the moment of the force about that point and is measured by multiplying the force magnitude by the perpendicular distance of its line of action from the point considered. For such a body to be in equilibrium, the sum of the moments of forces tending to cause rotation in one direction must be equal to the sum of the rotating influences in the opposite direction. This is the principle of moments.

For equilibrium, the forces applied to a body must have a zero resultant and a net moment of zero about any point, and the application of these conditions to various practical applications, for example, the design of bridges and skyscrapers, forms the basis of statics.

In addition to any external applied forces, most practical problems in statics involve the force caused by Earth's gravitational attraction acting on the body and frictional forces at the points of contact between the body and contacting objects. The weights of the constituent particles comprising any body form a system of parallel forces that can be effectively replaced by a

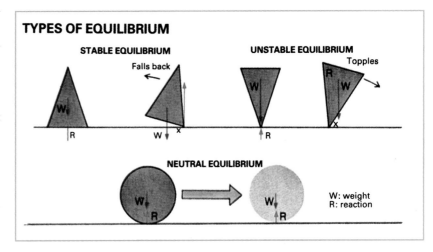

TYPES OF EQUILIBRIUM

STABLE EQUILIBRIUM

Falls back

W
R

W
X

UNSTABLE EQUILIBRIUM

Topples

W

R
W
X

R

NEUTRAL EQUILIBRIUM

W
R

W
R

W: weight
R: reaction

single force. For this to be an effective resultant of the system, it must act through some specific determinable point, which is known as the center of gravity of the body. The position of the center of gravity is of fundamental importance in determining the stability of an object when disturbed from equilibrium.

If the line of action of the force of gravity acting through the center of gravity remains within the base of the object when disturbed (as in an upright cone), it exerts a turning moment that restores equilibrium. The body is then said to be stable. The equilibrium is described as unstable when the vertical through the center of gravity

▲ An upright cone is in stable equilibrium. A rolling cylinder does not change its center of gravity, so it is in neutral equilibrium.

▼ Statics is very important in the design of bridges and other structures, enabling the structural engineer to calculate the maximum loads that the structure can withstand.

◄ All fluids have weight, so they exert a force per unit area (or pressure), which increases with increasing depth of fluid. This diving bell remains intact on the seabed or in the atmosphere because the forces acting on it are always in equilibrium.

▼ Forces can be resolved to give a resultant. Forces in opposite directions are subtracted; those in the same direction are added. Forces at an angle are resolved by the Parallelogram Law. The product of a force and the distance through which it acts gives a moment, or a turning force.

falls outside the base of the object (as in an inverted cone), because the moment exerted by the force of gravity then causes the object to topple. If the position of the center of gravity relative to the base remains unchanged by a disturbance (as in a horizontal cylinder), the equilibrium is said to be neutral.

The frictional force between objects in contact is brought into play when the two objects tend to move relative to each other, this force providing a resistance to such motion.

An important branch of statics concerns the study of forces acting on structural frameworks. These frameworks are normally triangular arrangements—a triangle being the only geometric shape that cannot be altered without deformation of the components in the framework. In practice, all structures experience deformation but are considered to be rigid if the deformation is negligible. If forces are assumed to be applied at the ends of the structural rods, they must act along the length of the rods to balance each other. If these forces tend to extend the rod, then such a rod is termed a tie, and if the rod is in compression, it is referred to as a strut.

FORCES IN EQUILIBRIUM

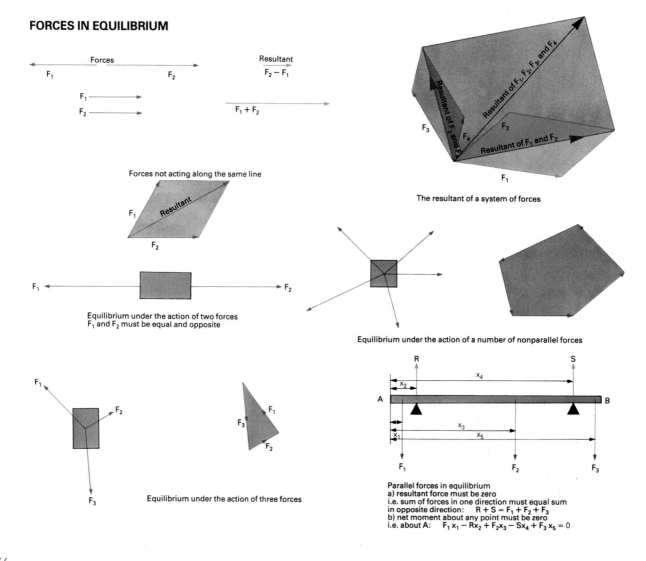

Forces

F_1 F_2

Resultant

$F_2 - F_1$

F_1 ——→
F_2 ——→

$F_1 + F_2$

Forces not acting along the same line

F_1 Resultant

F_2

The resultant of a system of forces

F_3 F_4 F_2 F_1

Resultant of F_3 and F_4

Resultant of F_1, F_2, F_3, and F_4

Resultant of F_1 and F_2

F_1 ←——→ F_2

Equilibrium under the action of two forces F_1 and F_2 must be equal and opposite

Equilibrium under the action of a number of nonparallel forces

F_1 F_2 F_3

Equilibrium under the action of three forces

F_3 F_1 F_2

R   S

x_4

x_2

A   B

x_1 x_3

x_5

F_1 F_2 F_3

Parallel forces in equilibrium
a) resultant force must be zero
i.e. sum of forces in one direction must equal sum in opposite direction: $R + S = F_1 + F_2 + F_3$
b) net moment about any point must be zero
i.e. about A: $F_1 x_1 - Rx_2 + F_2 x_3 - Sx_4 + F_3 x_5 = 0$

HYDROSTATICS

The theory of statics can be extended to deal with the equilibrium of fluids and of bodies immersed in fluids, where a fluid is considered as a material whose constituent particles act upon each other with forces normal (perpendicular) to their common surface—the plane at which they meet.

Because hydrostatics concerns the study of fluids in equilibrium, the cohesive forces within the fluid that are responsible for fluid viscosity can be ignored. The term *fluid* applies to liquids or gases, a liquid being defined as a fluid that is practically incompressible, whereas a gas is easily compressed and is capable of indefinite expansion. The density of a fluid is the mass of a unit volume of that fluid. A fluid has weight, so it exerts a thrust on any surface in contact with it. If the system is in equilibrium, the thrust is exerted at 90 degrees to the contact surface.

The thrust acting per unit area of contact surface is termed pressure, and it increases with increasing depth in the fluid. The pressure exerted by a fluid also depends on its density. At any point in the fluid the pressure is equal to the depth multiplied by the density. The pressure exerted on Earth's surface by its atmosphere at sea level is about the same as the pressure exerted by a column of water 34 ft. (10 m) high. The density of mercury is 13.6 times greater than that of water, and consequently, an equivalent pressure is given by a much shorter column of mercury (30 in., 760 mm). The rate at which the pressure in a fluid varies with height—the change in pressure divided by the change in height—is equal on Earth to the acceleration of Earth's gravity (9.8 m/s^2) multiplied by a constant.

The pressure at any depth in a fluid acts equally in all directions and at right angles to the surface of any object immersed in the fluid. This pressure within a liquid plays an important part in many branches of engineering.

Pascal's Law is an extremely important law in hydrostatics—it states that pressure applied to a liquid in a closed, completely filled container is transmitted equally to all parts of the container in contact with the liquid. The pressure is exerted in a direction perpendicular to the walls of the container. This principle is the basis of operation of many types of hydraulic devices, such as presses, jacks, and braking systems.

Another important principle is that discovered by the Greek mathematician Archimedes. He found that an object submerged in a fluid is acted upon by an upward force equal to the weight of the fluid that the object displaces. The volume of fluid displaced by a submerged object is equal to the volume of that object. If the mass of that volume of fluid is greater than the mass of the object (if the object is less dense than the fluid in which it is placed), the upward force exerted by the fluid causes the object to float.

HYDROSTATIC PRESSURE SYSTEMS

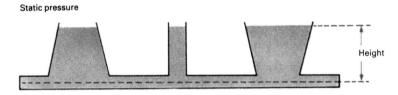

Static pressure

Height

HYDRAULIC SYSTEMS

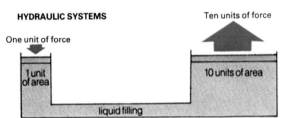

One unit of force

1 unit of area

liquid filling

Ten units of force

10 units of area

▲ Pressure within a fluid varies according to depth (left) not according to the shape of the vessel containing the fluid. A hydraulic jack (right) gets its lifting force from the difference in area over which the fluid acts. A small amount of force applied to a small surface area will result in a larger force being exerted by the larger surface area. The displacement of the small surface area, however, will be greater than that of the large surface area.

The rules of statics provide the means of calculating, and so predicting, the forces acting in the structural members of any such construction. This information, allied to a consideration of the strength of available construction material, enables the planning and building of structures suitable for the intended application.

Many modern buildings and engineering structures display the distribution of forces in their latticework of struts and ties. One particularly clear example is the geodesic dome, an idea originally developed by the U.S. engineer and mathematician Richard Buckminster Fuller and now used throughout the world for a variety of structures, including exhibition halls, private homes, conservatories, greenhouses, and arenas. These domes use the bare minimum of material to cover the maximum volume, reducing the structure to a grid made of triangles or polygons formed from ties and struts that distribute the tension and compression forces, and can thus be made of comparatively lightweight materials.

SEE ALSO: BRIDGE • DYNAMICS • ENERGY, MASS, AND WEIGHT • GEODESIC STRUCTURES • GRAVITY • NEWTON'S LAWS

Statistics

◀ Statistics are used in gambling to estimate the chances of someone winning a bet. Here bookmakers at the Irish Derby take bets on the basis of statistical odds that a particular horse will win a given race.

Statistics is a branch of mathematics concerned with the collection, presentation, analysis, and interpretation of numerical data. Throughout history, for example, whenever a society has become sufficiently organized, it has attempted to carry out surveys of its population—what we now call a census. The science of statistics is concerned with deriving general characteristics or trends from such large amounts of accumulated data.

The analysis of census data is one, perhaps the first, application of statistics, but out of it has grown a mathematical discipline that has evolved general techniques for the analysis of large amounts of numerical data. Today these techniques are used, for example, to analyze the results of scientific experiments, in quality control in industry, and in physics, where a new branch called statistical mechanics has evolved.

Basic concepts

There are two distinct types of analyses to which statistics is applicable, but they can both be treated in a similar way. In the first, it is assumed that a definite figure exists, although no measurement will be exactly correct, because small errors occur in any experiment. An example is a scientific experiment in which the frequency of oscillation of a pendulum is to be found. The objective is to determine the most accurate answer possible, by combining the results from several repetitions of the experiment, as well as a number that represents the possible uncertainties or errors in it.

In the second type of analysis, no unique answer is expected—as in a program to find the number of defective items from a production line. In this example, the desired dimensions of the product will have been specified and a figure attached representing the acceptable tolerance above which the item is considered defective. Ideally, the average dimensions and the deviation from this for any one item will be no greater than the maximum tolerance.

The mean

The mean, or average, is the simplest single figure that describes a collection of data on a given subject. For example, to determine the oscillation time of a pendulum, it will be easier and more accurate to time ten oscillations and divide the result by ten—giving the average time per oscillation. Repeating the experiment six times may give results such as the following:

Session	Time for ten oscillations	Time for one oscillation
1	9.8	0.98
2	10.1	1.01
3	10.0	1.00
4	9.8	0.98
5	10.1	1.01
6	10.2	1.02

The mean time per oscillation for a total of all six sessions is

$(0.98 + 1.01 + 1.00 + 0.98 + 1.01 + 1.02)/6 = 1$ second.

In general, the mean, m, of n measurements, $x_1, x_2, x_3 \ldots x_n$ is

$$m = (x_1 + x_2 + x_3 \ldots + x_n)/n$$

Tolerance

There are several ways of obtaining a figure that represents the closeness of a set of measurements about their mean value. The easiest is tolerance, and it is obtained by searching for the two numbers that differ most above and below the mean. From the above example of the pendulum, the smallest figure obtained is 0.98 seconds and the largest is 1.02 seconds. Thus there is a tolerance of ±0.02 seconds about a mean value of 1 second. As a percentage, this tolerance is written as ±2 percent. A final statement of the measured oscillating time is therefore 1 second ±2 percent. The larger the tolerance, the less accurate the result.

Variance and standard deviation

Another technique is to determine the mean deviation of the measurements about their mean value. The mean deviation is found by summing the differences between each individual measurement and the mean and dividing by the number of measurements. All differences are taken to be positive. Again, from the above example, the differences from the mean are (changing the sign to positive or negative when necessary): 0.02, 0.01, 0, 0.02, 0.01, 0.02. The mean deviation is therefore given by the following equation:

$$(0.02 + 0.01 + 0 + 0.02 + 0.01 + 0.02)/6 = 0.0133$$

The mean deviation is then 0.0133 (or 1.3 percent).

The mean deviation, however, is not easily manipulated mathematically and is consequently of little use. For this reason, the variance is used, and it is defined as the mean of the squares of deviations from the mean. Mathematically, the variance, δ^2, is defined as

$$\delta^2 = [(x_1-m)^2 + (x_2-m)^2 + (x_3-m)^2 \ldots + (x_n-m)^2]/n$$

and the square root of the variance, δ, is called the standard deviation. From the pendulum example,

$$\delta^2 = [(0.02)^2 + (0.01)^2 + 0 + (0.02)^2 + (0.01)^2 + 0.02)^2]/6$$

$$\delta^2 = 0.00023$$

The standard deviation is therefore $\delta = \sqrt{0.00023} = 0.0152$.

The standard deviation is extremely important in the application of statistics because it provides a measure of the range in which most of the measurements lie. If it were to be calculated about any other point than the mean, m, it would have a larger value. This point leads to yet another definition of the mean—that figure about which the standard deviation is a minimum.

Frequency distributions

Consider a group of 200 people whose heights are known. No two individuals will be exactly the same height, so it is useful to group everyone into classes—each class relating to a certain interval in height (say, at one-inch intervals). The number of people that fall into each class is called the frequency—meaning the frequency of occurrence of

◀ When a coin is flipped several times, the probability of any outcome is determined by binomial expansion. The area under the graph is unity. In a normal distribution, when the number of possibilities or outcomes is large, the curve is smooth. The area under the graph is still unity.

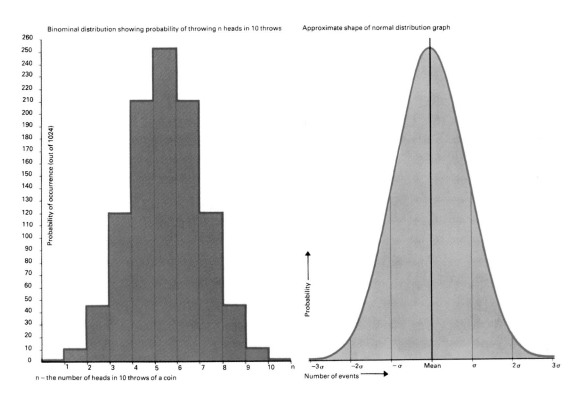

Binominal distribution showing probability of throwing n heads in 10 throws

Probability of occurrence (out of 1024)

n – the number of heads in 10 throws of a coin

Approximate shape of normal distribution graph

Probability

Number of events

-3σ -2σ $-\sigma$ Mean σ 2σ 3σ

people in that class. A table presenting this class-frequency information is called a frequency distribution, and an example is shown below.

Class	Frequency
5' 2" – 5' 3"	1
5' 3" – 5' 4"	4
5' 4" – 5' 5"	10
5' 5" – 5' 6"	20
5' 6" – 5' 7"	35
5' 7" – 5' 8"	43
5' 8" – 5' 9"	48
5' 9" – 5' 10"	28
5' 10" – 5' 11"	8
5' 11" – 6' 0"	3
	——
	Total: 200

This information can be plotted graphically, the classes on the horizontal axis and the frequency on the vertical axis. On one type of graph, called the histogram, a series of rectangles are constructed, their width equal to the class intervals and height equal to the frequency of that class.

When the number of classes is large and the corresponding class intervals become small, the frequency distribution may be smooth enough to plot with a continuous line. It is then usual to plot on the vertical axis not frequency but proportional frequency (as a proportion of the total sum of frequencies). In the case of the height–frequency distribution, the total sum of frequencies is 200 (the size of the population sample being studied). It should be noted that when using pro-portional frequency–distribution curves, the area under the curve must be unity, because the sum of all the various proportions in each class must be unity. From frequency–distribution curves, several things stand out clearly. Usually there is one class where the frequency is a maximum—this class is called the mode. The more pronounced the hill of the curve, the closer the classes are clustered and the smaller the standard deviation.

Another point of interest on the graph is the median. The median is another kind of average; it splits the population sample in half. From the graph on heights, 100 people are smaller and 100 larger than the median, which is just under 5 ft. 8 in. (1.7 m).

From either of these graphs, the mean average height of the 200 people can also be determined. If the midvalues of every class are $x_1, x_2, x_3 \ldots x_n$ (n classes in all) with frequency distribution in each of $f_1, f_2, f_3 \ldots f_n$, then

$$\text{mean height} = \frac{f_1x_1 + f_2x_2 + f_3x_3 + \ldots + f_nx_n}{f_1 + f_2 + f_3 + \ldots + f_n}$$

where we already know that the sum of all frequencies ($f_1 + f_2 + f_3 + \ldots + f_n$) must equal the population in question (200).

Probability theory

When a coin is tossed, there is a 50 percent chance of heads and a 50 percent chance of tails. If we toss the coin 100 times, the most common result to be expected is 50 heads and 50 tails. But 100 heads is not impossible—just highly

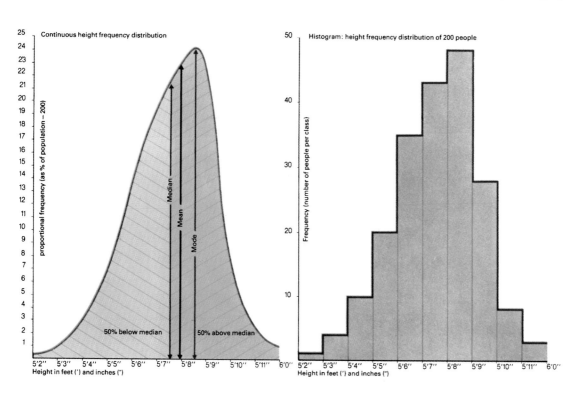

◀ The histogram (near left) shows the number of people in each one-inch-height class; the colored area under the graph equals the population sample of 200 people. Dividing the histogram classes into smaller subclasses eventually gives a smooth distribution curve, which can be plotted with a continuous-frequency graph (far left). The area under the graph is unity.

unlikely—99 heads and one tail is also unlikely but slightly more probable than 100 heads. If various combinations of heads and tails are plotted on a graph against the probability of each combination occurring, a curve is obtained that resembles the height–frequency distribution curve, except that it is symmetrical.

Other probability curves are possible, depending on the relative size of the two variables involved. The important ones have been given special names because they are known to occur frequently in certain physical problems. Their likeness to certain frequency distributions is not accidental. After all, if there is one height class where more people are situated than in any other class, then the probability of any one individual belonging to that class is also higher.

◄ Random sampling is an effective quality-control method often used by manufacturers; the goods from a small random sample are tested, and if they are satisfactory, there is a high probability that the entire batch will be up to standard.

Statistical mechanics

The statistical mechanics branch of physics sets out to describe the gross, or macroscopic, features of the physical world in which we live from the knowledge that it is composed of a large number of microscopic particles. All of the objects that are encountered in everyday life consist of millions of billions of billions of atoms and molecules. Although it is impossible to experimentally keep track of such large numbers of particles, the macroscopic systems they compose obey very simple laws. Such laws are of a statistical or approximate nature. However, the numbers of particles involved are so large that, for all practical purposes, they are exact. For example, the assumption that the molecules of a gas do not interact strongly, leads to an accurate prediction of the connection between pressure and volume.

One of the most far-reaching results derived by statistical mechanics is the Second Law of Thermodynamics in terms of molecular behavior. This law states that the entropy, or disorder, in a system always increases. For instance, it is easy to break a glass, but it requires a lot of energy to put it back together. Similarly, heat will only flow from a hot system (with lots of agitated atoms) to increase the disorder of a cold one (in a relatively organized state). The ultimate result of this law is that the Universe is running down and that it will end with everything at the same temperature.

Quantum mechanics

In quantum physics, the laws that apply to everyday objects must be modified. One reason for this modification is that when working with such small particles, the very act of observing the phenomena under investigation changes the results found. This concept is summarized in Heisenberg's Uncertainty Principle, which states that the uncertainty in the position of a particle multiplied by the uncertainty in its momentum (momentum is the mass of the particle multiplied by its velocity) can never be less than a certain very small number. In addition, the position of a particle is given as a probability based on a statistical likelihood that the particle will be in a particular place at a particular time.

Criminology and chemistry

An early use of statistics in criminology was the introduction of fingerprint identification in the 1890s. Statistics showed that no two people had the same fingerprint patterns. A century later, in 1984, a British scientist, Alec Jeffries, found that individuals can be uniquely identified by measuring the lengths of certain stretches of their chromosomes, or DNA sequences. This technique, called DNA fingerprinting, has been refined so that all that is needed are microscopic quantities of body tissue or fluid. If a sample from a suspect matches one found at the scene of a crime, the chance that it did not come from the suspect (or a blood relative) is less than one in a billion.

A major task in analytical chemistry is to determine the concentration of a particular substance in samples of raw material. One technique for achieving this goal is near-infrared (NIR) spectroscopy, in which the sample is exposed to a large number of infrared wavelengths, and the amount of radiation reflected at each wavelength is recorded. The information needed can then be extracted by routine statistical methods involving comparisons with samples of known concentrations.

 SEE ALSO: LOGIC • MATHEMATICS • NUMBER THEORY • QUANTUM THEORY • THERMODYNAMICS

Stealth Technologies

In military terms, stealth is the ability to avoid or prevent hostile forces from detecting aircraft, land vehicles, missiles, and other strategic objects. Stealth is achieved by the application of electronic countermeasures and by the use of designs and materials that minimize vulnerability to visual observation and detection by systems such as radar and heat-detecting infrared cameras.

Jamming techniques

Jamming techniques constitute a major part of the armory of electronic warfare (EW). They use the basic premise that radio-frequency systems—radar and radio-communications systems included—are vulnerable to degradation or total disruption by electronic interference.

Jamming was first used on a large scale by the British Royal Air Force in an attempt to defeat the *Knickebein* (dogleg) radio bombing system used by the German Luftwaffe in its Blitzkrieg (lightning war) bombing campaign of 1940–1941 against British cities. Thereafter, jamming became an increasingly important aspect of modern warfare in direct response to the proliferation of military electronic systems.

Jamming techniques are divided into active and passive types. Active systems use transmitters to produce signals that either swamp a target system's receiver, making it impossible to interpret incoming signals, or they deceive the system with false but intelligible signals. Active jamming systems are also called electronic countermeasures,

▲ A 35th Tactical Fighter Wing F-4 Phantom aircraft passes over the Saudi desert while on a training flight during operation Desert Storm. The airplane is carrying an AN/ALQ-131 electronic countermeasures pod on its right inboard wing pylon that is used for jamming enemy radar.

or ECMs. Passive systems do not transmit signals, but they provide false targets for hostile detector systems, helping friendly targets evade detection.

Brute-force jammers. Jamming systems that use electronic noise to swamp hostile detectors are described as brute-force jammers. In this context, noise is defined as any unwanted electric signal that affects an electronic apparatus and results in spurious signals occurring at the output. In a radar system, for example, the use of radio-frequency noise as a jamming agent produces obscuring spoke traces (the spurious signals) on the radar's display (its output). These traces prevent the operator from discriminating a true target amid a host of ghost targets on the screen.

Brute-force jammers are relatively simplistic pieces of equipment. They are produced in a number of distinct forms, the most common of which are the barrage and spot types. Barrage jammers broadcast electronic noise over a range of target frequencies. They have the advantage of being effective against various types of systems within their frequency ranges. Barrage jammers are useful in aerial combat, when an airborne attacker may be prone to detection by a multiplicity of radars; they are also useful where the attacker may anticipate being confronted by an unexpected type of electronic threat.

The disadvantage of barrage systems lies in the breadth of their frequency coverage, which reduces the power output available for use against a specific system. In order to be effective, a noise jammer must emit a signal around 10 times stronger than that emitted by the detector system. However, the wide coverage of the barrage unit often reduces this ratio unfavorably, allowing some elements in a multitype radar system the chance of seeing through the jamming because of the relative weakness of the disruptive signal. This limitation is overcome by spot jammers, which tune to specific target frequencies and can therefore concentrate their outputs against individual systems. Of course, a single spot jammer is unable to counter a multitype detector system; multiple spot jammers must then be used, each one targeting a specific subsystem. This approach requires extensive knowledge of hostile detector systems—information that is not always available—so spot jammers are of little use where an unexpected radar system could be in use.

Sweep-lock jammer. The individual limitations of barrage and spot jammers led to the development of a third type of system, sometimes called a sweep-lock jammer. Such systems are capable of broadcasting over a broad range of frequencies, and that range is monitored—manually or automatically—for incoming signals from hostile

detector systems. When threat signals are identified, the entire available jamming output is directed against them. Sweep-lock jammers therefore have more flexibility than spot jammers, and greater efficiency than barrage jammers.

The sweep-lock jammer illustrates a key maxim of electronic warfare—that the electronic "battlefield" is a constantly changing environment. Under such circumstances, no single measure can be fully effective or retain its effectiveness indefinitely in the face of an ever-changing threat.

Deception jammers. Deception jammers are more complex than the three types of brute-force jammers. As their name suggests, deception jammers are designed to deceive rather than to blind, and they are used primarily against radars. Their effect is achieved by carefully monitoring the hostile radar's signal and matching the jamming signal to it so that the spurious input is perceived by the radar as being a genuine response.

Having achieved this goal, the fake signal can be adjusted to provide the radar with range and target data advantageous to the attacker. In this way, the radar displays more than one target

◀ This helicopter is seen carrying Sea Skua missiles. The effectiveness of such missiles lies in the stealthy way in which they approach their targets.

▼ After launch, the Sea Skua drops to just above the sea surface, making it difficult for the hostile radar to detect. Close to the target, it uses its own radar system to lock onto the unsuspecting vessel.

trace—the true target plus the deception signal. The radar system is therefore deceived into "detecting" a particular target farther away or nearer than is actually the case. This technique, known as range-gate stealing, depends on capturing the radar's range-measuring circuitry range gate by presenting a fake signal strong enough to attract it away from the true echo signal. Once the range gate has been deceived in this manner, the phase of the deception signal can be subtly changed so that the signal appears to emanate from a location other than its real source.

Deception jammers incorporate receivers that monitor hostile radar emissions; these receivers work in tandem with circuits that either produce a matched signal that appears real to the radar and is powerful enough to attract it away from true radar echoes or amplify and modify the received signal for retransmission. The great advantage of deception jammers over brute-force jammers is that the former do not appear to be jamming at all and are therefore harder to overcome.

Aircraft-borne jammers

Jamming equipment for modern warplanes can be internal or external to the fuselage. Internal installations are used on both strategic and tactical aircraft, and large strategic craft have what are known as jamming suites to provide protection against a wide range of possible threats. An example of such a suite is that carried by the U.S. Air Force's B-52G and H aircraft, which carry no less than 20 separate jamming transmitters.

Although internal installations are becoming more common on smaller tactical aircraft, such as fighters, the more usual jamming cover for such craft is still the externally mounted jamming pod of the type used since the mid-1960s. The simplest jamming pods take the form of aerodynamically shaped housings mounted on one of the aircraft's underwing store stations. Such pods contain one or more jamming transmitter systems together with a cooling system. Such setups are called "dumb pods," since they act only in response to instructions from the pilot. The pilot issues control instructions when a radar warning receiver (RWR) or radar warning and homing system (RHAWS) signals the need for jamming.

More sophisticated "smart" pods have integral processor units that control their function automatically. Some such units also have their own receiver equipment to monitor the threat spectrum; others receive data through an interface with remote RWR or RHAWS equipment. All are capable of both noise and deception jamming.

Jamming pods have the twin disadvantages of creating aerodynamic drag and taking up valuable pylon space that could otherwise be used to carry

▲ Electronic countermeasure systems are portable for use in the field of battle. This radio operator can monitor signal transmissions and implement automatic jamming equipment from the back of a Landrover.

munitions. For this reason, there is an increased tendency for the use of miniaturized internal jamming equipment as used for larger aircraft.

Land-based and seaborne jammers

Land-based active jammers target communications links, which are vital for the control of troops. Such equipment is deployed in a number of forms, ranging from large static sites down through vehicle-mounted units to handheld sets for use by infantry soldiers. Some systems are mounted on airborne platforms, such as helicopters and fixed-wing aircraft. The increasing use of radar on the battlefield for gun or mortar fire control, as well as for personnel detection, calls for effective jamming cover in these respects.

Jamming also plays an important role in marine warfare, which is increasingly dominated by radar-guided antishipping missiles. As such, the world's navies provide both active and passive jamming equipment to protect their vessels from such missiles and to degrade their opponents' capacity for radar surveillance during battle. In some cases, such as that of the the U.S. Navy's carrier air group, dedicated jamming aircraft protect both fleet operations and aerial maneuvers.

Passive jamming: chaff

Before the development of active-jamming technology, the only available means for confusing hostile radar systems was the deployment of chaff. In essence, chaff is an antiradar material that forms a radar-reflective cloud when dropped from a plane or launched from a ship in a small missile that bursts to release the chaff. When a radar beam crosses a cloud of chaff, the multitude of reflections fills the radar set's display, obscuring true targets. Chaff is available in a number of forms—from foil strips, cut to a ratio of the target radar's wavelength, to coated glass-fiber needles.

UNDERWATER STEALTH COMMUNICATION

In 2001, Geoff Edelmann of the Scripps Institution of Oceanography, San Diego, demonstrated a system that could have a major impact on military submarine communications. It is a system that allows sound signals to be received in a single position, making them totally immune to interception by hostile receivers.

The system functions using reflection and other underwater acoustic effects. When a submarine's sonar emits a ping, for example, that sound reflects off the surface and bed of the sea, so the sound detected by a remote hydrophone (underwater microphone) combines the sound that travels directly from the sonar with echoes from the bed and surface. The exact composition of this combination varies with the location of the hydrophone.

Edelmann's demonstration used 32 hydrophones on a vertical cable to measure the influence of acoustic effects on a 1 kHz signal from a remote source near the shore. Each hydrophone received a signal at a slightly different time lag from transmission, indicating differences in the path lengths taken by the sound waves.

Using this information, the array was then used to transmit a ping to the source. The signal was split so the hydrophones transmitted in the opposite order to that in which they received the signal.

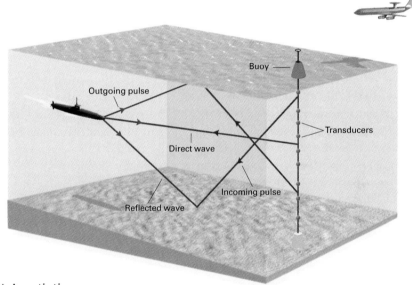

▲ Acoustic time reversal was tested as a secure means for transmitting to submarines in an experiment performed off the coast of Italy. The research group was led by Geoff Edelmann. The experiment used an array of 32 hydrophones mounted on a 262 ft. (80 m) cable. The cable was suspended from a boat and held taut by a concrete block. The array communicated with a hydrophone located near the shore, 6 miles (10 km) from the transmitter array.

Because the sound waves followed the same paths as the original signal, albeit in reverse, they all reached the remote hydrophone at the same time. There they combined to make a single ping. In any other location, sounds would be detected in random order, making them incoherent to potential eavesdroppers.

The system also has potential for the secure transmission of digital signals through water. In digital mode, the 1s and 0s of the digital information would be differentiated by reversing the phase of the signal, but maintaining the same sequential timing of transmission from each of the hydrophones.

Although chaff is easy to deploy, it has many disadvantages when compared with active jamming measures. Chaff clouds are susceptible to interference from meteorological conditions, such as wind speed and direction, which can cause the reflective cloud to bloom incorrectly after the initial dispersal. Furthermore, chaff is useless against Doppler radar, which identifies the relative speeds of objects by the frequency shifts of their radar reflections. Such a radar negates the effect of chaff by using circuits that ignore low-speed objects—drifting chaff, for example—while highlighting fast-moving aircraft and missiles.

Stealth aircraft

When approaching hostile territory, aircraft and missiles can evade radar detection to some extent by maintaining altitudes at which there is poor propagation of high-frequency radio and microwave frequencies—the radiation used in radar beams. Low altitude also provides cover: since radar is a line-of-sight device, it cannot see over the horizon or through mountains. Cruise missiles also use these strategies to maintain the element of surprise in their attacks.

An alternative approach, one taken in the design of the U.S.A.F. B-2 stealth bombers, is to use a design that renders the aircraft almost invisible to radar, even within its detection range. The B-2 achieves this with its flying-wing design, in which all surfaces are smoothed over and covered in radar-absorbing paint. Right angles are scrupulously avoided, since they promote reflection of radio waves, and all onboard systems are screened to prevent telltale leaks of electromagnetic radiation. Finally, the external skin is of graphite, rather than the more conventional aluminum, since graphite is a poor reflector of radio.

A small radar profile is not the only element in stealth design, however. The jet engines of the B-2 are contained within the fuselage, and their exhaust streams are mixed with cold air before discharge through vents above the wing, thus reducing the noise that can be heard from the ground and susceptibility to detection by infrared sensors and heat-seeking missiles, which home in on the hot exhausts gases of the jet craft.

Defense suppression

In modern warfare, it is usual to preempt general attacks with strategic attacks aimed at knocking out radar and communications installations. Subsequent attacks can then proceed without fear of detection by hostile radar systems.

The means of destroying such installations are usually cruise missiles or stealth bombers, which use the methodology already discussed to avoid detection until the last few moments before striking. An alternative approach is to use antiradar missiles, or ARMs. Rather than avoiding radar beams, an ARM locks onto a hostile radar beam and follows it to its source—the radar station.

Electronic countercountermeasures

When threatened with attack by hostile forces, it is important to have a line of defense against their jamming devices—their electronic countermeasures, or ECMs. The devices that provide protection against ECMs are known as electronic countercountermeasures, or ECCMs.

One form of ECCM is antijamming circuitry, which identifies jamming signals and filters them out of the signals from radar detectors, leaving the genuine signal intact. Another approach, used principally to protect radio communications from disruption by jamming, is frequency hopping. In this technique, the transmitter and receiver change through a preset sequence of frequencies,

▼ Stacks of circuit boards containing advanced miniaturization technology and components make up the heart of an AN/ALQ-135 airborne radar-jamming electronic countermeasures system. The modular design of hardware and software in the system allows it to be upgraded to meet evolving threats.

the two apparatuses remaining synchronized throughout. Attempts to jam using a single frequency affects only those fragments of the transmission that occupy the jamming frequency, so little information is lost. Similarly, an interceptor tuned to a single frequency will detect only tiny snippets of data that are too small to be useful.

In addition to automatic systems, operators trained in mockup electronic warfare scenarios are invaluable in determining which form of ECCM to use. Furthermore, if all radar systems are knocked out, they can resort to visual observation, sometimes with the aid of binoculars, heat-sensitive infrared cameras, or image intensifiers.

Electronic reconnaissance

Electronic reconnaissance is vitally important to electronic warfare. It is a useful tool for general military intelligence and also provides information for the design of ECM systems.

Electronic reconnaissance derives its effectiveness from the fact that no transmitted signal can be completely hidden from a suitably positioned and configured receiver system, be that system friendly or hostile. Analysis of signals traffic can provide a great deal of information about the types of equipment in use by a hostile force, since specific systems—the various types of radar, for example—produce quite distinct electronic fingerprints. Such information is invaluable in choosing and developing the types of electronic countermeasures necessary. In the general intelligence role, electronic reconnaissance provides vast amounts of information about such things as operational procedures and equipment locations.

Elint. Electronic reconnaissance has developed a number of distinct subdivisions, one of which is elint (*el*ectronic *int*elligence). Elint is the collection and analysis of signals from noncommunications sources, such as radar systems. As such, elint is the branch of electronic reconnaissance most closely allied to the development of effective new electronic countermeasures.

▲ The Tier III–UAV (unpiloted air vehicle), known as DarkStar, was designed to perform reconnaissance while circling at more than 45,000 ft. (13,700 m) above its target. Unlike most stealth aircraft, which are designed to be least visible from the front, Darkstar was designed to be least visible along its wings—the profile presented during its circling maneuver. The DarkStar project was halted in January 1999.

Telint. Telint (*tel*emetry *int*elligence) is the study of the control signals and instrument responses associated with the testing of weapons systems, such as missiles. These signals are often intercepted from radio remote-control communication, and they provide information on the status of new developments in weaponry.

Rint. Rint (*r*adiation *int*elligence) examines the background electromagnetic radiation generated by the movement of electrical current in power-distribution networks, giving a useful indication of industrial and military activity based on an analysis of electrical power usage.

Comint. Comint (*com*munications *int*elligence) is the interception and analysis of communications signals; it is also called sigint (*sig*nals *int*elligence). In the overtly military context, comint is concerned with the interception of commands and strategic information. Occasionally, such information is communicated "in clear" (rather than in code); usually, however, sensitive information can be extracted only after an intercepted signal has been decoded by cryptographers.

Increasingly, comint is being used to impede terrorists and drug traffickers, who use public telecommunications networks to send messages. Such messages can be retrieved from the microwave links between relay antennas and between satellites and ground stations. Suspect messages are pinpointed using software that acts like an Internet browser, picking telephone conversations, e-mails, and faxes that contain certain keywords. These keywords may be the names of suspect persons or locations or known codes for drugs, and they change on a weekly basis. A similar approach can be used to glean politically or commercially sensitive information, and many diplomatic offices are believed to house comint stations that monitor their host countries.

SEE ALSO: AIRCRAFT-CONTROL ENGINEERING • AIRCRAFT DESIGN • CRYPTOLOGY • ELECTRONIC SURVEILLANCE • MISSILE • RADAR

Steam Engine

The steam engine is a machine for converting the heat energy in steam into mechanical energy by means of a piston moving in a cylinder. More than any other machine, the steam engine made the Industrial Revolution possible. It was a source of power unrestricted by limitations such as water supply, wind, and space for draft animals. The steam engine dominated industry and transport for 150 years, and it is still useful in certain applications because it can use any fuel or source of heat and develops its full torque at any speed.

The basic steam engine was developed from the atmospheric engine in the last quarter of the 18th century by the British engineers James Watt and Richard Trevithick. However, the basic design soon evolved into diverse forms for different applications in the hands of many others. Like the Stirling engine, the steam engine is an external combustion engine—the fuel is burned outside the working cylinder, so atmospheric pollution by the combustion gases can be kept to a very low level, unlike the internal combustion engine, which causes more pollution.

Cylinder action

Most rotative steam engines are double acting—there are two power strokes for each revolution of the flywheel. Steam is admitted to one side of the

▲ Steam traction engines were once a common sight at fairgrounds, where they were used to power rides, and in the construction industry, where they were used to pull heavy pieces of machinery, such as road rollers.

piston, and simultaneously, steam is exhausted from the other side by means of valves as the piston moves to-and-fro. The sequence of events at one side of the piston during one revolution of the flywheel is as follows: First, steam is admitted just before the end of the previous stroke to cushion the piston; next, the inlet port is closed (cut off) and further movement of the piston is effected by expansion of the steam; then the exhaust valve opens just before the end of the power stroke (release); and finally, the exhaust valve closes, and the remaining steam is compressed into what is called the clearance volume. The same sequence occurs on the other side of the piston, but 180 degrees out of phase.

The sequence of events can be conveniently shown as a graph of pressure against volume for the different positions of the piston. Such graphs can be plotted mechanically while the engine is working by an indicator connected to the cylinder, and changes in graph shape show the need for adjustments or repairs.

In most engines, the whole sequence of events is effected by a single D-slide valve, invented in 1802 by Matthew Murray of Leeds, England. This valve is driven by the valve gear, which—in marine and reversible stationary engines—is usually a variant of the Stephenson link motion used in early locomotives. A piston valve, also a locomotive feature, in which a piston alternately opens and closes the inlet and exhaust ports, is used where high-steam pressures would cause excessive friction in a D-valve. Other types of valves, usually separate ones for each event, are worked by trip motions to give rapid operation when very early cutoff is needed in large stationary engines, such as those used in spinning mills.

The to-and-fro motion of the piston can be used directly only for pumping or hammering and must be converted to rotary motion for other uses. Rotary motion is achieved by some form of crank handle driven by a connecting rod. Early rotative engines had the piston rod linked to a beam, and the connecting rod pivoted to the other end of the beam. This mechanism made a very bulky engine, and it was soon replaced for most purposes by the guided crosshead invented by Trevithick. A still more compact arrangement was the oscillating engine in which the cylinder rocked about a trunnion so that the piston rod could be directly attached to the flywheel crank. Steam was admitted and exhausted through the trunnion. This form of engine was often used in early screw steamers.

There are two positions in each revolution when the piston rod and the connecting rod are in line with the crank arm and have no turning effect. The inertia of the flywheel must be used to carry a single-cylinder engine past these dead centers. The great majority of engines with more than one cylinder avoid this problem by having suitable angles between the cranks.

Boilers and furnaces

The limited strength of early boilers restricted the steam pressure to about 1 psi (0.07 bar) above atmospheric pressure, and thus, a steam engine with a useful power output had to have very large cylinders. It was also difficult to provide a large enough heating surface to get the heat efficiently into the boiling water, so a large part of the energy generated by burning the fuel went up the chimney. The first successful attempts to avoid these limitations were made by Trevithick and his U.S. correspondent, Oliver Evans of Philadelphia. They made cylindrical boilers of inherently stronger construction with a single internal furnace and flue. They were often set in brickwork containing return flues that heated the outside of the boiler shell, and they became known on both sides of the Atlantic as Cornish boilers. The Lancashire boiler, seen in many surviving steam plants, is very similar but has two furnaces and two sets of return flues.

Modern boilers have a greater heating surface, are less bulky, and enable steam to be raised more quickly than did early designs. They are either of the fire-tube or water-tube type. In the fire-tube boiler, the hot gases from the furnace pass through steel tubes surrounded by water, as is the case in the locomotive boiler. In water-tube boilers, the water flows through tubes situated above the furnace combustion chamber. Although this type of boiler is more expensive to build, it can be operated at higher pressures than fire-tube boilers and is significantly safer. Water-tube boilers are commonly used today to generate steam for marine and power-plant turbines.

Steam boilers do not always need burning fuel, and many are heated by the waste gases from metallurgical furnaces or the exhaust gases of diesel engines. Any combustible substance can be used as fuel, including waste materials such as sawdust, sugar-cane refuse, or oil-refinery residues. Combustion takes place at atmospheric pressure to reduce pollution.

Compound engines

Higher steam pressures allow a higher ratio of expansion from cutoff to release, but in a single-cylinder engine, this pressure often demands an impracticably early cutoff and gives rise to an excessive variation in the cylinder wall temperature. Better results were obtained by arranging for a small, high-pressure cylinder to exhaust into a larger, low-pressure one. Such a combination is called a compound engine and came into general use when mild steel allowed higher steam pressures in the 1860s.

Multiple expansion engines

Several forms of compound engine were widely used, particularly the tandem compound with two cylinders on a common piston rod and crank, the cross compound with its cylinders on either side of a rope drive pulley (often used in textile mills), and the marine compound with two vertical cylinders side by side. The first two types were usually horizontal and had drop valves (reciprocating valves that move into and out of contact with annular valve seats) or Corliss valves (rotary valves that oscillate to and fro through a small angle about the axis of rotation).

◀ Valve gear for the low-pressure cylinder of an engine used in a 19th-century mill.

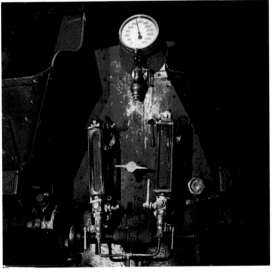

◀ The front of a Lancashire boiler, with coal hoppers on each side of the firebox.

Uniflow engines

Uniflow engines were designed to allow full expansion of high-pressure steam in one cylinder by avoiding the losses that had led to the adoption of compound and multiple-expansion engines. The expanded steam was released through a ring of ports uncovered by the piston that afterward compressed the remaining steam to boiler pressure. Steam was admitted by quick-acting drop valves loaded with powerful springs to give a cut-off of about 10 percent of the stroke at full load. This percentage was reduced for light loads.

The first successful uniflow engines were developed by a German engineer, Johann Stumpf, in 1908. The construction of large engines was simplified by avoiding compound working, but greater precision in manufacture was essential, and serious problems in designing the valve gear had to be overcome.

Many very large, horizontal, stationary engines were built on the uniflow principle in Germany, Switzerland, Britain, and the United States during the subsequent 45 years, and they included the most powerful steam engines ever built. Some in the United States developed 25,000 horsepower (18,650 kW) from four uniflow cylinders working in parallel, and a German five-cylinder engine of the 1930s developed 30,000 horsepower (22,380 kW). These large engines were designed for driving rolling mills. The uniflow engine was very successful in the United States, where one manufacturer built more than 2,000 of them between 1913 and 1958.

Marine uniflow engines appeared in the United States about 1930. They had from two to five vertical cylinders arranged in parallel. Such engines were a feature of U.S. steamers built

THE PRINCIPLE OF THE UNIFLOW STEAM ENGINE

Steam input on first stroke

Exhaust port

Steam input on return stroke

◄ In the uniflow engine, first developed in 1908, steam is admitted at each end in turn, driving the piston up and down the cylinder and escaping through the exhaust ports.

between 1930 and 1955, and they powered many of the liberty ships and small aircraft carriers of World War II.

High-speed engines

Most types of steam engine had a simple drip-feed lubrication system that was unsuitable for speeds over about 150 rpm. These speeds were too low for direct electricity generation, and early power plants were equipped with speed-increasing rope drives at great cost in space and complexity. The high-speed engine overcame this difficulty by having the crossheads, connecting rods, and valve gear lubricated by circulating oil under pressure inside a closed crankcase. Working was either compound or triple expansion with pis-

▼ The uniflow engine's inlet valves are at each end of the cylinder, with the ring of exhaust ports halfway along. The stream enters by means of spring-loaded, quick-acting drop valves.

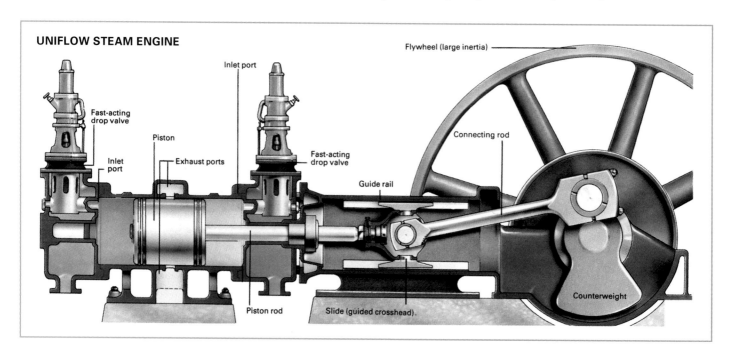

UNIFLOW STEAM ENGINE

Flywheel (large inertia)

Inlet port

Fast-acting drop valve

Piston

Inlet port

Exhaust ports

Fast-acting drop valve

Connecting rod

Guide rail

Piston rod

Slide (guided crosshead).

Counterweight

ton valves and a fixed cutoff in each cylinder, the engine being governed by throttling the steam supply. The cylinders were separated from the crankcase by distance pieces longer than the stroke so that oil on the piston rods would not be drawn into the cylinder to contaminate the exhaust. Such engines ran at about 500 rpm and could be coupled directly to a dynamo.

The larger, condensing engines were superseded by steam turbines, but a back-pressure engine, in which the steam is exhausted at above atmospheric pressure, is still made for electric outputs up to about 500 kW.

Steam cars

It is generally accepted that the first automobile ever built was a three-wheeled steam-powered vehicle constructed by a French inventor, Nicolas Joseph Cugnot, in 1769. It traveled for 20 minutes at a speed of about 2 mph (3.2 km/h) carrying four passengers. In the next 100 years, numerous steam carriages and traction engines were built, particularly in England. It was not until the end of the 19th century, however, that the first steam-powered vehicles recognizable as forerunners of the modern automobile were produced.

The most successful steam car was that built by the Stanley brothers in the United States—more than 60,000 were made between 1897 and 1927, and some remained in ordinary service until 1945. A Stanley steam automobile broke the world speed record in 1906 with a speed of 127 mph (204 km/h). The Stanley automobile had a two-cylinder noncondensing engine with direct drive to the rear axle and a special type of fire-tube boiler under the hood. Its range was limited because it needed a full tank of pure water every 20 miles (32 km) at full speed. A condensing model was made between 1915 and 1927.

Condensing-steam cars had a much greater range but were troubled by cylinder oil contaminating the feed water, and upsetting the boiler and controls. The most successful of these cars was one built in the United States between 1900 and 1911. It had a compound engine under the hood behind an air-cooled condenser. A spiral-tube boiler was under the driving seat. The usual fuel in steam cars was kerosene, and elaborate automatic controls were needed to ensure that the supply of steam matched the driving conditions without burning out the boiler or starting a fire from excess fuel. Steam cars went out of favor when electric starting for gasoline engines was introduced to replace the crank.

▲ A cutaway model of George Stephenson's *Rocket*, showing the piston, cylinders, steam valve, and connecting rod.

SEE ALSO:	Gas laws • Locomotive and power car • Pressure • Stirling engine • Valve, mechanical • Vapor pressure

Steering System

The simplest form of steering is the type that was used for centuries on horse-drawn vehicles. This system consists of a beam axle, pivoted in the middle and with a wheel on each end. When cornering at high speeds, it is unstable because of the difference in track (the distance between the front and rear wheels).

In 1818, a German carriage builder, Georg Lankensperger, took out a British patent on a system of steering in which the front wheels are separately pivoted at the ends of the shaft. As a result, all four wheels follow a true radius about a single point on a line that includes the rear axle. The geometry was named for Lankensperger's patent agent, whose name was Rudolph Ackermann. In 1878, a method for making this geometry more precise was invented by a French carriage builder, Charles Jeantaud. The combination of Lankensperger's and Jeantaud's ideas is today referred to as Ackermann steering.

Steering column

The steering wheel in an automobile is made of a steel skeleton covered with hard plastic or leather. The hub is splined to the steering column (splines are longitudinal grooves similar to gear teeth). The steering column extends from the interior of the car down to the front end where the steering gear is located. Today both the hub of the steering wheel and the column itself are made to be energy absorbing or collapsible for safety reasons: to reduce the risk of chest damage in the event of an accident.

Steering box

At the lower end of the steering column is the steering box. The purpose of the steering box is to provide leverage, or mechanical advantage, to turn the front wheels. There are four types of boxes.

The worm-and-peg (or worm-and-nut) system consists of a coarse thread (the worm) on the end of the column and a peg mounted on a cross-rocker shaft or a meshing nut surrounding the worm and fastened to the rocker shaft. As the column is rotated, the peg or nut rides up and down in the worm, so turning the shaft. The cam-and-roller system is a variant of this system, in which the peg is replaced by a cam (a sort of V-shaped roller) that meshes with the worm. The recirculating-ball gear is a more elaborate variant. A bearing casing takes the place of a nut, and instead of threads, ball bearings ride in the coarse groove of the worm. The bearing casing can have one or two threads, which are connected end-to-end by a tube (or tubes) to allow the balls to recirculate back to the end of the worm thread when they have in effect rolled off the edge. The rack-and-pinion system consists simply of a pinion gear on the end of the column meshing with a rack (a flat section of gear teeth).

All but the last type of box require a system of linkages to take the movement created by the drop arm (attached to the steering-box rocker shaft) to the steering arms on the wheels. Each manufacturer designs an appropriate system that gives the correct linkage geometry, allows the links to follow vertical wheel movement (for example, when the wheels hit bumps in the road), and fits into the available space. It requires a combination of several pieces of linkage: the operating arm, idler arm, and steering rods (tie rods). The rack-and-pinion system scores highly because its linkage is simple—a steering rod from each end of the rack connected to the steering arms on the wheels. Its main disadvantage is that the rack bridges the center of the car, getting in the way of a front engine.

Steered wheels

The attitude, or angle, of the wheel and axle to the road is important in steering. Caster is the term given to the interaction of the contact patch of the tire on the road, about which the wheel swivels, and the axis of the kingpin, or swivel pin, which creates a self-aligning torque that keeps the wheels pointing straight ahead when traveling in a straight line. Inclining the kingpin has the effect that, as the wheel is turned, it lifts the car slightly (like a door on rising hinges) so that, in addition to the turning torque required, an extra load has to be applied—and thus, steering becomes self-centering. Camber is the inclination of the wheel to the vertical—the angle is called the camber angle. Today automobiles have camber angles of less than one degree, and camber is usually positive (the tops of the wheels are tilted outward). The purpose is to prevent the wheels from tilting inward too much because of heavy loads or wear resulting in play in the kingpins or wheel bearings. If the camber of the two steered wheels is not equal, the steering of the vehicle will have a tendency to wander, and tire wear will be uneven.

Power steering

As automobiles became larger and heavier, with wider tires and more engine weight on the front wheels, the effort needed for steering increased considerably. At the same time, congested traffic conditions made driving more tiring. Various approaches were tried to make steering easier. One solution was to increase the ratio of the steering gear to give a better mechanical advantage with less effort needed to turn the wheel. However, this meant that more turns of the steering wheel were needed to turn the road wheels from one extreme to the other. Another solution was to use some form of power assistance.

Power-assisted steering was first developed in the 1920s; one of the first devices was developed by an engineer at Pierce Arrow, a U.S. maker of luxury automobiles. The Cadillac division of General Motors was going to offer power steering as optional equipment on some models in the early 1930s, but the depression interfered with development. During World War II power steering was fitted to military vehicles; in 1952, Chrysler began offering it on domestic cars. It is now standard equipment on many automobiles.

Electric devices were tried, but modern automobile power-steering systems are hydraulic. Compressed-air systems are also used on some heavy commercial vehicles, especially where the compressed air is also used for the power brakes. In hydraulic automobile systems, the necessary oil pressure, of up to 1,000 psi (70 kg/cm²), is supplied by a pump driven by the engine. The system is a servomechanism, or servoloop, which makes a correction to compensate for the torque applied to the steering wheel by the driver. It consists of an actuator and control valve. The actuator is a hydraulic cylinder with a piston, or ram, which is free to travel in either direction from the center. The function of the control valve is to respond to the torque from the steering wheel by actuating smaller valves at each end of the cylinder. The system is designed to assist the steering linkage rather than to replace it, and it does not do all the work of steering but leaves some of it for the driver. Thus, if the hydraulics fail, the automobile can still be steered, though with greater effort, and at all times, the feel of the road is mechanically transmitted from the front wheels to the hands of the driver on the steering wheel, an essential element of safe driving. Power steering makes a positive contribution to safe driving in that if the driver hits a small obstacle in the road or has a flat tire at speed, the power unit makes it easier to keep the automobile under control.

The power-steering system includes a reservoir to hold the oil. Oil pressure is always pro-

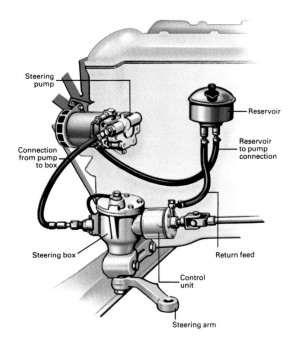

◀ A power-steering layout showing how the hydraulic pump, reservoir, and steering box are mounted independently.

Steering pump

Reservoir

Reservoir to pump connection

Connection from pump to box

Steering box

Return feed

Control unit

Steering arm

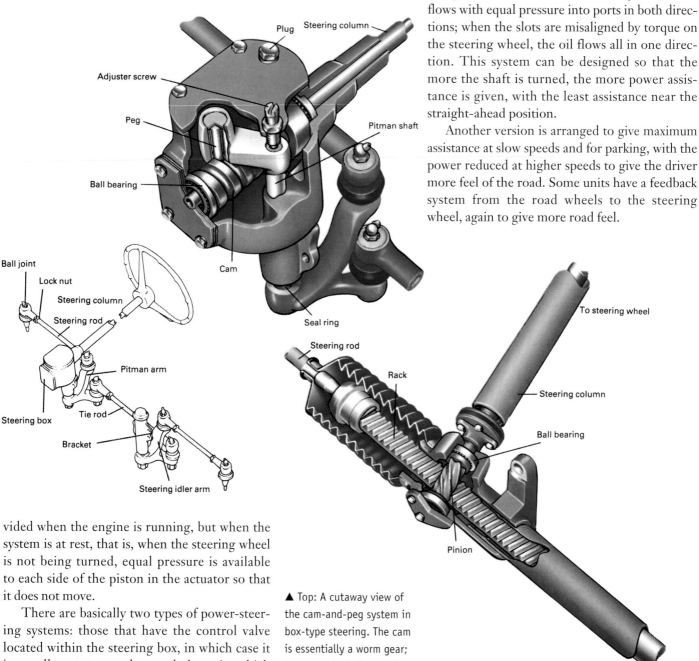

being turned, the slots are lined up so that oil flows with equal pressure into ports in both directions; when the slots are misaligned by torque on the steering wheel, the oil flows all in one direction. This system can be designed so that the more the shaft is turned, the more power assistance is given, with the least assistance near the straight-ahead position.

Another version is arranged to give maximum assistance at slow speeds and for parking, with the power reduced at higher speeds to give the driver more feel of the road. Some units have a feedback system from the road wheels to the steering wheel, again to give more road feel.

vided when the engine is running, but when the system is at rest, that is, when the steering wheel is not being turned, equal pressure is available to each side of the piston in the actuator so that it does not move.

There are basically two types of power-steering systems: those that have the control valve located within the steering box, in which case it is usually a rotary valve, and those in which the valve is integral with the actuator, when it is an axial spool valve.

Rotary valve

In a rotary-valve system, the valve is integral with the steering column and operated directly by rotation of the steering wheel. In some systems, the actuator is part of the steering linkage; in rack-and-pinion systems, the actuator is normally mounted on the rack itself. In others, the actuator as well as the valve is integral with the steering box and operates the drop arm, which connects the end of the steering column to the steering linkage between the front wheels. A rotary valve is an input shaft inside a valve sleeve, with longitudinal slots machined on the shaft and to the inside of the sleeve. When the steering wheel is not

▲ Top: A cutaway view of the cam-and-peg system in box-type steering. The cam is essentially a worm gear; in one variant, the peg is replaced by recirculating ball bearings. Above left: diagram showing the basic Ackermann steering principle, in which the front wheels adopt different angles to travel on a circular course. Above right: the rack-and-pinion steering gear, the simplest and most positive system, is fitted to most modern small cars.

Axial spool valve

An axial spool valve, which reacts laterally, is usually integral with the actuator in the steering linkage, particularly on commercial vehicles. The axial load, fed into the steering linkage by turning the steering wheel, actuates the valve. In these systems, the actuator is often connected at one end to the cross piece of the steering linkage with the piston and connected to the frame of the automobile so that the actuator in effect pushes or pulls against the frame when it is activated.

 SEE ALSO: AUTOMOBILE • CAM • GEAR • HYDRAULICS • RUDDER • SERVOMECHANISM • VALVE, MECHANICAL

Stereoscopy

Each of a pair of well-functioning human eyes receives a slightly different view of any given object by virtue of the horizontal separation of the eyes. This is an example of an effect called parallax. When the brain combines the two images, it can estimate distances of up to around 300 ft. (91 m). It can also perceive the viewed surface of an object in three dimensions by the slight differences in the distances between various points on the surface and the eyes.

In a normal photograph, these subtle differences are lost because the lens of a normal camera views scenes from a single perspective. Consequently, a person viewing such a photograph can estimate the distance from his or her eyes to the photograph but not the distance between the photographer and the scene at the time when the photograph was taken. In some cases, an impression of three-dimensional form can be gained from the way shadows fall within the image or from differences in focus. However, a flatly lit image, taken using a wide aperture to give an infinite depth of field, reveals no such information: the image appears totally two-dimensional.

Stereoscopy aims to preserve information about the three-dimensional (3-D) forms of objects by capturing images from two slightly different perspectives. These images then reveal the three-dimensional image when viewed separately but simultaneously by the corresponding eyes.

Basic stereoscopes

The principles of stereoscopy were first described by a British physicist, Charles Wheatstone, in 1832, but stereoscopes were not widely used until Sir David Brewster, another British physicist, showed one at the Great Exhibition of 1851. Queen Victoria was impressed, and there was a craze for stereoscopy for some time after.

A simple stereoscope has two lenses—one for each eye—with a separate image behind each lens. A central partition ensures each eye sees only one picture, and the lenses enlarge the image and make them appear more distant, thereby helping the eyes to focus correctly.

The images are usually photographs taken by two cameras 2.5 in. (6.4 cm) apart—the average distance between human eyes—so that each eye sees the view it would have had at the original scene. Alternatively, the pair of images may be printed using computer software that produces stereoimages from virtual 3-D screen images.

An even simpler form of stereoscopy uses a sheet of cardboard placed perpendicular to the

gap between a pair of stereoscopic images. The card separates the images and helps ensure they are viewed from an appropriate distance; the lack of lenses provides no help in focusing the eyes, although practiced viewers of such images have little difficulty in focusing on them.

Simple stereoscopes are rather bulky and can be used by only one person at a time. Other stereoscopic viewing techniques overcome these limitations by using relatively flat image viewers or projectors that can show stereoscopic movies.

One compact form of combined stereoscopic image and viewer is the 3-D postcard. Photographs taken from two viewpoints are cut into fine vertical strips that are then laid out with alternating strips of left-eye and right-eye shots. The print is then covered with a plastic layer whose surface is embossed so as to form a large number of tiny cylindrical lenses. These lenses are positioned so that from any direction only one of the original photographs is visible.

Stereoscopic movies

Three-dimensional films are made by two synchronized cameras recording the same scene; the 3-D image is then recreated by two synchronized projectors that illuminate a single screen. There must also be some way of ensuring that each eye

▲ This custom-built stereo camera, built from two Nikon FMs, simultaneously takes two photographs from the perspectives of the left and right eyes. A three-dimensional image of the original scene is obtained when the developed images are viewed in a stereoscope.

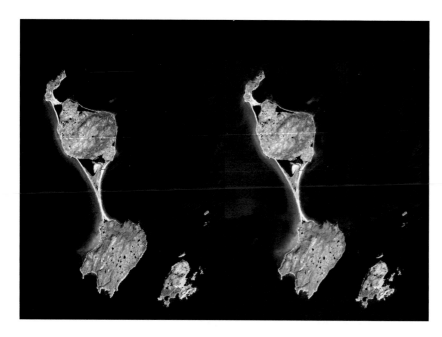

sees the image from only one projector, as has been achieved by the anaglyph system for monochrome (black-and-white) films, and the more modern light-polarizing system for color films.

In the anaglyph system, one film would be projected through a red filter, the other through a green filter. The images would then be separated for the viewers by eyeglasses that had one red and one green filter, which transmitted only the light from the appropriate projector to each eye.

The light-polarization system uses clear polarizing filters in the projectors and in the eyeglasses. The projector filters polarize the light from the two films in perpendicular directions, and the glasses transmit only the appropriate polarization to each eye. Although this system can be used for color films, it has several drawbacks. When the viewer tilts his or her head, for example, the polarizing filters in glasses lose their alignment with the projector filters, and some mixing of images occurs, so the quality of the three-dimensional effect decreases and the image appears blurred. Furthermore, a certain type of screen must be used to maintain the polarization of light when it is reflected. The projectors must also be synchronized to within one-hundredth of a second to maintain a three-dimensional image.

Stereoscopy in computing

Software designers—particularly games designers—have sought to achieve three-dimensional effects since the introduction of high-resolution graphics made possible the realistic portrayal of scenes and objects. At first, it was done by using rendering programs to calculate the fall of light within a scene, to hide background objects when foreground objects obscure them, and to add haze to create the impression of distance.

▲ Viewed through a stereoscope, this pair of images produces a three-dimensional impression of an airborne view of Grande Miquelon (top left), Petite Miquelon (bottom center), and Saint Pierre (bottom right), islands located south of Newfoundland, Canada. The images were created by superimposing images from the *Landsat 7* satellite on an elevation model generated by the Shuttle Radar Topography Mission aboard NASA's *Endeavour* space shuttle.

The first truly stereoscopic computer images were generated using a screen that alternated rapidly between the two images of the stereo pair and eyeglasses that transmitted alternately through the left and right filters in synchronization with the changing images. The eyeglass filters were sandwiches of cross-polarized film with a liquid-crystal filling, and electrical signals from the computer controlled their transparency. Such systems were prone to flicker caused by insufficient refresh rates of the screen and glasses.

More recent displays are autostereoscopic: they do not require the use of special eyeglasses. The three-dimensional effect is produced by illuminating each pixel (picture element) with two light sources, each angled at a single eye through its own LCD (liquid crystal display) element. The system requires users to keep their heads within a small range of positions, but it suffers none of the flicker inherent to the earlier systems. In August 2001, the Heinrich Hertz Institute of Germany demonstrated a computer system that combined such a screen with video cameras that tracked the positions of the head, eyes, and hands. Users can manipulate virtual three-dimensional objects floating in the space between them and the screen, and the tracking cameras provide the information for the computer to take commands or move those objects in response.

Other applications

One of the oldest uses of stereoscopy is in aerial surveying for resources and in military reconnaissance work. In hyperstereoscopy, or exaggerated stereoscopy, a combination of magnification and large camera separations creates stereo images that appear to have been taken from close to the ground, when in fact, they were taken from an aircraft flying at high altitude. In an extension of this technique, satellites now take stereo images of Earth's surface, revealing features such as mountain ranges and valleys in photographs that give strikingly good three-dimensional impressions.

The medical profession also makes use of stereoscopy. In stereoradiography, for example, stereoscopic images from body scanners help in diagnosis by providing three-dimensional information on the positions of tumors and injuries within the body cavity. Optical stereoscopy is also useful in recording surgical procedures, giving students a clearer impression of the positions of organs and surgical tools than could be achieved using normal two-dimensional photography.

SEE ALSO: Aerial photography • Camera • Eye • Lens • Mapmaking techniques • Polarization • Surveying

Stethoscope

The stethoscope is an instrument that enables physicians to listen to the sounds of internal organs. It is also used with the sphygmomanometer to measure the blood pressure indirectly. It was invented by the French physician René Laënnec, who worked among the poor in Paris and was interested in tuberculosis, a disease from which he died at an early age. He used a wooden cylinder to transmit sounds to the ear. In 1828, another Frenchman, Poirry, modified this very basic instrument by adding an earpiece and a trumpet-shaped chest piece. The design of the instrument remained the same until about the beginning of the 20th century, when a New York City physician, P. G. Cammann, produced the binaural stethoscope (with two earpieces) that is still in use today.

Acoustic stethoscopes

Acoustic stethoscopes are used to investigate the condition of the respiratory, circulatory, and digestive systems. Most sounds of interest to a doctor, especially heart sounds, have frequencies in the range 60 to 600 Hz, but some mitral diastolic murmurs (irregular sounds heard over the heart during expansion of the heart and indicating an abnormality in the mitral valve) have frequencies below 60 Hz, and a few sounds, such as crepitations (cracking sounds heard over the chest in some diseases of the lungs), have frequencies of up to 1,400 Hz. Acoustic stethoscopes do not amplify sound, they merely convey it to the ear, via rubber tubes, as efficiently as possible.

A typical acoustic stethoscope has a combined bell and diaphragm chest piece made of stainless steel. The bell section of the chest piece is open, has a diameter of 1.13 in. (28.7 mm), and is 0.25 in. (6.4 mm) deep. When this side of the stethoscope is in use, the patient's skin acts as a flexible diaphragm across the mouth of the bell to transmit the sound. The diaphragm section has a diameter of 1.72 in. (43.7 mm) but is only 0.13 in. (3.3 mm) deep. It is covered by a rigid linen–bakelite diaphragm. The doctor can select either side of the chest piece by rotating it relative to the collecting tube that connects it to the earpiece tubing. The bell side of the instrument will normally be used by the doctor to listen to relatively low-pitched sounds in the range of about 30 to 500 Hz, whereas the diaphragm side of the chest piece is designed as a high-pass filter to filter out or block the lowest sounds but pass or transmit the highest frequencies in the range 200 to 1,400 Hz. Stereophonic stethoscopes are also available

◀ The bell and diaphragm chest piece of one of today's stethoscopes. The bell-shaped piece is used for listening to the lower frequencies. The chest piece is resting on the diaphragm section.

in which the diaphragm or bell are split into two halves enabling the doctor to hear time delays and phase shifts between the left and right channel.

The stethoscope tubing is made of a flexible plastic material. The interior of the tube has a very smooth surface so as not to impede the flow of sound. The earpiece tubes are generally made of stainless steel and tipped with plastic earpieces. The design of the plastic tips for the earpieces is very important: they must be as large as possible, usually with a diameter of from 0.50 to 0.63 in. (12.7–16 mm), so that external sounds are blocked from the ears—a leak only five times the diameter of a human hair has a very marked effect on the performance of the stethoscope, particularly at low frequencies.

Fetal stethoscope

A fetal stethoscope is a funnel-shaped piece of metal, open at the top and tapering to the base, that has a small hole in it. The open part of the instrument is placed on the abdomen of a pregnant woman, and the listener, by placing an ear to the base, can hear the heart sounds of the baby.

SEE ALSO:	BODY SCANNER • ELECTRONICS IN MEDICINE • HEART • LUNG • SKIN • SOUND • SPHYGMOMANOMETER

Stirling Engine

The Stirling engine was invented in 1816 by the Reverend Robert Stirling, when he was a junior Presbyterian minister at Kilmarnock, Scotland, but its early development was hampered by the lack of materials with sufficient strength and corrosion resistance at high temperatures and the lack of suitable materials and techniques for gas sealing. For this reason, it was unable to compete with the steam engine or internal combustion engine—even though it is capable of higher thermal efficiency, can be powered by various energy sources, is much quieter, and can be designed to produce far less atmospheric pollution.

▲ This Gotland-class Swedish submarine is powered by a Stirling engine. With a Stirling engine, submarines like this are almost noise and vibration free and do not need air for the combustion reaction, which allows them to stay underwater longer.

Stirling cycle

In contrast to the internal combustion engine (in which fuel is burned inside the main engine cylinders) the Stirling engine is an external combustion engine—with the heat being transferred to the working gas through the cylinder walls or through a heat exchanger in contact with the heat source. The working gas normally remains permanently within the engine and goes through a closed cycle of heating and cooling to convert the thermal energy into mechanical work.

There are four stages in the theoretical Stirling cycle: isothermal (constant temperature) compression, heating at constant volume, isothermal expansion, and cooling at constant volume—the thermal efficiency of the cycle being the maximum allowed by the Second Law of Thermodynamics. This theoretical cycle can be applied in a number of ways, the most common approach using a displacer moving in a cylinder to control the movement of the working fluid between a hot expansion space (heated by the external source) and a cold compression space. Power output is produced by a piston working in the cylinder below the displacer, with the relative motions of the piston and displacer being controlled by a linkage.

At the start of the cycle the displacer is at the top of the cylinder and the piston at the bottom of its stroke, with the working gas filling the cold space between the piston and displacer. The piston moves up to compress the gas in the cold space, and then the displacer is moved down to transfer the compressed gas to the hot space at the top end of the cylinder. This transfer takes place through channels that link the hot and cold spaces and incorporate regenerators. As the compressed gas passes through the regenerator, it takes up heat, and further heating takes place while it is in the hot section of the cylinder. The heated gas then expands, moving down the displacer to contact the piston, which makes a power stroke under the pressure of the hot gas. At the end of the power stroke, the displacer starts to move upward and transfers the expanded gas back through the regenerator to the cold space between the displacer and piston. As the hot gas passes through the regenerator, it gives up its heat, which is stored in the regenerator for release to the compressed gas on the next cycle.

A complex linkage is required to give the required movement of the displacer. The actual cycle achieved does not correspond to the theoretical one because the individual stages blend into one another owing to the continuous motion of the piston and displacer. Another departure from the ideal cycle lies in the fact that the compression and expansion of the working gas are not isothermal. Thus, the efficiency of practical engines is significantly lower than postulated by the theoretical cycle, but it is generally higher than that of other heat engines working between the same temperature limits.

In early engines, the working gas was air at about atmospheric pressure, but today in most engines, the pressure is higher (in some cases, several hundred times that of the atmosphere), and air is replaced by helium or hydrogen—because these gases are better conductors of heat, they greatly simplify the problems of rapidly heating and cooling the gas.

Under given conditions, the power that can be produced with a given volume of working gas is proportional to the difference between the upper and lower extremes of temperature that occur in the engine cycle. It is therefore advantageous to make the temperature of the hot end of the engine as high as the properties of the construction materials will allow, and most engines now operate in the 842 to 1382°F (450–750°C) range.

Regeneration

An important feature of the Stirling engine is its use of regenerators to recover heat from the working gas after expansion and then apply it to heat the compressed gas on the next cycle. This feature avoids wasting the heat in a cooling system (the working fluid has to be cooled before compression) and helps increase the overall efficiency. In a regenerator the gas is made to flow through a porous material such as fine metal mesh, or through narrow passages in a matrix, thus ensuring good thermal contact and maximum heat transfer between the gas and the regenerator, both when cooling and when heating.

◄ The heat generator section of a Stirling engine. This device prevents heat wastage.

Development

The engine arrangement in which the displacer and power piston work together in a cylinder was the one adopted for the original Stirling engine, which had a power output of around 2 horsepower (1.5 kW). These two pistons were coaxial—hot over cold—and the hot space was surrounded by a ring-shaped regenerator. This arrangement, which has been widely favored, poses the problem of keeping the pistons in phase with each other. Of the many mechanisms designed, one of the most elegant is the rhombic drive, invented by the Philips company, which involves contrarotating,

▼ United Stirling's V160 engine, one of many variations on the basic Stirling theme, has one hot piston and one cold. The working fluid (helium or hydrogen) passes between them, alternately expanding and contracting to drive the hot piston.

THE STIRLING V160 ENGINE

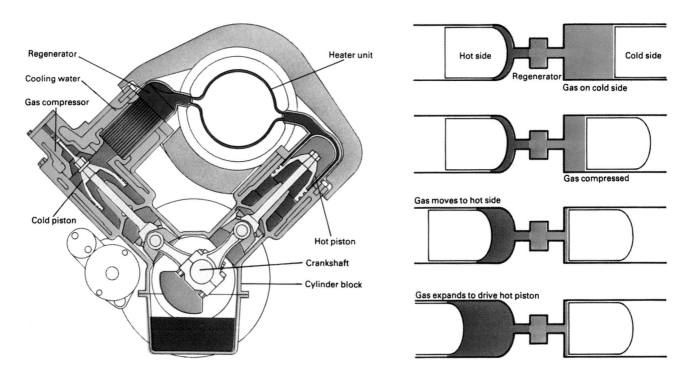

Regenerator
Cooling water
Gas compressor
Cold piston
Heater unit
Hot piston
Crankshaft
Cylinder block

Hot side
Cold side
Regenerator
Gas on cold side

Gas compressed

Gas moves to hot side

Gas expands to drive hot piston

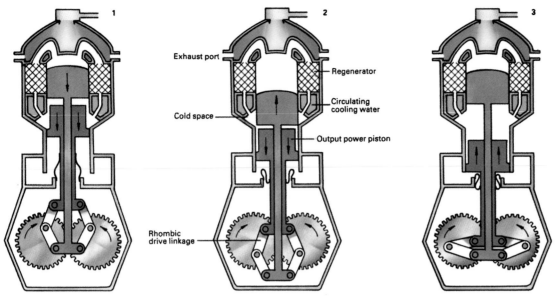

◀ One operating cycle of a Stirling engine. (1) Heated by the burner, gas in the hot space expands, pushing down the power output piston and displacer. (2) The gas, almost fully expanded, continues to push the piston down. The displacer begins to move up to transfer gas from the hot to the cold space. (3) The displacer nears the top of its travel; the gas has been transferred to the cold space, where it contracts, drawing up the piston. The cool gas is then transferred back to the hot space, and the cycle begins again.

geared-together crankshafts connected to each other by a rhombic drive linkage.

A number of other arrangements are possible, including designs with separate displacer and power cylinders and multicylinder types, but the same working principle is applied. Stirling engines were made in many forms during the 19th century, from very low powers up to about 35 horsepower (26 kW). They were used for driving pumps and, to a lesser extent, crushers, grinders, churns, and so on. They were more efficient than the steam engines of that period, but burnout of the hot ends of cylinders was a major problem.

The engine was little used in the 20th century, but continuing research has resulted in engines with higher efficiency and similar output power for a given weight and size to gasoline and diesel engines. Efficiency of combustors and regenerators has been raised, and fueling control is more effective than it was owing to the capability of varying the pressure of the working fluid.

New materials

One reason that Stirling engines were slow to develop is that for a long time the materials available for their manufacture were insufficiently durable. Now, acceptable standards of durability and reliability are attainable using traditional materials as well as a newer range of materials, such as ceramics (silicon nitride), for example. The chief benefit of ceramics is that they have a greater resistance to high temperatures than most metals. Such resistance is of fundamental importance in the Stirling, since its efficiency and fuel consumption depend on the difference between the minimum and maximum temperatures occurring during the cycle. The ceramics—used on the hot side—enable maximum temperatures to be raised.

The main barriers that prevent the adoption of the Stirling principle for high-power engines are the well-established position of traditional piston engines and the relatively high cost of the heat exchangers required for passing the large amounts of heat into and out of the engine. Research continues, however, to investigate cheaper and more efficient options that may make Stirling engines more economically competitive. A particular advantage of the Stirling engine lies

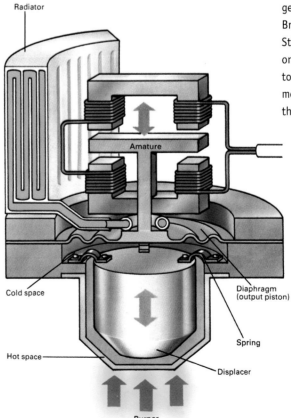

◀ This thermomechanical generator, developed in Britain, is a scaled-down Stirling engine, needing only a small power supply to operate. A vibrating metal diaphragm acts as the power-output piston.

in the fact that it is an external combustion engine and can be arranged to work on a wide range of fuels, while the combustion process can be arranged to give very low pollution levels. Application of a suitable means of heat transfer, such as a heat pipe, even allows the use of less conventional heat sources, such as nuclear reactors and solar power.

Another promising application of the Stirling principle lies in its reversibility. If a Stirling engine is driven by externally applied mechanical power without the application of a heat source, the engine continues to draw in heat at what would normally be its hot end, thereby cooling it, and to reject heat at what would normally be its cold end, thereby heating it. In this mode of operation, it has been demonstrated as a particularly efficient refrigerator for temperatures in the range of about –76 to –292°F (–60 to –180°C). It could also be used as a heat pump, for example, to draw in heat from the outside environment for heating buildings.

Further developments

Toward the end of the 20th century, much research was conducted on improving the performance of Stirling engines. Sweden's FFV group, for example, developed a compact, 20-horsepower engine called the V160. It has one compression and one expansion piston and can deliver 6.5 kW at 1800 rev/min. It runs on helium. This design has since been improved and updated by SOLO of Germany to produce the V161, used, for example, to generate power in solar arrays.

Britain's Atomic Energy Research Establishment developed an ingenious device derived from the Stirling engine. This device, named the Fluidyne, has no solid moving parts or any rotating mechanisms, the orthodox Stirling pistons being replaced by oscillating columns of liquid, normally in a U configuration. This oscillation can be arranged to provide a pumping action, so the Fluidyne is attractive as a simple powered pump.

In the 1970s, it seemed as though the Stirling could be developed to rival the traditional piston engine for vehicle duties. Large amounts of money were directed toward research by the Ford Motor Company. Ultimately the bulk, weight, unit cost, and driveability problems of Stirling engines continued to overshadow their environmental and fuel-saving advantages. Despite these disadvantages, there are still possible road-transportation opportunities for the Stirling engine. These engines may be useful for powering buses and delivery trucks for city work, where the balance between pros and cons would make the Stirling a genuine competitor to the diesel engine.

Today Stirling engines have a broad range of practical applications. Stirling Energy Systems manufacture solar power units that use arrays of mirrors to direct solar power toward a Stirling engine. The Stirling engines used in this situation employ hydrogen as the cylinder gas. An array of around 37 ft. (11 m) in diameter is capable of providing enough solar heat to produce 60,000 kW of energy annually. Such systems are already in use in parts of California and are more cost effective than those that obtain power from photovoltaic cells.

Kockums of Sweden are a manufacturer of naval vessels, and some of the submarines they produce are powered by Stirling engines. These submarines have the advantage of being almost noise and vibration free and are also air independent, being powered by diesel and liquid oxygen. Other manufacturers produce Stirling engines for cryocooling to cool such devices as lasers, microprocessors, and biological materials.

Stirling engines have also been designed for use in cars with hybrid engine systems. These engines combine the advantages of internal combustion engines with the quietness, efficiency, and low emissions of the Stirling engine.

▼ Stirling engines, such as the United Stirling V160, are still being developed for use in automobiles, but its future off the road is more promising, with electricity generation, underwater applications, and rail locomotives as possibilities for its application.

SEE ALSO:	Gas laws • Heat engine • Heat exchanger • Heat pump • Refrigeration • Thermodynamics

Stone Cutting

Although it is not certain when people first made stones into decorative ornaments, the Neolithic (c.8000–3500 B.C.E.) technique of rubbing down stone tools and weapons to give them sharper, cleaner edges could have led to the art of gem cutting and polishing. Archaeologists have found a jade Neolithic ax with a good polish, for example, that is about 10,000 years old.

Early jewelry making

Bracelets of amethyst, lapis, and turquoise set in gold have been found in Egyptian tombs dating from 3000 to 2780 B.C.E. The exquisite treasures found in the tomb of the Egyptian boy king Tutankhamen show that by about 1000 B.C.E., most of the goldsmithing processes had been developed, such as casting, soldering, piercing, chasing, engraving, enameling, and setting stones in collets or as inlay. The gemstones that were rounded or carved would have been worked with bronze tools and abrasives, such as silica, powdered garnet, corundum (which is second in hardness only to diamonds), and—some authorities think—even diamonds.

The earliest colored stones to be polished would have been the softer materials, such as turquoise and lapis lazuli, and they would simply have had their roughness removed. As techniques developed, shaping of beads and cylinders and drilling and carving would have followed—together with the use of harder stones such as chalcedony, chrysoprase, onyx, agate, bloodstone, jasper, and amethyst. Finally, people discovered that spectacular results could be obtained in transparent stones by cutting facets to reflect light and produce brilliancy and fire.

◄ Quartz is one of the most widespread silica minerals found in Earth's crust. Many of its forms, such as amethyst and agate, can be cut and polished into semiprecious stones for use in jewelry.

▼ The stages of cutting a brilliant diamond. (1) A pyramid is cut from one end of an octahedral crystal using a saw. (2) The table (top) facet is produced by rotating the stone against a lathe or another diamond to form a conical-cylindrical shape (3). (4 and 5) The first four facets are cut on the crown and pavilion. The position of these facets is the most critical stage of diamond cutting. Other facets are then cut onto the crown, pavilion, and girdle (6 and 7). The finished diamond (8) will display a play of colors based on the reflections produced by the facets.

Styles of cutting

Cut stones may be divided into two broad categories—those with curved surfaces, such as beads, cabochons, carvings, and baroque shapes, and those with flat facets.

The earliest, simplest, and cheapest method of fashioning gemstones is to polish just the surface of the rough (uncut) gemstone, which still retains the original shape. A classic example is the Black Prince's ruby in the British Imperial State Crown, which is actually a fine red spinel about 2 in. (50 mm) long and of a polished irregular shape.

A cabochon is a stone with a rounded top surface that may be oval, round, or drop-shape in outline. The top may have a high, medium, or low dome; the back, often left semipolished, may be of similar curvature to the front—flat or even hollow (to lighten the color of a dark stone, such as almandine carbuncle, a form of garnet).

Although the cabochon style was previously used for precious stones such as emeralds, rubies, and sapphires, it is now reserved either for material that is not clean enough (sufficiently free from flaws) to warrant faceting or for translucent and opaque stone such as jade, agate, turquoise, and opal. It is also used to bring out optical effects in some stones—for example, chrysoberyl (cat's eye) and corundum (star stone). Since the 1960s, a great deal of rough has been tumble polished in revolving barrels, producing highly polished stones with baroque, or irregular, contours.

Faceting was originally used to enhance the surface reflection and give more interesting shapes. In the 14th century, the natural faces of the diamond octahedra were polished to give point stones, and one corner of the octahedra was ground off and polished to give the table cut.

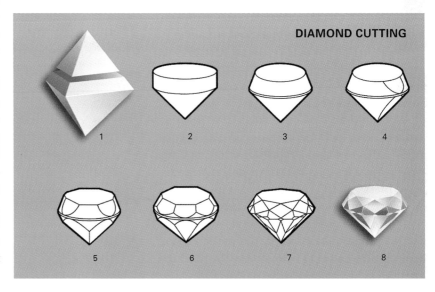

DIAMOND CUTTING

A fine blue rose-cut sapphire in the British regalia is the St. Edward's sapphire, said to have been worn in a ring by Edward the Confessor (king of England from 1042 to 1066) in 1042. A typical rose cut is the Dutch Rose, consisting of a symmetrical arrangement of 24 triangular faces terminating in a point and on a flat base. This cut has been used for small diamonds, Bohemian garnets, and pale Sri Lanka zircons.

The brilliant cut consists of 33 facets above the girdle (the thin ridge dividing the upper part, or crown, from the base) and 24 facets below (25, if a culet, a flat facet at the apex, is cut). The brilliant cut is especially suitable for colorless stones of high dispersion—for example, diamonds and zircons—because it reveals the full fire of such stones. The cut is also used for colored stones such as ruby, sapphire, blue zircon, red and green garnets, and spinels.

Colored rough should be oriented to show the best color through the crown. The facets must be accurately placed and polished to a high degree of flatness to achieve maximum brilliancy. The angle between the girdle and pavilion (back) facets must be such that the maximum amount of light is reflected back from the back facets by total internal reflection to emerge through the crown. The correct angle varies from one gem species to another, but in general, it is about 40 degrees, and the lower the refractive index of the stone, the deeper the stone must be cut.

It is also necessary to take into account directions of easy cleavage, flaws, and fractures; variation of hardness; and brittleness. Often a compromise has to be made when starting with awkwardly shaped rough or when the color is so strong or so pale that ideal proportions are not practicable. Often with stones cut in Sri Lanka and India, the main consideration is to conserve weight, because the cutters are paid by the carat (5 carats equal $^1/_{25}$ oz., or 1 g). Stones cut by native cutters in these countries are often too deep and dull by Western standards.

There are many variations on the brilliant cut, including double brilliants for large stones; shapes include marquise, or navette (boat shape), pendalogue (teardrop shape), oval, and cushion.

The step, or trap, cut is the most suitable cut for stones relying on color for their beauty. It consists of a four-sided table facet with oblong quadrilateral facets cut parallel to its edges. The rectangular form with truncated corners giving an eight-sided outline is so frequently used for the emerald that it is known as the emerald cut. The angles producing total internal reflection are important, but the overriding consideration is definitely depth of color. Deep-colored stones will have a shallow profile, but pale ones will have a deep cut to enhance their color. Many variations of this cut are possible, including baguette (long rectangular), kite, lozenge, keystone, hexagonal, and octagonal shapes.

◀ Transforming diamonds from their rough, natural state to the sparkling, polished gemstones that adorn the most expensive jewelry is a long and delicate process. Top left: cleaving the raw crystal. Top right: rounding on a lathe to form the table. Bottom left: bruting the stone into a conical-cylindrical shape. Bottom right: polishing the finished stone on a wheel coated in diamond dust and olive oil. Diamonds are cut and polished to expose their hidden quality of light reflection, which was revealed in about 1670, when Perruzi of Venice developed the full brilliant cut.

Cutting processes and equipment

Most stoneworking equipment is powered by electric motors, although there are still some parts of the world where cutters drive their laps by hand or by foot. A lap is a flat polishing table that usually rotates. Many of the processes are similar for both cabochons and faceted stones.

A diamond is first cleaved, or sawed, to remove outcroppings or to break it up into smaller stones. The cutter makes a groove in the surface in the direction of the grain by inserting a steel knife and striking a sharp blow on the back of the knife. Traditionally, the next process was bruting, or roughly shaping two stones by rubbing them together. Today diamonds are sawed with a diamond-edged revolving wheel. They are shaped by inserting a dop stick (holder) containing one diamond into a lathe that revolves it against a stationary diamond. The facets are cut by a revolving wheel impregnated with diamond dust.

For gemstones other than diamonds, the cutter is known as a lapidary. The first process for rough occurring in large pieces—for example, jade, citrine, agate, and lapis—is to produce slabs or small pieces of rough by cleaving with diamond-edged wheels. The wheels revolve at speeds of hundreds to thousands of revolutions per minute, depending on their diameter, which may vary from a few inches to several feet. The desired area is then selected and unwanted pieces are removed by a small trim saw.

Cabochons are shaped and preforms for faceting are produced by holding the rough

▲ When uncut, gems look dull and cloudy. However, as soon as they have been polished, their brilliance is quite breathtaking. Gems are made of crystalline minerals, which is what allows them to be cut into geometric shapes along cleavage planes. The crystal structure of the gem determines the type of cut the stone is given. Colored stones are sometimes cut to give them a depth of color rather than to maximize their reflections.

against vertically revolving water-cooled wheels of silicon carbide or sandstone that may be several feet in diameter. Automatic machines that produce preforms mechanically often have diamond-impregnated wheels.

The traditional method of grinding is to fix the preform to a dop stick with wax or shellac; the cabochons are then wet sanded on silicon carbide disks to produce a smooth contour. Facets are put on by grinding the preform, attached to its dop stick, on horizontally revolving flat laps. Professional cutters get the correct angles for the facets by using a jamb peg—a block of wood covered with small depressions into which the sharp back end of the dop stick is located. This process requires great skill and practice. Faceting machines used by amateurs and some professionals have faceting heads that set the angles and elevations by notched wheels and angle quadrants.

There are as many polishing techniques as there are lapidaries, but commonly, cabochons are polished on laps of hard felt, leather, or wood. Facets are polished on tin, tin alloys, or copper. Many other laps have been used in the past, including plastic, wood, and artificial-fiber cloths stretched over a hard backing. Polishing powders include rotten stone, aluminum, silicon, iron, cerium oxides, and diamond dust down to 4×10^{-7} in. (0.01 micron).

FACT FILE

■ An aquamarine discovered in Brazil in 1910 weighed in at 520,000 carats, or 229 lbs. (104 kg). It eventually produced 200,000 carats of gem-quality stones.

■ A 2,302-carat sapphire found in Queensland, Australia, in 1935 was cut into a portrait head of President Abraham Lincoln. In the 1950s, another large sapphire was made into a bust of General Eisenhower.

■ Since the 1950s, the most precious of the world's gemstones has been the ruby. A broken stone weighing 3,421 carats was discovered in 1961, but the largest cut stone is a star ruby of 138.72 carats, on display at the Smithsonian Institution in Washington, D.C.

SEE ALSO: ABRASIVE • CRYSTALS AND CRYSTALLOGRAPHY • DIAMOND • LUBRICATION

Stone Monument

Stone monuments occur throughout the world as far apart as the Sudan in Africa and the island of Sumatra in Indonesia. They are called megaliths, from the Greek words for "great stone," or menhirs, in the case of single standing stones. Any structures made partly or entirely of massive stones are megalithic, but the word is most commonly used to describe structures erected between 5000 B.C.E. and 1500 B.C.E. by the Neolithic (late Stone Age) and Bronze Age peoples of the western Mediterranean and Atlantic Europe. Megaliths have been featured frequently in the scientific press, and there have been many conflicting theories about their origins and functions.

The most common megalithic monuments in Europe are dolmen—burial chambers of upright stones with flat stones laid across them to form a roof. The best known are probably the stone circles that are found in the hundreds and in widely varying sizes across the British Isles and in continental Europe from Denmark to Sardinia and from France to Czechoslovakia. Long lines of standing stones, called alignments or avenues, are also widespread in Europe.

Stonehenge

By far the best-known prehistoric monument is Stonehenge on Salisbury Plain in southern England. This legendary stone circle—once believed to have been created by Merlin, King Arthur's magician, and later regarded as a temple of the Druids, the Celtic priests at the time of the Roman invasion—is one of the most significant of all the British prehistoric solar and lunar observatories. Studies of its features suggest that it must have been used primarily for astronomical purposes—and archaeological evidence suggests there was not just one celestial observatory but several at the same site. It is thought that the site would also have been used for tracking lunar movements.

Excavations and radiocarbon dating show that work on Stonehenge was most likely begun several hundred years before the end of the Neolithic period (about 2800 B.C.E.) and covered a span of 1,000 years, continuing until the end of the early Bronze Age about 1600 B.C.E. Professor Richard Atkinson's division of the periods of construction into three main phases has enabled scientists to make some sense of the site's conflicting orientations and geometric relationships.

Stonehenge I consisted of a circular bank and ditch 320 ft. (97 m) in diameter and of a concentric circle of 56 holes 10 ft. (3 m) inside. These Aubrey holes (named for John Aubrey, an antiquary who discovered them in the 17th century) were 2 to 4 ft. (0.6–1.2 m) deep. Outside the entrance, in the northeastern part of the bank, is the Heel Stone, a large, unshaped standing stone.

▲ Modern day Druids carrying out midsummer rites at Stonehenge on Salisbury Plain in England. The Heel Stone leans forward, lowering the sight line, but as the ground level is now lower, the line still works.

Stonehenge II, built many centuries later by an early Bronze Age people, consisted of a double circle, each comprising 38 stones, with an entrance facing the Heel Stone. The smaller, inner group of bluestones (named for their blue–gray color) were brought from the Preseli Mountains in Wales, 135 miles (217 km) away, but after three-quarters of them had been set up, they were removed to make way for Stonehenge III—the massive remains seen today.

All the stones in Stonehenge III, called sarsens, were transported from the Marlborough Downs 20 miles (32 km) to the north; scientists calculated that it would have taken 1,500 men 10 years to move all 81 stones. They were up to 30 ft. (9 m)

▼ Some significant alignments at Stonehenge. Only stones that are still standing are shown. In addition to the central axis alignment, the Station Stones point to the farthest north and south lunar positions. Eclipses can occur when the Moon rises or sets along these lines (compare with sky sphere below), suggesting that the ancients could calculate the next eclipse.

long and 56 tons (50 tonnes) in weight. The stones were arranged in two concentric structures, the outer consisting of 30 upright stones supporting an unbroken circle of lintels 14 ft. (4.3 m) above ground and the inner comprising a horseshoe arrangement of five arches of three stones each (trilithons), two on each side of the axis of the monument, with the fifth—and largest—on the end of the axis opposite the Heel Stone. Carbon-dating evidence showed the structure was erected about 2100 B.C.E. Later, some of the bluestones used in Stonehenge II were reerected in a circle within the sarsens, and a massive sandstone slab (the Altar Stone) was placed in the center.

Because the axis of Stonehenge points over the Heel Stone to the horizon where the Sun rises on Midsummer Day, it was long assumed that Stonehenge was a temple for solar worship— but the religious significance of the arrangement of the various stones is now doubted by scientists. According to one theory, the monument served to mark the most northerly and southerly risings of the Sun, indicating the occurrence of the midsummer solstice and the midwinter solstice. This function would have given the Neolithic and early Bronze Age farmers a calendar to sow their crops.

Others disagree, suggesting that the purpose of the Heel Stone would more likely have been to mark the rise of the Moon at the midpoint of its 18.6-year cycle. The four Station Stones that stood at about the same distance from the center as the Aubrey holes may have been used to locate the extreme points of the Moon's motion, and according to one theory, the 56 Aubrey holes may have been used to predict the years during which there would be an eclipse at one of the lunar solstices. Because such eclipses occur three times in a period of almost 56 years, it would have been possible to forecast each one by spacing three stones equally around the Aubrey holes and moving a stone within the holes one hole ahead each year.

Archaeoastronomy

The study of the astronomical practices of the preliterate peoples are usually called astroarchaeology or archaeoastronomy. Various theories about the astronomical and geometric functions of megaliths have been propounded by Alexander Thom, a retired Scottish pro-

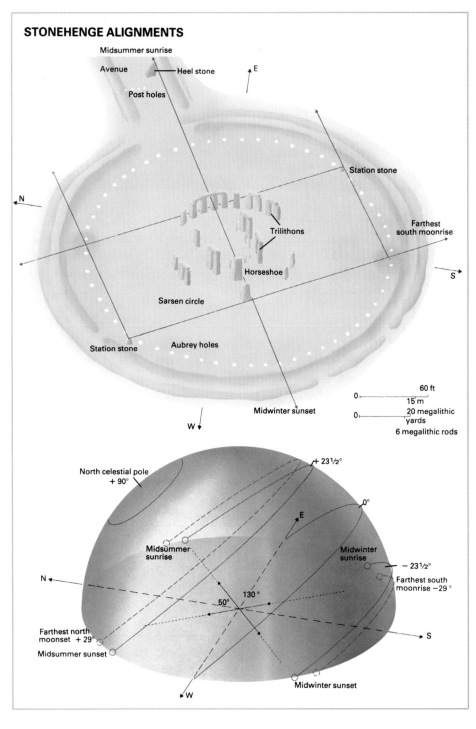

STONEHENGE ALIGNMENTS

fessor of engineering, who accurately surveyed several hundred megalithic sites across the British Isles and, later, many in Brittany, France. Thom's researches have proved that all 900 or so stone circles in the British Isles were built using a common unit of measurement, the megalithic yard, which is 2.72 ft. (0.83 m) in length.

Confirmation for the astronomical function of megaliths may be found in Central America where the Maya, and others, built monuments to serve as places of worship and also as astronomical devices and calendars. One of the most famous is the pyramid known as the Temple of the Plumed Serpents at Xochicalco, Mexico. Beneath the ruins, there is a large rectangular cavern supported by three pillars of natural rock. A half-yard wide tube leads from the ceiling to the ground, about 23 ft. (7 m) below. Just before noon between May and the middle of August, the Sun—almost overhead—sends a shaft of light directly down the tube onto the cave floor every day for 105 days.

Another well-known stone monument in Central America is the great ceremonial complex of Chichén Itzá at Uaxactún in Guatemala. The best-known of the many structures—the circular El Caracol Tower—has four outer doors facing the cardinal points of the compass. Near its top is a flat area with three horizontal rectangular openings—suggested alignments for the extreme setting positions of the Moon and Venus declinations for about 1000 C.E.

Intriguing among the megaliths of the Americas are the medicine wheels of the Plains Indians in the United States, which may have served as celestial calendars. For instance, the Big Horn Medicine Wheel in northern Wyoming is an imperfect circle of loose stones about 80 ft. (25 m) in diameter, with the central cairn as the hub from which 28 unevenly spaced spokes may act as a lunar-month counter—though several of the alignments can be interpreted as showing the solar solstice rising and setting points.

Other theories

In 1973, a British dowsing expert, Tom Graves, surveyed the Rollright stones in Oxfordshire, England, to test for energy reactions. He found that sometimes the pendulum rotated in one direction, dubbed positive polarity, and sometimes in another, so-called negative polarity. He also found that all but a dozen of the stones reversed polarity, usually from hour to hour.

Animals possess a mechanism that enables them to navigate by the invisible patterns of electromagnetic energy that surround the Earth. Scientific investigations have suggested that humans, too, possess such a mechanism—a thin layer of magnetite (a metallic deposit that responds to the Earth's magnetism) in the bony walls of the sinuses. This discovery led Tom Graves to conclude that our ancestors—more sensitive to Earth's magnetism—constructed stone circles at focal points of the energy.

In 1980 a British engineer, Charles Brooker, tested Rollright stones with a magnetometer. He was able to establish a series of lines (which he called ley lines) that registered on the magnetometer as it passed over them. Brooker found that the lines converged on the geometric center of Rollright. He also found that sight lines from the stones across the landscape were marked with churches, standing stones, and burial mounds.

In 1978, a group of scientists from various disciplines—ranging from archaeology to electronic engineering and calling themselves the Dragon Project—decided to investigate the site's magnetic phenomena with a wideband ultrasonic detector. They picked up a pulsing ultrasound signal around the Kingstone, which stands some way outside the circle, and were able to determine that over a period of a year, ultrasound activity peaked at the equinoxes and remained at the background level at the solstices. In 1980, they carried out a month-long monitoring of the site's radioactivity. They found that at certain points readings on a Geiger counter were much higher than the background radiation level, whereas around the Kingstone, radiation was below the background level.

From the evidence they gathered, the scientists concluded that these emissions are governed in some way by phases of the lunar cycle. This finding would seem to indicate that most ancient stone circles were indeed astronomical devices—even if they were also used as places of worship.

▼ The Temple of the Plumed Serpents—a centerpiece of Mayan culture in around 800 C.E.—at Xochicalco, about 62 miles (100 km) south of Mexico City. The temple is decorated with several eclipse symbols and ornamental glyphs relating to the calendar and planetary activity.

SEE ALSO: Archaeological technologies • Eclipse • Magnetism • Magnetometer • Pyramid

Streetcar

◀ Double-deck streetcars are peculiar to Britain and its former colonies. This car operates along the seafront at Blackpool, a resort in the north of England. It gains power through an overhead cable, which is collected by a pantograph.

The world's first street railroad was built in New York in 1832—it was a mile (1.6 km) long and known as the New York & Harlem Railroad. There were two horse-drawn cars, each holding 30 people. The one-mile route had grown to four miles (6.4 km) by 1834, and cars were running every 15 minutes. The idea spread quickly, and by the 1880s, there were more than 18,000 horse cars in the United States and more than 3,000 miles (4,800 km) of track. The building of streetcar systems required the issuance of construction contracts and the acquisition of right-of-way easements and was an area of political patronage and corruption in many city governments.

The advantage of the horse car over the horse bus was that steel wheels on steel rails gave a smoother ride and created less friction. A horse could haul on rails twice as much weight as on a roadway. Furthermore, the streetcar had brakes, but buses still relied on the weight of the horses to stop the vehicle. The American example was fol-

lowed in Europe, and the first tramway in Paris, France, was opened in 1853—appropriately styled after the "American railway." The first line in Britain was opened in Birkenhead in 1860. It was built by George Francis Train, an American businessman who also built three short tramways in London in 1861. The lines used a type of step rail that protruded from the road surface and hindered other traffic, so they were taken up within a year.

Self-propelled cars

A steam car was tried out in Cincinatti, Ohio, in 1859 and in London, England, in 1873. The steam car was not widely successful, because tracks built for horse cars could not stand the heavier weight.

The solution to this problem was found in the cable car. Cables, driven by powerful stationary steam engines at the end of the route, were run in conduits below the roadway with an attachment passing down from the car through a slot in the roadway to grip the cable; the car itself weighed no more than a horse car. The most famous application of cables to streetcar haulage was the Scottish engineer and inventor Andrew S. Hallidie's 1873 system on the hills of San Francisco—still in use today and a great tourist attraction. This system was followed by others in U.S. cities, and by 1890, there were some 500 miles (800 km) of cable car track in the United States. In London, there were only two cable-operated lines. Edinburgh, Scotland, and Melbourne, Australia, had extensive cable systems.

The ideal source of power for streetcars was electricity, which was clean and flexible but difficult at first to apply. Batteries were far too heavy—a converted horse car with batteries under the seats and a single electric motor was tried in London in 1883, but the experiment lasted only one day. Compressed-air-driven cars, the invention of an Englishman, Major Beaumont, had been tried out in London between Stratford and Leytonstone in 1881. Between 1883 and 1888, streetcars hauled by battery locomotives ran on the same route. A coal-gas-driven car was even tried in Croydon, England, in 1894.

Electric streetcars

In early experiments, especially in the United States and Germany, electricity from a power station was fed to a streetcar in motion. The first useful system employed a small two-wheel carriage running on top of an overhead wire and connected to the streetcar by a cable. The circuit was completed via the wheels and the running rails. A route on this system was working in Montgomery, Alabama, as early as 1886. The converted horse cars had a motor mounted on one of the end platforms with chain drive to one axle. Shortly afterward, there were trials on a similar principle in the United States and Germany, but using a four-wheel overhead carriage known as a troller.

Real success came when an American engineer, Frank J. Sprague, left the U.S. Navy in 1883 to devote more time to problems of using electricity for power. His first important task was to equip the Union Passenger Railway at Richmond, Virginia, for electric working. It was there that he perfected the swivel trolley pole that could run under the overhead wire instead of above it. From this success in 1888 sprang all the subsequent streetcar systems of the world, and by 1902, there were nearly 22,000 miles (35,000 km) of electrified railroads in the United States alone. In Britain, there were electric streetcars from 1890.

Except in Britain and countries under British influence, streetcars were normally single-decked. Early electric cars had four wheels, and the two axles were quite close together so that the car could take sharp bends. Eventually, as the need grew for larger cars, two undercarriages were used, one under each end of the car. Single-deck cars of this type were often coupled together with a single driver and one or two conductors. Double-decked cars could haul trailers in peak hours, and for a time, such trailers were a common sight in London.

The two main power collection systems were from overhead wires, as described above—though modern streetcars often use a pantograph collecting device held by springs against the underside of

CURRENT COLLECTION DEVICES

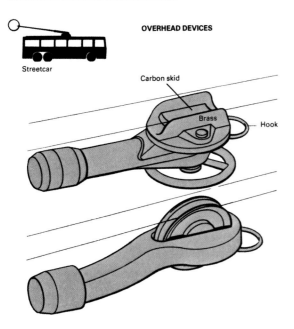

OVERHEAD DEVICES

Streetcar

Carbon skid

Brass

Hook

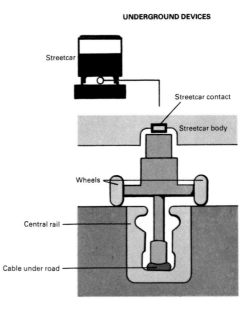

UNDERGROUND DEVICES

Streetcar

Streetcar contact

Streetcar body

Wheels

Central rail

Cable under road

◀ Streetcars can collect power either from overhead devices, such as pantographs and trolley poles, or a conduit system, where the current is carried beneath the ground and picked up by a contact shoe.

the wire instead of the traditional trolley—and the conduit system. This system is derived from the slot in the street used for the early cable cars, but instead of a moving cable, there are current-supply rails in the conduit. The car is equipped with a device called a plow that passes down into the conduit. On each side of the plow is a contact shoe pressing against one of the rails. Such a system was used in inner London and in other European cities, as well as in New York and Washington.

Cars were driven through a controller on each platform. In a single-motor car, this system allowed power to pass through a resistance as well as the motor, the amount of resistance being reduced in steps by moving a handle as desired, to feed more power to the motor. In two-motor cars, a different control was used. When starting, the two motors were connected in series so that each motor received power in turn. As speed rose, the controller was notched up to a further set of steps in which the motors were connected in parallel so that each received current direct from the power source instead of sharing it. The U.S. streetcar revival in the 1930s resulted in the design of a new streetcar, known as the PCC after the Electric Railway Presidents' Conference Committee that commissioned it.

San Francisco

San Francisco's century-old streetcar system—the Muni, from San Francisco Municipal Railroad—is the world's last using cable propulsion. No. 1.,

▲ The ALRV (Articulated Light Rail Vehicle) at the Neville Park loop in Toronto, Ontario, is typical of modern streetcar designs. Among its principal features are twin chopper control and pneumatic brakes. Some systems, such as the Docklands Light Railway in London, are fully automated and do not have drivers on board.

Muni's first streetcar, began service in 1912 and is the oldest operating streetcar built for a publicly owned and operated transit system in the United States. The system—refurbished in the early 1980s—was designed with the cables buried under the street and with the cars hooked onto them. During refurbishment, new materials, such as Teflon, were introduced to increase the life of the new components. To save on maintenance, stainless steel has been used beneath street level.

Developments

Since the 1970s, interest in streetcars has revived in the United States because they use less energy and create less pollution than cars or buses do. Modern streetcar lines are often called light rapid transit systems. Trains can run as single units, in articulated or linked units, on tracks set beside or in the middle of streets, or on their own tracks. On segregated tracks, the rail vehicles do not interfere with automobile traffic, unlike streetcars that run down the middle of the street. In many of the new systems, braking and speed are controlled by a computerized control system.

In Hannover, Germany, urban planning has led to the development of a hybrid vehicle that is used on railroad track in tunnels or on tracks buried in the roadway in a more traditional streetcar role. The cars can use existing streetcar tracks and railroad tunnels.

The streetcar seems assured of a place in many of the world's cities as a part of their transportation systems. However, as the Hannover system suggests, the streetcars of the future may be rather different from those of a generation ago.

FACT FILE

- Streetcars had not run in Portland, Oregon, since the 1950s. Like many U.S. cities, though, Portland is reviving the streetcar, and the first new streetcar line was opened in 2001.

- In addition to the famous streetcar system in San Francisco, streetcars operate in a number of U.S. cities, including Boston, Cleveland, Dallas, New Orleans, Newark, Philadelphia, Pittsburgh, San Diego, Portland, and Seattle.

- Light-rail systems are in use in the United States, Canada, Britain, Australia, Germany, Hong Kong, and the Netherlands. In London, England, the Docklands Light Railway (DLR), an automated system, opened in 1987.

SEE ALSO: CABLE TRANSPORT SYSTEMS • COG RAILWAY • MASS TRANSIT AND SUBWAY • MONORAIL SYSTEM

Stringed Instrument

The history of stringed instruments goes back so far that no accurate data are available as to when they were first made. The emperor Nero is supposed to have fiddled while Rome burned, but the truth of that is not easy to discover. It is not even known when a bow was first used. In modern times, the most important family of stringed instruments played with a bow is the violin family.

Violin family

The basic design of the violin includes a fingerboard and a resonator chamber. Four strings are strung above the resonator by means of a bridge and pass closely along the length of the fingerboard so that the fingers can stop the strings in various places, selecting the desired pitch. The string is resonated by drawing a bow of horsehair across it close to the bridge. The strings are attached at the body end to a tailpiece that is held to the violin by a loop fitted over a tail pin. At the other end, the strings are wound around tuning pegs that fit in holes in the side of the peg box. The peg box is usually ornately finished off into a scroll.

The peg box is connected to the body of the instrument by the neck, which is fastened to the body by means of a top block and a back button. The fingerboard extends from the peg box nearly halfway down the length of the body but without actually touching the body.

The body, or resonating chamber, consists of a belly, or upper, and a back joined around their perimeter by a 1.5 in. (38 mm) rib strengthened by corner blocks and linings. Inside the body, there is a sound post between the belly and the back, to the right of center and just below the bridge, and a bass bar that runs to within 2 in. (50 mm) of each end of the body under the left-hand string. The presence of the sound post increases the effective soundboard area and is also used to phase out any natural resonances that the chamber may possess.

The strings can be made from a gut center, but today the three lower strings are usually covered with fine wire, and the highest string is usually a fine steel wire. The bow, which dates in its present form from the work of the French violinmaker François Tourte toward the end of the 18th century, is incurved logarithmically. (Earlier bows had a convex rather than a concave shape.) The string is first pulled sideways by the rough horsehairs and then pulled back by its tension.

▲ Stringed instruments constitute the major part of professional orchestras. Included in the family are violins, violas, cellos, and basses, which cover a wide range of octaves between them. Other stringed instruments such as harps, pianos, and guitars may sometimes be included if a piece demands it.

◄ The modern harp has 46 or 47 strings with the C strings colored red and the F strings colored blue. When all its pedals are in their upright position, the natural key of the instrument is C-flat. Depressing the left pedal by one or two notches raises the pitch first to C and then to C-sharp.

The violin family has four members that in descending order of pitch become larger in size: the violin, the viola, the violoncello (or cello), and the double bass. The two smaller instruments are held under the chin, and the other two are rested by means of an end pin on the floor. The cellist plays the instrument while seated, holding it between the knees; the double bass player plays while standing or seated on a high stool. The bass is to some extent an odd-man-out—it has sloping shoulders somewhat like those of the viol family, and also like the viols, its strings are tuned in fourths. Like the violin, however, it has no frets, and because of its construction in thicker wood and its higher string tension, its sound is closer to the violin than the viol family.

The modern violin differs from its Baroque (c.1600–1750) ancestor in a number of ways. In the late 17th century, modifications began to be made in order to increase the volume of sound at some expense to clarity and color. The Baroque violins of the Italian Stradivari, Amati, and Guarneri violin-making families would have had a slighter bass bar than do today's violins, on which the bass bar has to support a greater tension and slightly greater length and thickness of the strings. The modern instrument is pitched a semitone higher and has a neck about 0.5 in. (12 mm) longer. Its bridge is more highly arched, leading to a corresponding increase in the angle at which the neck is thrown back. The high esteem in which the Stradivarius violin, for example, is held is due in some degree to the better response it gave to these modifications, which in the case of other violins, often led to harm to the instrument.

Viol family

The instruments in the viol family rose to importance during the 15th century and were most widely used during the Renaissance. There are four members of the viol family—treble, alto, tenor, and bass. In consort music, where several players play together but with separate parts rather than in unison, the alto was often replaced by a second tenor. The large body of music that survives for the viols is a reflection of their popularity and of the fact that ownership of a chest of viols containing all of the family was widespread.

The important features distinguishing the viols from the violin family are as follows: the back of the viol is less bulging and has deeper ribs, the shoulders are sloping rather than rounded, the sound holes are C-shaped instead of F-shaped, the viol usually has six strings instead of four, and all viols are played resting on or between the knees. Most important, the viol has frets of gut around the fingerboard that serve as markers for the player's fingers. The frets are placed to mark the notes a semitone apart, but their real function is to produce a sharpness in the quality of the sound by providing a hard platform for the stopping finger. The thinner wood of the viols, the thinner strings, and the lower tension in the strings and in the general construction of the instrument all give the tone quality a distinct sound—reedy and less assertive than that of the violin.

Plucked string instruments

Plucked string instruments include the harp, lute, and guitar. The harp is constructed so that the plane of the strings is perpendicular to the soundboard. Harps are triangular in shape and have three basic elements: resonator, neck, and strings. European harps are of the frame type: a fore pillar or column connects the lower end of the resonator to the neck, adding support to the structure and helping bear the string tension. Most other types are called "open harps."

Harps may have from one to more than 90 strings. The resonator has a wooden soundboard or skin sound table on top and a string holder to which one end of the strings is attached. The other ends are attached either directly to the neck or indirectly to pegs or tuning pegs. Mechanisms to alter the pitch of the strings range from hooks operated by hand to pedal-activated systems.

VIOLIN CONSTRUCTION

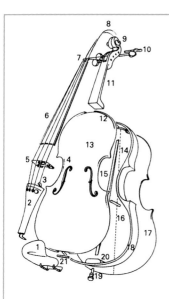

Violin

Viola

▲ The parts of a violin. (1) chin rest, (2) tailpiece, (3) E-adjuster (fine tuner), (4) F-hole, (5) bridge, (6) fingerboard, (7) nut, (8) strings, (9) scroll, (10) peg, (11) neck, (12) purfling, (13) top plate, or belly, (14) lining strips, (15) bass bar, (16) soundpost, (17) back plate, (18) rib, (19) end button, (20) bottom block, (21) saddle.

By the early 18th century—the era of the master artisans of the violin, such as Antonio Stradivari—the instrument already had a history stretching back 200 years. Though one or two refinements have since been added (such as the chin rest in 1820), its basic design has proved resistant to major improvements. Foremost in the string family, the violin is the most versatile and has the widest acoustic scope. Its brother, the viola, is similar in design but with a lower range.

◄ The craftsman who produces stringed instruments has many criteria to consider while working. The size, shape, weight, thickness of wood, and type of string will all affect the volume, clarity, and color of the sound it produces. Centuries of modification and refinement of techniques—as well as technological developments, such as electric amplification— have all contributed to the virtuosity of individual instrumentalists and, indeed, the scope of modern composers.

The Western concert harp, or double-action pedal harp, has 47 strings. The pedals allow each string to be shortened, raising the pitch by one or two semitones, giving the instrument a full chromatic range of six-and-a-half octaves. Harps are played in six basic positions; the player plucks, strikes, or strums the strings with the fingers or a plectrum. The harp was introduced to the New World by the conquistadors and is played in Argentina, Mexico, Paraguay, Venezuela, and Peru. It is widely used in rituals in many African countries and is also played in Asia.

The European lute is descended from the Moorish instrument, and it was an important instrument in Western music from the late Middle Ages to the 18th century. It has a half-pear-shaped body built from separate ribs that are shaped, bent, and glued together. The soundboard features an ornate sound hole and the fingerboard has tied gut frets. A peg box with tuning pegs is attached at almost right angles to the neck, and the other end of the strings are attached to a bridge at the lower end of the soundboard. There are six or more courses of double strings. Like the guitar, the lute is played by plucking or strumming the strings with the fingers of the right hand and stopping the strings with those of the left. The lute was mainly used as a solo instrument and to accompany singers.

The guitar is a plucked string instrument probably also of Moorish origin. The modern Spanish guitar has a flat back, a wooden resonator with a figure-of-eight shape, a round sound hole, a fretted fingerboard, and six strings. The strings are attached at one end to a bridge on the soundboard and tuned by rear pegs that activate a geared mechanism. The guitar's range encompasses more than three octaves, and music for it is written an octave higher than it sounds.

In the 20th century, the influence of the Spanish guitarist Andrés Segovia helped turn the guitar into a respected concert instrument. The evolution of jazz, folk, blues, and rock music in the 20th century required guitars that had greater volume and penetration than the classical guitar. They include the dreadnought (larger and broader), acoustic, and electric guitars.

Electrified instruments

The most commonly electronically amplified stringed instrument is the guitar. Electric guitars were first manufactured in the 1930s. There are two main types: jazz musicians favor the hollow-bodied (or semi-acoustic) guitar, while rock musicians prefer the solid bodied. One or more pickups on the guitar convert the vibrations in the metal strings into an electric signal that is passed to an amplifier. A standard electric guitar has six strings and has the same tuning as an acoustic guitar. Electric bass guitars have four strings, which are tuned like a double bass.

Other instruments

The rebec dates from the 13th century and included a family of four instruments. Its back was shaped like half a pear, and its fingerboard and peg box were integral parts of the body. It did not have a sound post and, consequently, had a softer and slightly nasal tone quality. It had only three strings, usually tuned in fourths like the viol, but was unfretted.

The lyre family was often called the *lira da braccio* (lyre on the arm) to distinguish it from the classical harplike instrument. It looked not unlike a violin and had a sound post. It was held under the chin, but its nearly flat bridge allowed the soft bow to play all five strings at once. The top string played the melody, while the other four produced a drone in fifths and octaves, rather like a bagpipe. During the Renaissance, the bridge was arched and the number of strings was increased.

The Welsh *crwth*, of ancient origin, had a number of similar features but had a rectangular shape of which one half formed the sound box while the other was indented to allow the stopping hand to pass through. It was played resting downward and varied in its number of strings. The Renaissance fiddle had five strings, one a drone, and was constructed like a violin with a separate fingerboard and neck, but it was oval or nearly square in shape and was usually fretted. The pegs were fixed from the front into a heart- or leaf-shaped box.

The *violino piccolo* was tuned higher than the violin, usually by a fourth or a minor third; music was written for it by the German composer Johann Sebastian Bach. A smaller version, called the kit, or *pochette*, was supposedly carried in the pocket and was a popular instrument of dancing masters. There was a five-string violin called the quinton and a six- or seven-stringed *viola d'amore* played like a violin. Other variations in size and tuning were the *viola pomposa*, the *viola da*

spalla (shoulder), the *violoncello piccolo*, and the *viola di fagotto*, which allegedly derived a tone like a bassoon (*fagotto*) from its wire-covered strings.

Physical principles

When a stretched string vibrates, the distortion travels backward and forward between the two fixed ends, creating a standing wave motion. Between about 30 and 30,000 Hz (cycles per second), the displacement of air is audible. These sound waves are small and must be amplified, perhaps electrically, as in the electric guitar, but traditionally by forcing a soundboard to vibrate at the same frequency and stimulating resonant frequencies in an air-filled cavity, as the body of a violin. Design and construction, type of wood used, and even the varnish on the wood affect the tonal quality of the instrument. Both soundboard and cavity have fundamental, or primary, tones (frequencies) of their own, but the latter is allowed to enrich the sound with its own inherent overtones. Sympathetic vibrations occur when vibration of one string excites vibrations in others nearby, as in the *viola d'amore*.

Pitch

The pitch, or fundamental tone, of a string is proportional to its tension but inversely proportional to its length, thickness, and density.

▼ Contemporary popular music makes great use of the electric guitar. Acoustic pickups enable the sound of the strings to be fed to an amplifier and magnified to such an extent that a single plucked string can be heard at the back of a huge auditorium.

The higher the tension, the higher the note, but the longer, thicker, or denser the string, the lower the note. Harps, pianos, and similar instruments have one or more open strings for each note (an interesting exception is the clavichord). Most smaller stringed instruments have a smaller number of strings and raise the pitch by manual stopping—shortening the string by pressing it against a fingerboard.

Overtones

The fundamental, or primary, tone is produced by vibration of the entire string. At the same time, overtones, or upper partials, are produced. They are an exact multiple of the fundamental frequency—the acoustic properties of a string cause it to vibrate in one, two, three (and so on) equal portions separated by invisible nodes (points along the string where no movement occurs). These partials, of which the fundamental note is the first, form the harmonic series; their mixture

◀ Steps in the construction of a rebec. The body and neck were made by gouging a bowl out of a solid piece of wood. Most stringed instruments are made from separate pieces that are glued and blocked to give them strength.

enon is illustrated by the *tromba marina*, a single-string instrument that is played by lightly touching the string and bowing the string above the finger. The sound is slightly brassy, hence *tromba*, which means trumpet.

The midpoint node divides the string into two equal parts, each vibrating at twice the fundamental frequency to give an octave above. Touching the node at one-third the length divides the string into three equal parts, each vibrating at three times the fundamental frequency, or one-and-a-half times the octave. Because the interval between notes having the ratio 3:2 is a fifth, this harmonic must be the fifth note in the scale above the octave of the fundamental. The values of the other harmonics can be similarly calculated. Stopping the strings so as to raise the fundamental by a given amount will raise the harmonic series by the same amount.

String harmonies do not, like those of brass and other wind instruments, constitute the bulk of available notes but are used as a contrast to the normal range of open and stopped notes.

is responsible for the timbre, or musical color, of the instrument. Overtones having a node at the point where the string is activated are absent from the series—for example, when a string is plucked at midpoint, all the even-numbered partials are absent because they all have a node at that point. The broader the plucking or bowing surface, the more overtones will be suppressed. Therefore, a finger makes a softer, less twangy sound than a sharp or pointed plectrum, and violinists have a number of tone colors in their bowing technique.

The loudness of overtones produced by plucking decreases rapidly at higher overtone frequencies. The continuous vibration created by a horsehair bow maintains the high-frequency overtones, resulting in a brilliance of sound that plucked instruments cannot produce.

Harmonics

Harmonics are overtones or partials produced in such a way as to exclude the fundamental. If a string is lightly touched at one of its nodal points, the note produced by activating the string elsewhere along its length will be the harmonic appropriate to that particular note. This phenom-

FACT FILE

- *Walking-stick guitars were made as novelties in the 19th century, usually with four strings and a long, narrow sound box. Walking-stick fiddles were also made, with a handle that doubled as a chin rest.*

- *The automatic harp was produced by the Wurlitzer company and was operated by a perforated mechanical roll. The pattern of perforations activated tiny fingers that plucked the harp strings.*

- *In the 17th and 18th centuries, musical craftsmen produced miniature fiddles known as kits. Narrow, with a long neck, these tiny instruments were popular with professional dancing masters, who used them to demonstrate tunes.*

- *The Chinese guitar-banjo is shaped like a guitar but has a circular section let into the front of the body, which is covered with a resonator, usually made from stretched snakeskin.*

SEE ALSO: BRASS INSTRUMENT • MUSICAL SCALE • PERCUSSION INSTRUMENT • PIANO • PICKUP, ACOUSTIC • SOUND • WOODWIND INSTRUMENT

Stroboscope

A stroboscope is a lamp that produces flashes of high-intensity light at precise, controllable frequencies, and it is primarily used to produce an optical illusion of slowed or stopped motion. This illusion is a result of the persistence of vision of the eye—the eye's ability to retain an image for a fraction of a second after it has disappeared.

For example, if a rotating disk has a mark painted near its outer edge, and it is viewed under stroboscopic light, when the frequency of the light flashes equals the rotational speed of the disk, the painted mark will appear to be stationary. In this case, the mark is at the same position every time the light flashes, and the persistence of vision of the eye retains the image of the mark at that position during the brief intervals between the flashes of light. If the disk is turning at 1,000 rpm, a flashing rate of 1,000 flashes per minute will make the disk appear to be stationary.

Stroboscopes (or strobes) have calibrated speed-control dials, and so the speed of a rotating object can be accurately determined by adjusting the frequency of the strobe until the object appears stationary, at which point its speed corresponds to the light frequency shown on the calibrated dial.

Electronic strobe

Most stroboscopes use a xenon-filled discharge tube lamp controlled by an oscillator and a trigger pulse generator. The frequency of the oscillator that drives the trigger pulse generator is varied by means of a potentiometer, which is turned by the calibrated control dial.

Low-energy pulses at a high voltage are produced by the trigger pulse generator and delivered to the trigger electrodes in the side of the

▲ The movement of a robot photographed using a strobe light. Strobe photography breaks down rapid movements into a chronological sequence of images, enabling the movement to be studied in detail.

◄ A Bosch diagnostic engine tester linked to a car engine via a diagnostic plug. The plug link-up uses a stroboscope to test the ignition timing—critical aspect of the engine's functions—without placing any load on the engine being tested. Compression, battery condition, and exhaust emissions are also checked by the engine tester.

xenon tube. This action ionizes the gas in the tube and creates a conductive path through the gas between the anode at one end and the cathode at the other. A capacitor, charged from a high-voltage circuit, is connected across the anode and cathode, and when the gas is ionized by the trigger pulses, the capacitor discharges through the tube creating a high-intensity flash of about one microsecond's duration.

Application

As already mentioned, an important use of the stroboscope is to measure rotational speeds. With a mechanically driven revolution counter (tachometer), the process of measuring the speed of a machine may actually cause the machine to slow down. A stroboscope, however, places no load upon a machine and there is therefore no risk of the machine being slowed as its speed is measured. This fact is an advantage in measuring the speed of devices such as small electric motors, which produce only a fraction of a horsepower and could be slowed greatly if a conventional tachometer were used.

In addition to freezing the motion of rotating objects, stroboscopic light can be used to freeze the motion of reciprocating objects, and so stroboscopes are also used in studying the behavior of machine parts with a reciprocating motion. In the textile industry, for example, stroboscopes are used to aid the adjustment of high-speed spinning and weaving machinery.

Strobe lamps are also used in high-speed photography, where the one-microsecond flash can freeze the motion of, for example, a rifle bullet. In most cases, it is only the very short duration and

◀ A strobe light used in photography to capture three stages in the take-off of a fly. Three consecutive flashes of up to $\frac{1}{25,000}$ of a second were used.

high intensity of a single flash that is used in photography, but by leaving the camera shutter open and setting the strobe to flash at a suitable frequency, a series of images can be produced on a single frame of film. Such pictures are useful for analyzing the motion of a machine, an animal, or a person. The movement of athletes, for example, may be filmed using stroboscopic light to analyze their technique.

Strobe lamps have proved to be of use in medicine, for example, in the study of epilepsy, which can be induced in some people by exposing them to light flashing at a certain frequency. The risk of induced epilepsy has led to recommended maximum exposure times for stroboscopes used in night clubs.

Other strobe effects

A common example of a stroboscopic effect is the apparent backward motion of spoked wheels in movie films. If the camera shutter frequency exceeds the rotational speed of the wheel spokes, the images produced on the film will give the impression that the wheels are turning slowly backward. If the shutter frequency is less than the rotational speed of the spokes, then the apparent motion will be forward.

Electric lighting from an AC supply flickers at the frequency of the supply, but this flickering is normally invisible to the eye except in the case of some types of fluorescent lighting. Before the introduction of CD players, this flickering effect was widely used in adjusting the turntable speed of many types of record-player decks and is still currently used by hi-fi enthusiasts. A small disk with a series of alternating black and white marks around its edge is placed on the turntable. When the

turntable is running and the disk is viewed under electric light, the disk will appear to be stationary when the turntable is running at the correct speed. Alternatively, the turntable may have a series of marks around its edge that serve the same purpose as the disk, and on some models, a small lamp is fitted to the base plate next to the turntable to provide illumination for the strobe marks.

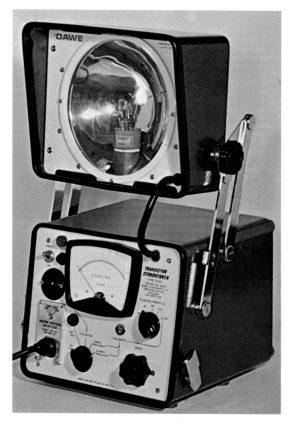

◀ An electronic strobe unit that uses a moving-coil meter to indicate the flashing rate.

SEE ALSO: HIGH-SPEED PHOTOGRAPHY • LIGHT AND OPTICS • OSCILLATOR • POTENTIOMETER • SPEEDOMETER AND TACHOMETER

Submarine

Although the principle of the diving bell has been known for 2,000 years, and Leonardo da Vinci produced drawings for underwater craft, it was not until an English naval officer, William Bourne, produced a treatise on the principle of underwater ballasting in 1580 that the practicalities were examined. By applying Archimedes' principle (a floating body displaces an amount of water equal to its own weight), it was possible to build a craft into which water could be admitted, increasing its weight sufficiently for it to submerge. The expulsion of the water would allow the craft to float back to the surface.

Using this basic idea, a Dutch mechanic, Cornelis van Drebbel, built what is believed to be the first boat that not only sank but also surfaced again. His craft was demonstrated in 1624 to King James I of England in the River Thames in London. It used an expanding leather bulkhead that admitted water safely into the body of the submersible, and when it was screwed back into position, the ballast water was expelled. Oars that protruded through the greased leather hull propelled the craft. A breathing tube led to the surface.

Early submarines

During the 17th and 18th centuries, a number of attempts were made to design more efficient underwater craft. In 1773, an Englishman, J. Day, sailed into Plymouth Sound, England, in a boat that relied on rocks for external ballast to destroy its buoyancy. The rocks were to be released from within to resurface. With no means of controlling his depth and possibly experiencing difficulty in jettisoning his ballast, it seems likely that Day and his craft were crushed by water pressure; he became the first submarine casualty.

Only three years later, during the Revolutionary War, David Bushnell, an American inventor, built the *Turtle* to attack British ships. It was an egg-shaped craft large enough for one person and driven by a propeller operated by a crank.

▲ The Ohio-class missile submarine USS *Michigan* begins a dive while undergoing sea trials before joining the navy on regular service.

It carried a charge of 150 lbs. (68 kg) of gunpowder that was fitted with a timing mechanism. In 1776, the first submarine attack was carried out on the British ship HMS *Eagle* in New York Harbor. The attack was unsuccessful. The screws securing the charge to the flagship's hull struck metal and would not penetrate.

In 1800, a larger and more ambitious submersible, the *Nautilus*, was built by the American inventor Robert Fulton. It succeeded in sinking ships in two trial attacks—by the French and the British—but was never used in action. With only hand propulsion, no means of accurate depth control, and a weapon that needed contact with the target, the submersible was not yet suitable for operational use.

In 1850, a German army corporal, Wilhelm Bauer, produced a boat with a cast-iron hull and a primitive trimming system in which weights were moved fore and aft. It was equipped with a hand-driven screw. In 1863, the French produced the *Plongeur*, which had compressed air stored in bottles to operate the engine and blow the ballast tanks. In the same year, steam-driven craft, the *Davids*, were used in the American Civil War.

From this time, various methods of propulsion—steam engines, electric motors, and gasoline engines—were employed. The greatest advances, however, were made by John Holland, an Irish schoolteacher who immigrated to the United States, and a designer, Maxime Laubeuf of France. The series of craft designed and built for the U.S. Navy by Holland incorporated the horizontal rudder. The ballast tanks of the *Narval*, which Laubeuf completed in 1899, were located between a double hull. These craft were the true forerunners of today's submarine fleets.

By the early years of the 20th century, all the major naval powers were forced to take an interest in this new form of warfare, and submarine design followed the general principles that have continued into the 21st century.

Craft design

The strength of the main pressure hull determines the depth to which a boat can dive. Constructed of steel, its plates were originally riveted together but are now welded. The description "cigar shaped" is probably accurate—the cross section should be circular to obtain maximum strength, and lengthwise it should be long, thin, and tapered for streamlining. This shape gives the maximum internal volume for the minimum surface area, minimizing friction as the submarine passes through the water.

The pressure hull is pierced by as few holes as possible. They are usually confined to access hatches, torpedo tubes, missile hatches, the sleeves for periscopes and masts, the engine exhaust system in diesel-driven craft, snort mast (snorkel) leads, some of the trim tanks, and the log (speed indicator). Each opening can be sealed, and the seal is tested to full depth pressure.

Outside the pressure hull are the conning tower, the casing, and the ballast tanks, which are either saddle tanks—great bulges hung from the main structure—or double-hull tanks, which lie under an extra skin around the pressure hull.

Each ballast tank must have two openings—one at the bottom to let the water in on diving (and out on surfacing, when it is expelled with compressed air) and a hole in the top to let the air out when the tanks are flooded.

Diving deep

Diving is achieved by having all Kingston valves open and then opening the main vents, so releasing the air pressure that has previously kept the

▼ Typical layout of a submarine carrying ballistic missiles. The missiles are stored in tubes in the center of the vessel. The submarine is powered by a nuclear reactor, which enables it to stay at sea for long periods.

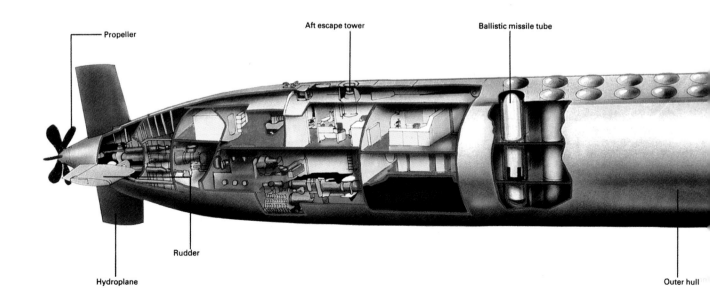

Propeller

Aft escape tower

Ballistic missile tube

Rudder

Hydroplane

Outer hull

◄ Forward view aboard USS *Ohio*, class lead ship, showing open Trident C-4 missile-launch tubes. Missiles are serviced after each patrol.

tanks dry. The submarine then achieves neutral buoyancy—the slightest downward force will cause the craft to sink. Sinking is achieved by the thrust of the propellers forcing the submarine forward while the hydroplanes, horizontal rudders situated two forward and two aft or on the conning tower, direct the bow downward.

Once below, the submarine must have weights within it so adjusted that, at the desired depth, it will remain static and horizontal. This position is achieved by transferring water into and out of trim tanks situated at either end and amidships. The deeper the submarine goes, the greater the compression of the hull and the less the displacement. As a result, more water must be expelled from the trim tanks to ensure that the submarine's displacement always equals its weight. Only then will the submarine be in the state known as stopped trim, in which it can hover at the desired depth without any mechanical assistance from the screws or hydroplanes.

Propulsion

The method of propelling submarines was not satisfactorily solved until the diesel engine was incorporated in the design. Steam propulsion,

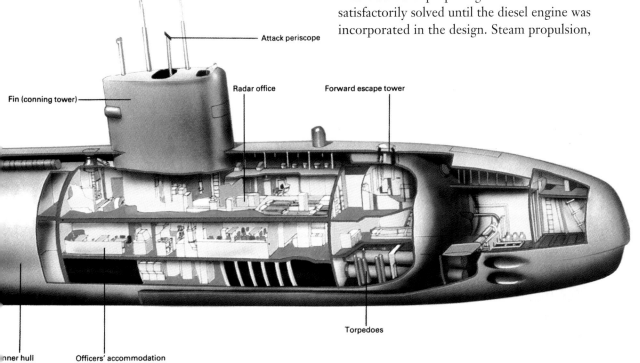

Communications mast

Attack periscope

Radar office

Forward escape tower

Fin (conning tower)

Torpedoes

Inner hull

Officers' accommodation

until it was used in concert with a nuclear reactor, presented major difficulties. Steam needed a funnel; shutting down the boilers delayed diving, and the residual heat of the boilers caused problems; and gasoline engines produced fumes that were occasionally explosive and presented the difficulty of storing a highly volatile fuel. The heavy oil engine, followed by the diesel, overcame most of these initial problems.

Propulsion on the surface or at periscope depth can be either by direct drive or by diesel-electric drive. In direct drive, the diesel is coupled through a clutch to the main electric motors and through a tail clutch to the screw. In diesel-electric drive, the diesel drives a generator that provides power for the main electric motors to rotate the propeller.

When below periscope depth, propulsion is by means of the main motors, which draw their power from large storage batteries below the main deck. These batteries are charged, when the diesels are running, either from the generators in a diesel-electric boat or from the main motors acting as generators in a direct-drive boat.

In nuclear submarines, a coolant liquid is pumped in a closed circuit between a nuclear reactor, where it takes up heat from the radioactive core, and a boiler heat exchanger, where it gives up its heat to a water feed, generating steam. The steam is conducted through valves to the main propulsion turbines and auxiliary turbines that generate power for subsidiary systems.

Subsidiary systems have many purposes. Hydraulic power operates the periscopes, the raising and lowering of the snort and other masts, the opening and shutting of the torpedo tube bow caps, the control of the main vents on the ballast tanks, and many other vital tasks. On modern submarines, nothing is hand operated, and most systems are electronically controlled.

Navigation

In the early days, navigation of submarines was described as "by guess and by God." The early submarines had no periscopes. When periscopes were introduced, some projected an inverted picture on a ground-glass screen. Later improvements, which allowed operators to examine the sky as well as the sea, included radar ranging and low-light television scanning in addition to periscope sextants for taking Sun and star sights.

A point of land for a periscope fix or a surfacing to allow the navigator to take a Sun, Moon, or star sight with a sextant is no longer needed. Submarine inertial navigation system (SINS), a complex of gyroscopes, allows a submarine to navigate underwater by keeping track of its movement from its starting point. The submarine still has to approach the surface occasionally to take periscope readings from external sources. Until

▼ Fore torpedo firing control panel on HMS *Trafalgar*; such submarines carry either Tigerfish torpedoes or Stonefish or Urchin mines.

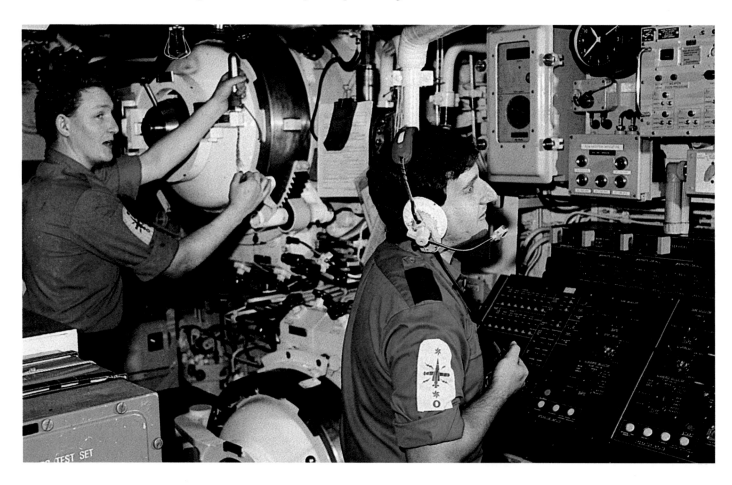

the early 1980s, long-range radio navigation (LORAN) shore stations provided updates. Since then, LORAN has been replaced by the global-positioning system (GPS), which uses satellites, allowing the navigator to know the boat's exact position in the ocean.

Armament

The submarine's weapons have improved beyond recognition over the years. The original screwed charge was replaced by the spar torpedo (an explosive charge secured to the end of a long spar). Robert Whitehead, a British engineer, perfected his mobile torpedo in the 1870s, and it soon became the natural equipment for underwater craft. Originally dropped from collars on the upper deck, these torpedoes were soon ejected from tubes projecting from the pressure hull that—provided the submarine had watertight bow caps—allowed reloading to take place.

Methods of aiming torpedoes progressed from shooting by eye and maneuvering the submarine to aim the torpedo to the computer-controlled system. Torpedoes equipped with passive or active homing heads as well as wire guidance are used. When they reach their target area, preprogrammed guidance devices home in on propeller sound, the magnetism of hulls, and other signs.

The onboard gun has now been superseded by the cruise missile, which can be launched from above or below the water and hug the wavetops, below radar level, until they strike their surface target. Tomahawk cruise missiles, which were first deployed in 1991 during the Gulf War, have a range of 1,000 miles (1,600 km).

Missiles that were part of the armory in the Cold War have now been withdrawn. The Subroc antisubmarine weapon, introduced in the mid-1960s, was withdrawn in the 1980s, and the Harpoon antiship missile was withdrawn recently.

Ballistic missile submarines carry intercontinental ballistic missiles (ICBMs). Polaris and Poseidon missiles have been replaced by Trident, which has a range of about 4,600 miles (7,360 km). Information to program and control these weapons comes from shore control, aircraft reconnaissance, and the submarine's own radar and sonar, as well as from periscope sightings.

Submarine operations changed radically when the first nuclear submarine, the USS *Nautilus*, was launched in January 1955. In many ways, it was the first true submarine, as opposed to a submersible that was dependent on the atmosphere for support. A nuclear-powered submarine can operate for years—and for up to 400,000 miles (640,000 km)—without refueling. It can manufacture its own air and fresh water, travel at fast, sustained speeds underwater (more than 25 knots), and remain submerged for periods impossible for diesel-driven boats.

Today 47 countries operate more than 700 submarines, approximately 300 of which are nuclear powered. All submarines in the U.S. Navy are nuclear powered, and Britain, France, China, and Russia have both nuclear- and conventionally powered submarines in their fleets.

▲ Regular maintenance is carried out on missile systems to ensure they are ready to be fired in hostile situations.

SEE ALSO: AIR LOCK • INERTIAL GUIDANCE • MISSILE • PERISCOPE • RADAR • SUBMERSIBLE • TORPEDO • WARSHIP

Submersible

A submersible is any relatively small vessel that operates beneath the surface of the sea. Generally, submersibles are designed to be used at great depths as protection rather than as undersea transportation if they carry crew or as a substitute for divers in dangerous environments. Some submersibles may be lowered from surface vessels; others, more complex, can be free swimming.

Size is often the only distinguishing factor between free-swimming submersibles and submarines, although submersibles are usually unarmed, while submarines carry weapons. A submersible is designed to let divers and scientists descend far below 165 ft. (50 m)—pressure would prevent an unprotected diver from descending beyond this depth. Submersibles—even those that are designed to be free swimming—depend on surface vessels for transport and support.

Submersibles are useful in shallower dives, too. Unlike free-swimming divers, crew members in submersibles are not prone to decompression sickness. This condition, also known as the bends, is caused by divers breathing in the oxygen and nitrogen mixture at a pressure equal to the water pressure at the depth at which they are working. If they return to the surface too quickly, the pressure

release leads to bubbles of nitrogen entering body tissue, which, in serious cases, can lead to brain damage or even death. Free-swimming divers must therefore "decompress" either by rising to the surface slowly or in a specially built chamber.

In a submersible, crew members receive their air supply at a pressure approximately equal to that at the surface. There is less risk to life, and trained crew members do not have to undergo lengthy depressurization procedures.

Deep-sea submersibles

The history of deep-sea submersibles started with the U.S. explorer William Beebe's bathysphere in the early 1930s. The craft was used for four years off Bermuda and dived to a depth of more than 90 ft. (27 m). Since then, submersibles have been used in a variety of fields applications: oceanography, ocean engineering (the oil industry and ocean salvage), archaeology, and fisheries.

Bathyspheres were tethered to the mother ship, so they were not very maneuverable. In the late 1940s, a Swiss-Belgian physicist, Auguste Piccard, developed the bathyscaphe. The name is derived from two Greek words: *bathys*, meaning "deep," and *skaphe*, meaning "boat." Piccard's

▲ The Japanese submersible *Shinkai 6500*, seen here being lowered into the water, is one of the deepest diving vessels in active service. It can reach depths of 21,500 ft. (6,500 m).

craft allowed the crew to descend several miles beneath the sea in a free-swimming vessel. Deep-sea submersibles came of age in 1960, when the bathyscaphe *Trieste* descended to 35,000 ft. (10,670 m) into the Mariana Trench in the Pacific Ocean, the world's deepest water. The design concept of the bathyscaphe has been the basis for all subsequent manned submersibles.

The *Trieste* was followed by a series of other craft. The U.S. Navy built two deep submergence rescue vessels (DSRVs), which can dive to more than 5,000 ft. (1,525 m) and rescue 24 people on each dive. Another U.S. Navy vessel is the *DSSV* (deep submergence search vessel). The *NR1* is the world's first nuclear-powered vessel designed for peaceful purposes—it can dive to depths of 20,000 ft. (6,100 m). As well as continuing to be used for deep-sea research, submersibles are also employed today for marine engineering projects and exploration.

Diving

The bathyscaphe has two main sections—a large float and a spherical cabin slung beneath it. The float, which is lighter than water and filled with gasoline, gives the craft positive buoyancy. It also contains iron shot, held in hoppers by electromagnets. On the surface, some of the compartments in the float are filled with air. For diving, these compartments are filled with water.

The gasoline-filled compartments are left open at the bottom. As the bathyscaphe dives deeper and the pressure increases, some water finds its way into the gasoline-filled compartments, equalizing the pressure inside and outside the float. This function allows the float to be constructed from much lighter materials than those used for the cabin.

Ballast is dumped when the vessel reaches the desired depth. Ballast-dumping ceases when the vessel achieves neutral buoyancy. A guide chain, an ingenious device for automatically adjusting the quantity of ballast when a submersible is near the bottom, is often used. A length of heavy-duty chain is hung from beneath the vessel. When the chain hits the bottom, the ballast is effectively lightened because the weight of some of the chain is being supported by the seabed. The vessel continues descending until sufficient chain touches the seabed for it to achieve neutral ballast.

Returning to the surface is simple. The electromagnets keeping the remaining shot in place are turned off. The ballast falls away, leaving the vessel to float to the surface, buoyed by the gasoline-filled compartments in the float.

The cabin must be able to withstand great pressures—at 10,000 ft. (3,050 m), the pressure is about 8 tons per sq. in. (124 MN/m²). The Plexiglas windows are carefully seated into the surrounding metal to give a perfect seal—at a great depth, even a small leak could prove disastrous. The portholes are constructed like a cone with the point sliced off and the base facing the outside. The Plexiglass portholes are glued into place. Electric conduits connecting the bathyscaphe to the surface are sealed using epoxy adhesive. Submersibles are normally equipped with external grabs to assist with research or salvage operations.

Life-support systems

Life-support systems used in submersibles are generally simpler than those found in larger submarines. Cost, size, and mission length have all had an influence on the design of these systems. Free-swimming submersibles usually have systems for both oxygen supply and carbon dioxide removal, but those lowered from surface vessels often economize by having only an oxygen-supply system. Consequently, dives are limited to an hour or two. Oxygen is usually supplied from cylinders, and carbon dioxide is removed by Barylyme (barium hydroxide) or lithium hydroxide scrubbers. Air pressure is carefully maintained at the level found at sea level, and the air is usually made up of the same ratio of gas constituents found in Earth's atmosphere.

Deep-sea submersibles normally hold two or more divers. Sufficient air supply for 24 hours is usually carried to avoid having to return to the surface if very deep dives are to be undertaken.

◄ An uncrewed, underwater, self-propelled television camera, nicknamed Snoopy. Linked flash units are used at depths that lack natural light. Remotely controlled vehicles such as this can be sent down to depths that would be difficult for divers to view for long periods of time.

Power limitations imposed by the batteries used in submersibles often mean that there are no heating and humidity controls on board, although silica gel has been used to absorb some of the humidity produced by breathing. Because of these restraints, submersibles are not always the most comfortable way for people to dive to great depths.

The first deep-sea submersible to carry passengers—a pilot and two observers—was *Alvin*, which has been in operation since 1964. It has been modified over the years, and is now capable of diving to a maximum depth of 14,764 ft. (4,500 m). In 1977, scientists using *Alvin* in the Pacific Ocean found the first hydrothermal vents.

Crew or no crew?

Submersibles may or may not carry crew, but the relative merits of crewing such craft are still debated. An uncrewed submersible, or remotely operated vehicle (ROV), is easier to construct—it does not need a life-support system, but the vessel must be sufficiently strong to withstand the pressures found at great depths in the sea.

Using ROVs also has many advantages to those involved in the work. Because the vessel does not have to come up for air, the mission has no time limit. The controlling crew can be changed on the surface, and the work can progress without disruption. Potentially hazardous environments and materials can be tackled with little danger. Finally, with only a surface crew, there can be no arguments about operational decisions.

ROVs are not without disadvantages, however. It is much easier to lose equipment under remote control. Economies of construction often mean that ROVs are simple structures that are prone to snagging in cables and other submerged obstructions. Many surface controllers find that because of the intense concentration demanded of them, they can operate ROVs for only two or three hours. In fact, vision problems are probably the greatest argument against the use of uncrewed vessels of this type. Without the detail and the dimensionality of on-the-spot vision, many potentially disastrous and expensive decisions can be made by the surface controllers.

ROVs were first used in industrial applications, such as inspecting pipelines and testing offshore platforms, and have also proved useful in scientific applications and ocean exploration.

ROPOS, or remotely operated platform for ocean science, is a remotely operated vehicle designed to undertake scientific exploration at depths of up to 16,400 ft. (5,000 m). In deep water, ROPOS is lowered to the required depth inside a large steel cage. It then leaves the cage and roams freely on 300 ft. (90 m) of tether. At

▶ Johnson Sea Link's two-man submersible has a six-inch-thick acrylic sphere for observation. Powerful lights can be mounted on the frame to illuminate the seabed, a particularly useful feature for underwater photography.

shallower depths, ROPOS operates without the cage. It is navigated with a sonar tracking system aided by a global positioning system (GPS).

ROPOS carries the standard onboard equipment—digital video cameras, manipulator arms fitted with sampling tools, and sonar—and can also be fitted with up to eight custom-designed observation tools, such as a chemical scanner or rock-coring drill. Although ROPOS is easy to operate, it requires at least four people in the control room to process and analyze the large amount of information it collects.

Autonomous vehicles

The newest submersibles are able to move without a pilot or a tether to a ship. The first of its kind, *ABE*, or Autonomous Benthic Explorer, is a robot preprogrammed to undertake a set of maneuvers, take photographs, and collect samples and data within a designated area. It then goes into "sleep" mode to conserve power and thus can repeat its programmed tasks for months.

Currently, the data *ABE* collects is accessible only when the robot is recovered. However, the development of underwater acoustic transmission systems will soon allow scientists to access video and data from *ABE* and even to control its movements from onshore laboratories.

SEE ALSO:

BOAT BUILDING • DIVING SUIT • OCEANOGRAPHY • PRESSURE • REMOTE HANDLING • SEA RESCUE • SHIP • SUBMARINE • UNDERSEA HABITAT • UNDERWATER PHOTOGRAPHY

Sugar Refining

Sugarcane grew in New Guinea 12,000 years ago and was cultivated in Egypt and the coastal lands of the Mediterranean about 3000 B.C.E. A soft, sweet, and thin-stemmed variety, known as *criolla*, was introduced to the West Indies in 1493 by the Italian explorer Christopher Columbus. During the 18th century, sugarcane plantations developed rapidly in the colonies of many European countries thanks to the cheap supply of slave labor drawn from the African continent. The modern varieties of sugarcane are hybrids of *Saccharum officinarum*, *S. robustum*, and *S. spontaneum*, which have been bred to resist mosaic disease and to give high yields.

The sugar-beet plant was discovered comparatively recently. As a weed, *Beta maritima*, it was found on Mediterranean seashores. The variety cultivated about 100 years ago contained only about 5 percent by weight of sucrose, but later varieties, such as *B. vulgaris*, contain up to 20 percent sucrose. Sugar beet is grown in temperate regions and accounts for about 40 percent of world sugar production. The rest is obtained from sugarcane grown in tropical regions. There is no difference between the sugar derived from cane and that from beet, although different manufacturers produce crystals of different sizes.

Chemical structure

Granulated sugar is more than 99 percent pure sucrose, which is a disaccharide with the chemical formula $C_{12}H_{22}O_{11}$. It can be broken down into two other sugars, glucose and fructose, by the addition of one molecule of water. This process of hydrolysis is called inversion and can be accomplished by heating a sucrose solution with a dilute acid or by the action of enzymes. The resulting glucose and fructose mixture is referred to as invert sugar and, unlike sucrose, is able to reduce copper in a Fehlings solution (an alkaline solution containing Rochelle salt and cupric sulfate) to a precipitate of cuprous oxide.

▲ Unloading sugar beet prior to refining. Most sugar comes from sugarcane and beet, although it is also found in foods such as milk and cornstarch.

◄ Transferring raw cane sugar from a bulk carrier. Cane sugar is imported from its main growing areas, the tropical and subtropical regions of South America and the West Indies.

Mature sugar beet contains mostly sucrose, but sugarcane may contain appreciable quantities of invert sugars. Fortunately, these invert sugars are at a minimum when the sugarcane crop is mature.

Raw-sugar production

Sugar-beet processing is a relatively simple process. The beets are washed and sliced up. Sucrose is extracted from the slices with hot water, and the solution obtained is purified by precipitating calcium carbonate in it. Impurities are trapped in the precipitate and filtered out. The process is repeated several times to give a clear solution. Vacuum evaporation is used to concentrate the solution, which is seeded and cooled so that the sugar crystallizes out.

Much of the world's sugarcane is harvested by hand cutting after burning the crop to remove the leaves. However, mechanical systems such as push-rake cutting and grab harvesting have come into use. The cane arriving at the raw-sugar factory is washed on conveyors to remove field mud, sand, and trash. The cane is nearly 90 percent juice, which was traditionally extracted by a combination of shredders and three-roll crushers that squeezed out the juice. This process gave 95 percent extraction of the juice, but the extraction

has been improved to greater than 97 percent by the introduction of diffusion processes. One system, known as the ring diffuser, prepares the cane by shredding it in hammer mills, operating at 1,000 rpm, which pound the cane with steel hammers. The shredded cane is fed to an annular, rotating perforated plate of the diffuser where sugars are extracted by recycled juice percolating through the cane at 160 to 165°F (71–74°C). The extracted cane, or bagasse, is removed from the diffuser by screw conveyors and can be used as a fuel in the steam-raising plant of the factory, which produces the steam used to heat the sugar and, in some factories, to drive the machinery.

Many of the impurities of raw cane juice are removed by adding a mineral-lime suspension to give a pH of 8.5 and heating to about 220°F (104°C), which is maintained for 20 minutes. Acids are neutralized, and the phosphates present are flocculated (coalesced) and adsorb coloring matter and colloids (suspended particles), which are subsequently removed by settling for about three hours in clarifying tanks.

Next the clarified juice is concentrated to about 65 percent by weight of sugar in a multi-effect (multistage) evaporator system. The juice temperature in the first evaporators is about 229°F (109.5°C), and the pressure in succeeding evaporators is reduced so that the juice boils at 153.3°F (67.5°C) in the fourth effect. Vapor generated in each evaporator is condensed in the heating tubes of the next effect, thus economizing on the use of steam.

The concentrated juice is then boiled to a supersaturated (highly concentrated) solution in vacuum pans. Crystallization is induced by seeding with a magnum of sugar and syrup to form a mixture of sugar crystals and liquor, known collectively as massecuite. The massecuite is discharged from the vacuum pans at 160°F (71°C) into water-cooled crystallizers, where further sugar crystals are formed by reducing the temperature to about 100°F (37.8°C) over a 48-hour period. The raw-sugar crystals are separated by reheating the massecuite to 122°F (50°C) to reduce the viscosity followed by treatment in basket centrifuges operating at 1,500 rpm. The residual syrup purged from the massecuite—a dark viscous liquid known as blackstrap molasses—is used in the manufacture of rum, industrial alcohol, and citric acid.

Refining raw sugar

The first stage of raw-sugar refining is called affination and consists of removing the molasses film coating the crystals by mingling the raw sugar in a U-shaped trough with a 73 percent sugar syrup.

◀ Purifying tanks in which sugarcane is clarified. The sugar is then concentrated and crystallized, leaving a black residual syrup used in the manufacture of rum and industrial alcohol.

molds of a cylinder that rotates against a stationary pressure bar to compress the cubes. The cubes are discharged onto a conveyor and dried in an oven at 140°F (60°C). Soft sugars vary in color from light to dark brown. They have an invert sugar content of up to 6 percent and a moisture content of 4 percent. Brown sugars can be either sticky browns or free-flowing browns.

Liquid sugar can be a pure sucrose syrup of 67.5 percent concentration or a mixture of sucrose and invert sugar. Some liquid sugars are blended with corn syrup. Powdered sugars, such as icing sugar, are prepared by grinding granulated sugar, and their tendency to cake is often overcome by incorporating 3 percent cornstarch.

Molasses and its uses

Molasses is the brownish liquid residue that is left after the heat crystallization of sucrose during refining. Molasses is often reprocessed to draw off more of the remnant sucrose. The better grades—such as New Orleans drip molasses—are unreprocessed and so are lighter in color and contain more sucrose. They are used in cooking and confectionery and in the production of rum. The lowest grade, called blackstrap, is added to cattle feed and is used in the production of industrial alcohol. Sugarcane is the main source of molasses; sugar beet yields inferior molasses.

The syrup is removed by centrifuging, and the affined sugar is melted in pure water at 190°F (88°C) to give a strength of 68 percent by weight. Up to 50 percent of the color can be removed by treating the refinery melt with phosphoric acid (H_3PO_4) to an equivalent dosage of 0.02 percent P_2O_5 and adjusting the pH to 7.3 with lime (CaOH). After heating to 195°F (91°C), flocculation of the impurities occurs, and they can be removed by flotation, often followed by filtration. Final color removal is achieved by adsorption in beds of granular carbon or bone char (carbonized bone particles) followed by filtration to remove the last traces of suspended matter. Today refineries use ion-exchange resins for decolorization.

The pale-yellow sugar liquor is concentrated to 75 percent in a double-effect evaporator, and crystallization is initiated in the vacuum pan by further evaporation and seeding with fondant sugar. The sugar recovered in the centrifuges contains about 1 percent moisture, which is removed by drying for 10 minutes in a 30 ft. (9 m) long rotary drier with an air inlet temperature of 220°F (104°C). After cooling to 110°F (43°C), the sugar is transferred to silos, where the air is kept at a humidity of 60 percent to avoid readsorption of moisture.

Cube sugar is produced by pouring a mixture of dry sugar and 1 percent sugar syrup into the

▶ A filter press used during the last stages of color removal in a sugar refining plant.

SEE ALSO: Agricultural science • Alcohol • Biofuel • Carbohydrate • Food processing • Spirit

Sulfur

Sulfur, chemical symbol S, has been known since antiquity, and its occurrence in its natural state in Sicily ensured its availability to the early Mediterranean civilizations. The Greek writer Homer mentioned its medicinal properties around 900 B.C.E., and the fumes of burning sulfur (sulfur dioxide, SO_2) have long been used for bleaching textiles and for fumigation.

The name can be traced to the Sanskrit word *sulveni*, which was the basis of the Roman word *sulphurium*. It is also known as brimstone from the German word *Brennstein* meaning "burning stone." To the alchemist, sulfur, along with mercury, was an essential ingredient of all metals, and it was not until the work of the French chemist Antoine Lavoisier in the late 18th century that it was classified as a chemical element.

Physical properties

In the periodic table (a table of the elements arranged according to the number of protons in the element, or the atomic number), sulfur is situated toward the end of the third period. Accordingly, it is a nonmetal and a good thermal and electric insulator. At room temperature, it is a yellow crystalline solid, tasteless, and odorless. There are two common crystalline forms, or allotropes—the more stable of these, known as alpha (α) sulfur, has an orthorhombic crystal structure and melts at 235°F (113°C). Above 203°F (95°C), however, the other crystalline form, designated beta (β) sulfur, is the more stable—it has a monoclinic crystal structure and melts at 246°F (119°C). The transition between the two forms takes place at a fairly leisurely pace so that α-sulfur heated rapidly will melt before any β-sulfur has time to form. Similarly, if the beta form is crystallized from the melt or if α-sulfur is held between 203°F (95°C) and 235°F (113°C) and then cooled rapidly to room temperature, the monoclinic crystals of β-sulfur will be preserved in a metastable (apparently stable) condition, although they will revert to the alpha form over a period of a day or so. Crystals of the alpha form can, however, be prepared directly by crystallization from a solution of sulfur in carbon disulfide, CS_2.

Plastic sulfur is made by pouring liquid sulfur at nearly its boiling point into cold water. It is noncrystalline, being a supercooled form of the viscous melt, and it reverts to the crystalline alpha form on standing. Other types of noncrystalline sulfur, known generally as amorphous sulfur, can be formed by the action of light on solutions of sulfur in carbon disulfide or by various reactions that precipitate sulfur from solutions of its compounds. Flowers of sulfur, prepared by sublimation, contain some of the amorphous form, which can be separated by dissolving out the crystalline component.

Occurrence and extraction

The occurrence of native sulfur (free sulfur rather than a sulfur-containing compound) is associated with regions of volcanic activity. Ores containing sulfur include the sulfates barite and gypsum and the sulfides chalcopyrite, pyrite, cinnabar, and galena. The deposits in Sicily contain about 20 percent sulfur, which is extracted by burning the rock with a limited supply of air in kilns. The fraction of the sulfur burned provides heat to melt out the remainder—it is cheaper to use sulfur itself as fuel than to import coal or oil.

The extensive deposits in the United States and Mexico are on average some 650 ft. (200 m) underground and cannot be mined by conventional methods. Instead, the sulfur is brought to the surface using a technique invented by a U.S.

chemist, Herman Frasch. A well with three concentric tubes is sunk into the sulfur-bearing strata. Pressurized superheated water at 356°F (180°C) is passed down the outer tube. It melts out the sulfur from the rocks surrounding the bottom of the well, and the molten sulfur is forced up to the surface as a froth through the central tube by means of compressed air. The sulfur is run out into large vats where it solidifies better than 99 percent pure and is suitable for immediate use.

Natural gas is an abundant source of sulfur in the form of hydrogen sulfide, H_2S, and the gas fields of France, the United States, and Canada produce a significant proportion of the total world requirements. The hydrogen sulfide is first concentrated using an absorption and regeneration process, and the sulfur is then separated from the hydrogen by catalytic oxidation, a technique called the Claus process. This process enables around 98 percent of the sulfur present in natural gas to be recovered.

Sulfur is also recovered from sulfur dioxide present in waste gases from metallurgical processes involving the reduction of sulfide ores and also from power station furnaces burning sulfur-containing coal. Normally the sulfur dioxide is concentrated by absorption in a chemical solution, such as basic aluminum sulfate, and then reduced to sulfur by white hot coke.

▼ At this plant in Sulingen, Germany, about 700 tons (630 tonnes) of sulfur a day are produced from natural gas.

Sulfur compounds

The most common sulfur-containing compound is sulfuric acid, H_2SO_4, from which are derived the sulfates, salts containing the ion SO_2-. Sulfuric acid is prepared from sulfur dioxide, and for this reason, about 85 percent of all the sulfur produced is burned to produce the dioxide:

$$S \quad + \quad O_2 \quad \rightarrow \quad SO_2$$

sulfur   oxygen   sulfur dioxide

It is then used for acid manufacture.

At first sight, therefore, the careful oxidation of the hydrogen sulfide found in natural gas to give sulfur rather than sulfur dioxide might seem rather pointless, but elemental sulfur is much easier to handle and cheaper to transport than sulfur dioxide (a pungent, poisonous gas at room temperature). Sulfur dioxide is also used as a refrigerant, as a bleaching agent in applications where the fiercer action of chlorine is undesirable, in food preservation to control the growth of spoilage microorganisms, and by the paper-making industry.

Hydrogen sulfide, H_2S, a poisonous gas with the odor of rotten eggs, is important in chemical analysis and can be prepared very easily by the action of an acid on a sulfide:

$$2HCl \quad + \quad ZnS \quad \rightarrow \quad H_2S \quad + \quad ZnCl_2$$

hydrochloric   zinc sulfide   hydrogen   zinc chloride
acid   sulfide

▲ Measuring the sulfur content of petroleum products. The samples are burned in test tubes, and the combustion gases given off are collected and analyzed so that the sulfur content of a product can be calculated. Sulfur compounds are a source of air pollution and must be kept to a minimum in motor fuels.

Sulfur is the crosslinking agent used in the vulcanization of rubber, and the process also employs aromatic sulfur compounds as accelerators. Many important antibiotics, particularly the penicillins, the cephalosporins, and the sulfonamides, are sulfur-containing compounds. Sulfur is also a component of a range of quick-drying cements, and sulfuric acid is used in batteries.

Sulfur and sulfur-containing compounds are present in small quantities in most fossil fuels, and during combustion of the fuel, they are converted to sulfur dioxide, one of the major atmospheric pollutants. The problem with sulfur dioxide is that it dissolves in water very easily to give sulfurous acid, H_2SO_3, which, although only a weak acid, will in time attack the stonework on buildings and adversely affect animal and plant life. Acid rain caused by emissions from power stations and industrial plants has been shown to cause extensive pollution in rivers and lakes, killing fish as well as slowly killing trees and other vegetation. This is an international problem because pollution caused in one country often affects another—Canadian forests, for example, are damaged by the sulfur dioxide from industrial plants in the United States—and the effects can be long lasting. Such pollution can be reduced significantly by the use of low-sulfur fuels and by the use of scrubbers to remove the sulfur from exhaust gases.

FACT FILE

- When a French company gained a monopoly over Sicilian sulfur in 1839, industrial nations like Britain and the United States were forced to develop their own sulfur resources. Sicily had produced commercial sulfur from the 15th century onward, and in the 18th century, sulfur was the island's major industry.

- In 1946, scientists discovered anaerobic bacteria capable of reducing sulfates in the cap rock of the saltdomes on the U.S. Gulf Coast. These bacteria are likely to be the origin of the crystal aggregates of sulfur that occur in the saltdomes. There are 329 of these domes, and 27 have been used to produce sulfur commercially.

- In the 18th century, sulfur was combusted in pottery, glass, and lead spheres and chambers for the production of sulfuric acid. By the end of the century, some of the lead chambers reached a size of 26 ft. (8 m) long by 16 ft. (4.8 m) high.

SEE ALSO:	ACID AND ALKALI • BATTERY • CHEMISTRY, INORGANIC • ELEMENT, CHEMICAL • PERIODIC TABLE • RUBBER, NATURAL

Sundial

average position and sometimes behind it. The difference between clock time and sundial time is called the equation of time—the word equation here meaning "that which is needed to make things equal." The variations in the equation of time are the same each year, so the correct time can easily be calculated.

A sundial at the center of Earth could be made to read the exact clock time always—if suitable corrections were made. One way of doing so would be to only read the time from the tip of the shadow stick (the gnomon) and to provide hour lines that, instead of being straight and radiating from the center, would be slightly curved with alternative markings for different times of the year. Then by reading off from the appropriate marking, the time correct to a few seconds could be obtained.

Setting up a real sundial presents a few more problems. A sundial can be laid out on any surface that catches the Sun, whether horizontal, vertical, curved, or angled in any way. The only important points to take into consideration are that the

To an observer at the center of a transparent Earth, time measurement would be no problem. Earth's rotation with respect to the Sun would make the Sun appear to move around once in 24 hours, and it would be clear that every 24 hours it crosses the same line of longitude—though it would be a little farther north or south each day with the changing season. All that would be needed to keep track of its movement is a card marked with 24 equal hours around a circle, aligned with the equator, with a central vertical stick to cast a shadow. Then, whatever the season, the shadow would point in the same direction at the same time each day.

By comparing the sundial time with a good mechanical timekeeper, however, it would be found that the Sun's motion varies throughout the year and that the sundial time would sometimes be up to about a quarter of an hour slow or fast, because Earth's orbit around the Sun is not a perfect circle. It is an ellipse—a slightly flattened circle, with the Sun offset from the center. As the German astronomer Johannes Kepler found in the 17th century, Earth moves faster when it is near the Sun, so the Sun is sometimes ahead of its

▲ The Tower of the Winds in Athens, Greece. Each of the eight sides faces a point of the compass and carries sundials. On top was a bronze figure of a triton that turned around to indicate wind direction. The top figures represent the wind gods.

▶ An armillary sundial, with equal markings on a ring set to the angle of latitude.

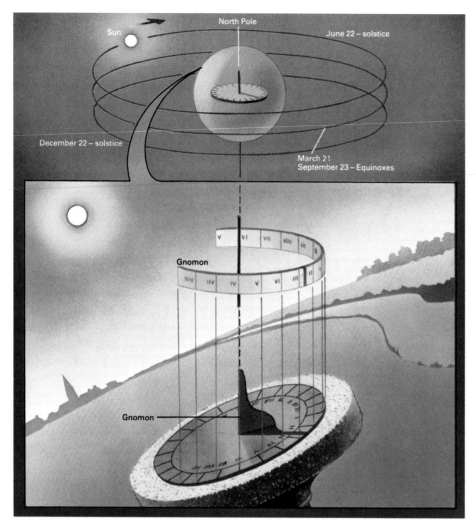

Gnomon

Gnomon

shadow stick should be parallel to Earth's axis—that is, pointing at the North Star in the Northern Hemisphere—and that the hour lines should be aligned parallel with those on the imaginary dial at Earth's center. To take into account the fact that the real surface is probably not parallel with the Equator, the markings must be projected down onto the real surface from an imaginary dial that is parallel with the Equator, as if illuminated from the direction of the North Star.

The simplest design of sundial is the armillary. It often looks like a skeleton globe with an inclined central axis. This axis is the gnomon, and the time is marked by equal divisions around a band at right angles to it. The gnomon is set up pointing north–south at the angle of latitude of its location. It will then be parallel with Earth's axis. The only disadvantage with this type of sundial is that unless the band is carefully designed, it will not work on a few days in March and September, the times of the equinoxes, when the Sun is exactly over the Equator—the band, aligned with the Equator, gets in its own way. For this reason, such bands are often incomplete or have a perforated design so that some light can shine through the holes.

▲ The function of a sundial. If the Sun went around Earth, instead of the other way around, it would appear to move along a different track each day. The top diagram selects three of these tracks and shows how the central sundial would indicate the time of day by the shadow of the central vertical stick. In practice, a ring dial must be aligned with the Equator or its markings projected down onto a flat dial, as shown.

▶ This sundial, scratched on a wall in Napon, England, gave only a rough indication of time.

Flat sundials are made by projecting the markings down, parallel with the gnomon, onto the surface desired. In this way, markings can be made on any surface, whether flat, vertical, or angled. Many buildings have sundials on walls that do not face the Sun exactly. In such cases, the gnomon also has to be aligned at an angle to the wall, so as to be parallel with the Earth's axis—unless the tip of the shadow only is to be read, in which case it can project at right angles to the wall.

Sundials have been used for thousands of years, the earliest known practical example being Egyptian. The Greeks went on to develop complex and sophisticated sundials including those found on the Tower of the Winds in Athens. Built in 100 B.C.E., this octagonal tower possesses eight sundials positioned around its walls. The Romans had hemispherical sundials, or skaphes; they also used portable sundials. A portable sundial should give an immediate reading, but lacking compasses, the Romans could not locate north during the day to align the dial on the meridian. Instead, the dials were designed to measure the length of a vertical gnomon's shadow. These dials could be used only at the latitude for which they were designed, and different scales were needed for different times of the year—at any given latitude the Sun is in the same spot in the sky on only one day each half year. Later portable sundials had compasses. These sophisticated devices also had provision for altering the latitude and for allowing for the equation of time.

 SEE ALSO: CLOCK • EARTH • SOLAR SYSTEM • STONE MONUMENT • TIME • WATCH, MECHANICAL

Supercharger and Turbocharger

With any internal combustion engine, there is only one way to extract more power—by burning more fuel. According to the laws of chemistry, when a given quantity of fuel is burned, an exact amount of oxygen is required if the mixture is to be burned without leaving any excess fuel or oxygen. Most gasoline engines have to operate at or near this chemically correct mixture, called the stoichiometric ratio, as do diesel engines at full load. To burn more fuel, it is necessary to increase the mass of air supplied to the combustion chambers. This goal can be achieved by the use of a supercharger, which effectively acts as a pump to force more air into the engine.

With aircraft piston engines, the power output falls off with increasing height—because of the decreasing air pressure and density, a smaller air charge is drawn into the cylinders. To maintain the power output, the amount of air supplied has to be increased, a job that can be done using a supercharger. There are two main types of superchargers—with the mechanically driven superchargers the power is taken directly from the engine; turbochargers, however extract energy from the exhaust gases, which turn the shaft by driving air through a volute, similar to that of a centrifugal pump.

Superchargers

Different types of mechanically driven superchargers include the vane supercharger, the Roots blower, and the centrifugal compressor. A typical vane supercharger has a cylindrical housing with a rotor mounted eccentrically within it. Vanes carried by the rotor extend to the casing and

▲ A Rickman Kawasaki KZ1000 motorcycle with a Magnum turbocharger.

▼ Mechanics at a Grand Prix working on René Arnaux's turbocharged Renault RE 30 B.

divide it into a number of separate chambers. The vanes are mounted so that they can slide radially into the rotor. Inlet and outlet connections are provided in positions that correspond to the largest and smallest of the chambers formed by the vanes. As the rotor revolves, centrifugal force keeps the vanes in contact with the outer casing to give a set of rotating chambers that reduce in volume as they move around. Air is taken in at the inlet, compressed as it is carried around, and expelled at the outlet.

The Roots blower consists of two rotors, each shaped like a figure eight in cross section, running in an oval-shaped housing on parallel shafts and geared together so that their lobes are always in line contact. Clearances between rotors and housing are kept to a fine minimum so that they do not actually touch (and therefore need no lubrication), but the gap is so small that little leakage of air takes place past the rotor tips. As the rotors rotate, they collect air at the inlet, carry it around the outside, and deliver it to the outlet. The volume of the chambers formed between the rotor and the housing is constant, so the air is not compressed during its passage through the blower (hence the name). However, compressions can be said to be taking place in the outlet region, because a larger volume of air is moved in than is taken out by the engine.

The basic centrifugal compressor fan is a platelike rotor with curved axial vanes—as the vanes rotate, they collect air at the center and, by centrifugal action, fling it toward their periphery into a volute, or spiral-shaped housing, which by its shape slows down the air and converts its velocity to pressure in a way similar to the action of a centrifugal pump.

Some mechanical superchargers can be coupled to the engine directly, but more often belt, chain, or gear drives are used. Both the vane compressor and the Roots blower are positive displacement units with a reasonable pressure boost being available at low speed, though the efficiency falls off at higher speeds. In contrast the centrifugal compressor has little boost at low speeds but the output rises sharply as the speed increases. Superchargers are normally used only on high-performance vehicles.

Turbochargers

If instead of the mechanical drive to a centrifugal compressor fan, another, similar device—a turbine—is attached back-to-back on the same shaft in a suitable housing and if the exhaust gases from the engine are directed into the volute, the gases will turn the blades of the turbine and so drive the compressor as well. This is the principle of the turbocharger—a more efficient way of supercharging, because the energy of the exhaust gases, which would otherwise be wasted, is made to do useful work.

Although the basic principles of turbochargers were known in the early years of the 20th century, the development of successful designs had to wait for modern materials. The inlet turbine, in particular, has to withstand a combination of high temperatures and mechanical stresses, and precision manufacture is essential. These requirements were met by high-temperature alloys, more recently, by ceramics, and by using fluid bearings to reduce the amount of friction occurring around the turbine shaft.

Turbochargers are used extensively in diesel truck engines, where great increases in power can be achieved for very little weight penalty, as compared with a standard engine—for the same power output, a turbocharged engine can be made significantly smaller. Turbocharging is also common on high-performance spark-ignition automobile engines, for both road and racing use.

Owing to the speed characteristics of the turbocharger, there is little boost effect at low engine speeds. Another drawback lies in the fact that the turbine output, and hence the boost provided by the compressor stage, depends on the flow of exhaust gases from the engine. A result of this dependency is that a lag occurs when the throttle is opened rapidly for maximum acceleration, while at high speeds, excessive boost may occur. Careful design can minimize these effects—small, low-inertia rotors, for example, are used to minimize lag effects, though these rotors may not produce enough additional air pressure at higher speeds. Alternatively, a combination of two turbochargers, one small and one large, may be used to take advantage of the properties of each, providing the necessary boost at both low and high speeds. Wastegates are also employed to dump excess exhaust gases away from the turbine when the required boost level has been achieved.

Another problem with turbochargers is that the increased air pressure produced in the cylinder may produce increased air temperature and thus can cause premature ignition of the fuel and result in noise and vibrations known as knocking. High-octane fuels may be used to reduce this effect.

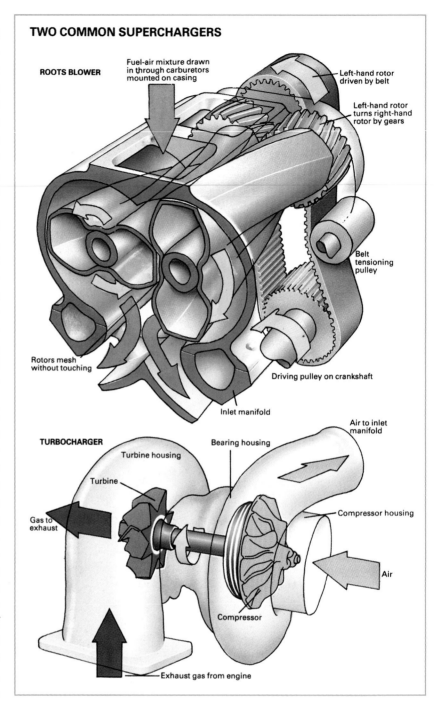

TWO COMMON SUPERCHARGERS

ROOTS BLOWER

Fuel-air mixture drawn in through carburetors mounted on casing

Left-hand rotor driven by belt

Left-hand rotor turns right-hand rotor by gears

Belt tensioning pulley

Rotors mesh without touching

Driving pulley on crankshaft

Inlet manifold

TURBOCHARGER

Turbine housing

Bearing housing

Air to inlet manifold

Turbine

Gas to exhaust

Compressor housing

Air

Compressor

Exhaust gas from engine

▲ Two common types of supercharger. The two vanes of the Roots blower (top) compress the air and drive it into two sets of ports, one for each bank of a V-8 engine. In the turbocharger version (bottom), exhaust gases (brown arrows) turn the shaft, driving air through a volute.

Intercooling

Increased air temperature as a result of compression also results in a less dense charge and therefore reduced efficiency. Reducing the temperature of the compressed air in an intercooler before it is passed to the engine increases the mass of the charge and so helps minimize the efficiency losses. Intercoolers are essentially heat exchangers, and the cooling effect may be provided by water or air. Efficiency can also be improved by using two or more compression stages, allowing each compressor to work at its most efficient pressure ratio.

SEE ALSO: COMPRESSOR AND PUMP • ENGINE COOLING SYSTEMS • IGNITION SYSTEM, AUTOMOBILE • INTERNAL COMBUSTION ENGINE

Index

Page numbers in **bold** refer to main articles; those in *italics* refer to picture captions.